Storytelling in Design

*Defining, Designing, and Selling
Multidevice Products*

Anna Dahlström

Beijing · Boston · Farnham · Sebastopol · Tokyo

Storytelling in Design
by Anna Dahlström

Printed in the United States of America.

Published by O'Reilly Media, Inc., 1005 Gravenstein Highway North, Sebastopol, CA 95472.

O'Reilly books may be purchased for educational, business, or sales promotional use. Online editions are also available for most titles (*http://oreilly.com*). For more information, contact our corporate/institutional sales department: (800) 998-9938 or *corporate@oreilly.com*.

Acquisitions Editor: Jennifer Pollock	**Indexer:** Angela Howard
Developmental Editor: Angela Rufino	**Cover Designer:** Karen Montgomery
Production Editor: Katherine Tozer	**Interior Designers:** Ron Bilodeau and Monica Kamsvaag
Copyeditor: Kim Cofer	
Proofreader: Sharon Wilkey	**Illustrators:** Jose Marzan Jr. and Rebecca Demarest

December 2019: First Edition

Revision History for the First Edition:

    2019-12-02   First release

See *https://www.oreilly.com/catalog/errata.csp?isbn=0636920051374* for release details.

978-1-491-95942-8

[GP]

[*Contents*]

It All Starts with "Once upon a time..."

I GREW UP IN a family where stories were always told. My dad, Ingvar, is a writer, and reading and writing played a big part in my childhood. I remember sitting next to my dad on the sofa with one of my brothers on the other side. Dad would read us the *Moomin* books, *The Chronicles of Narnia*, the Brothers Grimm, Hans Christian Andersen, and Astrid Lindgren, and we'd sit there completely absorbed.

The stories he read sent us on journeys to places we didn't know existed. They created worlds in our minds and sparked our imaginations by making us see things we'd never seen before. As with a dream you don't want to wake up from, we never wanted those reading sessions to stop. We wanted to know what would happen next, how it all began, and how it was going to end. Evening after evening, we'd get one step closer until the final page was turned and it was time to start a new chapter, sometimes in a new book.

Many of the classic fairy tales from our childhoods, like *Snow White*, *Rumpelstiltskin*, and *Hansel and Gretel*, start with one of the most widely known sentences in the world: "Once upon a time..." According to *The Oxford English Dictionary*, the phrase has been used in one form or another since at least 1380 to introduce narratives of past events, typically in the form of fairy tales and folktales. During the 1600s, it became commonly used as a way to begin oral narratives and often ended with "...and they all lived happily ever after."

Today a number of modern variants of "Once upon a time..." have been introduced, primarily through film and TV. One of the most famous ones is "A long time ago, in a galaxy far, far away...," which opens the *Star Wars* films. Other well-known variations are "In a land of myth, and a time of magic...," which is the opening line of the TV series *Merlin*, and "In the time before time..." from the movie *Bionicle*. Whether it's the classic "Once upon a time..." or one of the modern variants, these opening phrases signal that it's time to sit back because in one form or another, a story will follow. This book is the story of the role that storytelling plays in product design: telling stories with our work is essential for the people and contexts we now design for.

The Art of Storytelling

The art of storytelling has always been a well-respected skill, and those who were great at telling stories were often key figures in their communities. Great storytellers have always been particularly gifted at communicating in a memorable and effective way to not only convey a sequence of events, but also evoke emotions from the listeners. This was key for ensuring that whatever the tale was about—be it war, deeds, or events—wasn't forgotten and could be passed on. Today technology and print have solved the challenge of how to pass on information, but great storytellers remain key figures just as much now as in the old days.

In 2014, Raconteur published an article and infographic called "The World's Greatest Storytellers." It was the result of a survey that asked almost five hundred authors, journalists, editors, students, and media and marketing professionals who they considered to be great storytellers. The top five included William Shakespeare, J.K. Rowling, Roald Dahl, Charles Dickens, and Stephen King, but there was great diversity in the responses and the reasons behind their respective choices. The suggestions spanned continents, genres, disciplines, and mediums. Some picked influential people in their own fields. Others chose family members who'd influenced their love for writing and history. Yet others based their choice on their own definition of "great." What united them all was that, in one way or another, their stories had hit home. [1]

This points to some of the key aspects of a good story. However we tell or create a story, all good stories capture the audience's attention and resonate with them. At times they're almost spellbinding and draw us in so deep that we can't help but keep on turning pages to find out what happens next. Other times a gripping tale of faith connects with

---

[1] "The World's Greatest Storytellers," Raconteur, December 17, 2014. *https://oreil.ly/K4_Gh*.

us emotionally and moves us to excitement, or even rage—"This can't be right," "How could they let that happen?" All instances of good storytelling involve a bit of magic. The narrator draws the audience into the world they're telling a story about and, to some extent, holds them captive by building up the anticipation around how the story will end.

Why I Wrote This Book

While many stories in the form of film, TV series, plays, novels, and books tend to come with happy endings, storytelling is increasingly moving outside its traditional form. A quick search on Google for "storytelling" and "business" returns around 122 million results, and there is no doubt that storytelling has become a buzzword in the business world over the last few years. However, as this book covers, it's not without good reason. Stories have the power to make us see things, to move us emotionally as well as into action, and to make us process and remember facts. Responding to and telling stories is part of what makes us human.

As a business tool, storytelling is also incredibly important. We've all likely sat through horrific presentations that make us want to leave the room. Most of us have been impressed by someone who, on the other side of the spectrum, has delivered a great presentation and captured the attention of the whole room. Today, being a good communicator, which essentially is being a good storyteller, is an increasingly sought-after skill. It impacts our ability to communicate with clients, team members, and internal stakeholders, whether we're having day-to-day conversations or writing and giving great presentations. Being a good storyteller is something that is reflected in the work that we produce. It's also increasingly important when we look for that new role—from our own personal branding to the way we present ourselves and our work as well as in any portfolio. When it comes to work, we can all benefit from knowing how to tell a good story.

So what is it that sets a great story apart from an average or even a good one? What is it that makes the likes of *Star Wars* and *The Shawshank Redemption* become box office hits, and the likes of *Harry Potter* become such page turners? And what is it that makes certain TED talks the most watched of all time?

The question of what makes for a good story is what started the journey of this book. It's a question I asked my dad when I was preparing for my first-ever storytelling talk. I wanted to find out if there was a magical recipe or formula to follow, besides a beginning, a middle, and an end. While I wasn't expecting a "Well, yes there is!" answer, my dad's response and the research it sparked turned out to be far more interesting than I could have imagined. Everywhere you look and everywhere you go, there is a story to tell. Exactly what makes for a great one and how this is connected to product design is the story I aim to tell you through this book.

As the world we're designing for is becoming increasingly complex and automated, it is shifting what's required of us as UX designers, product owners, strategists, founders, marketers, and more. Not only does our T-shaped form—a metaphor used to describe cross-skilled people who have expertise in at least one area (vertical bar) and are also knowledgeable in related areas (horizontal bar)—need to stretch a bit wider, but we also hold greater responsibility. In the words of product designer Wilson Miner:

> We're not just making pretty interfaces; we're in the process of building an environment where we'll spend most of our time, for the rest of our lives. We're the designers, we're the builders—what do we want that environment to feel like? What do we want to feel like? [2]

To build and create great product experiences that deliver to both the user and to the business, we need to master Walt Disney's ability to get the bigger picture right as well as the small details. We also need to account for a growing number of eventualities and moving parts that need to be defined and designed so that they all come together. Just like a good story. By turning to traditional storytelling, we can draw on tools, principles, and methods to help us—from character development (to help identify and define all the actors that play a part, including when and where), to narrative structure, main plots, and subplots for defining and designing for all eventualities. Happy and unhappy ones. And then, of course, there are set, scene, and shot design, which help

---

2 Wilson Miner, "When We Build," Build, Vimeo Video, Recorded at Build 2011, *https:// vimeo.com/34017777.*

us bring particular parts of a product or service experience to life. This all helps to ensure that the people who are or will be using our products and services will be the heroes of our stories, and who the experience is about.

How the Book Is Structured

The purpose of this book is not to come up with new tools and methods to replace those that we and our clients are used to working with, but instead to take methods, tools, and principles from traditional storytelling and use them to complement and enhance the tools we're already using. There are increasing overlaps between the various disciplines and professions involved in product design, with each team member influencing the project, product, and the experience of the same in different ways. Because the products and services we are working on are no longer limited to just being experienced on a screen but increasingly offline as well, we benefit from looking broader afield in our approach. This is where turning to traditional storytelling can provide insight, inspiration, and practical tools to help us think about and approach product design differently.

The book is divided into three parts. The first part provides background and context around storytelling theory, its relevance for product design, and what we need to consider for the current state of digital experiences and where we are heading. It's less practical and more theoretical and forms the foundation of the book. If you feel you have a good understanding of some or all of what this part covers, jump ahead to Part 2.

CHAPTER 1: WHY STORYTELLING MATTERS

In this chapter, we look at the role of stories throughout history as a means to pass on information and instill moral values, and how storytelling has been highly regarded as a profession. We also look at how the medium of storytelling has evolved as well as the role of storytelling in our day-to-day lives before ending with the role of storytelling today and for product design.

CHAPTER 2: THE ANATOMY OF A GREAT STORY

Here, we look at some of the theory behind great stories, including Aristotle's seven golden rules, the art of dramaturgy, Aristotle's three-act structure, and Freytag's pyramid. We also start looking at what product design can learn from dramaturgy before rounding off with five key lessons from various types of storytelling.

CHAPTER 3: STORYTELLING FOR PRODUCT DESIGN

In the third chapter, we start by looking at seven areas in which traditional storytelling is changing, from the shift to on-demand, to transmedia storytelling. Hereafter, we turn the focus to the changing landscape of product design and what that means for those involved.

In the second part of the book, we look explicitly at what we can learn from traditional storytelling and how to apply those lessons to product design. Since I am a user experience (UX) designer myself, each chapter in this part of the book covers a key aspect related to UX design and draws parallels to traditional storytelling principles, tools, and methods.

CHAPTER 4: THE EMOTIONAL ASPECT OF PRODUCT DESIGN

The key to a good story lies in the emotional connection that it evokes from its audience. Without that emotional connection, we don't care. This connection is also where the persuasive power of storytelling lies. In this chapter, we look at why emotion in design increasingly matters and what we can learn from the way traditional storytelling evokes emotions in readers, listeners, and audiences.

CHAPTER 5: DEFINING AND STRUCTURING EXPERIENCES WITH DRAMATURGY

Just as any good story needs a good structure, so does a carefully considered product or service. Applying dramaturgy to the products and services we work on is a simple yet effective tool to help analyze both how things are and how they should be. It helps us to be explicit about and to define the desired narrative of the product or service experience we're working on. This chapter shows you how.

CHAPTER 6: USING CHARACTER DEVELOPMENT IN PRODUCT DESIGN

Characters together with the plot form the key part of any good story. If you fail to make your characters believable, the story will fall flat. Make your main character—the protagonist—the hero and pay close attention to the development of all the other characters as well, and your story is more likely to hit home. In this chapter, we look at what we can learn from traditional storytelling when it comes to defining the people we're building our product or service for. We also see how storytelling helps identify and define all the other characters and actors that increasingly are a part of the product and service experiences that we define; for example, in the form of bots and VUIs.

CHAPTER 7: DEFINING THE SETTING AND CONTEXT OF YOUR PRODUCT STORY

Setting is one of the main elements in traditional storytelling. In this chapter, we explore what setting and context mean, the role they play in traditional storytelling, and how that translates into product design in terms of the environment and context of the product experience.

CHAPTER 8: STORYBOARDING FOR PRODUCT DESIGN

Storyboards are widely used in film and TV, and to some extent they're also used in product design. Here, we look at storyboarding and how to incorporate storyboards into the product design process.

CHAPTER 9: VISUALIZING THE SHAPE OF YOUR PRODUCT EXPERIENCE

Most of the world's stories follow one of a few well-known storylines. In this chapter, we look at what the shapes and structures of typical stories can teach us about product design. Mapping out the visual shape of the experience with our products and services can help us not only define and design better products, but also ensure we increase buy-in for our projects.

CHAPTER 10: APPLYING MAIN PLOTS AND SUBPLOTS TO USER JOURNEYS AND FLOWS

In traditional storytelling, more than one storyline often runs through and makes up the narrative. In this chapter, we look at the role that main plots and subplots have as a mechanism in traditional storytelling, as well as why and how main plots and subplots can be applied to product design.

CHAPTER 11: THEME AND STORY DEVELOPMENT IN PRODUCT DESIGN

In all good stories, things happen for a reason. Part of the glue that makes a story come together is its theme. In this chapter, we look at theme in relation to traditional storytelling as well as its role for product design. This is also where we study how to develop your story.

CHAPTER 12: CHOOSE-YOUR-OWN-ADVENTURE STORIES AND MODULAR DESIGN

In choose-your-own-adventure (CYOA) stories, the reader is an active participant making decisions about how the story should unfold. In this chapter, we look at the similarities this has with product design and what we can learn from CYOA when it comes to modular design.

CHAPTER 13: APPLYING SCENE STRUCTURE TO WIREFRAMES, DESIGNS, AND PROTOTYPES

Every chapter in a book and every episode in a TV show is a story in and of itself, and so are the pages and views in the products and services we design. In this chapter, we look at how to apply storytelling principles to help narrate the layout of pages and views across various devices and sizes, as well as make everything come together using the tools discussed in the previous chapters.

The third part includes the last chapter of the book and provides an introduction to the importance of telling and presenting your story.

CHAPTER 14: PRESENTING AND SHARING YOUR STORY

In the last chapter we look at the role of purposeful storytelling. We also look at and how we can use storytelling to inspire, ensure we get buy-in for our products and services, and as a way to identify and tell the right story behind data. Additionally, great storytellers know how to adapt their story to the audience. For us to have the desired impact in the workplace, we ought to adapt our story presentations to our audiences as well, from clients to team members and internal stakeholders. We'll discuss how to go about that as well as some key tips for both visual and verbal presentations.

Who Should Read This Book

I started writing this book with an intended audience of other UX designers and practitioners like myself. While this book will especially speak to UX designers, projects and products in this day and age are always the result of many people and disciplines coming together. All of us, regardless of whether we have "UX" anywhere in our job title, have an impact on the user experience of the products and services that we work on. As the book will make clear, everything is an experience, and the tools, methods, and theories that are covered are valuable for service designers, product owners, strategists, visual designers, developers, marketers, and startups. In fact, they are valuable for any type of experience, not just digital ones.

The book will be of particular interest to those with a few years of work experience, but it will still be a valuable read with useful tools for those who are more junior or simply new to digital. With the references to traditional storytelling and the latest developments in technology, the book will hopefully also be an enjoyable read for those who have an interest in the intersection of these two fields.

How to Use This Book

Though the chapters build on each other and ideally should be read in order, that's not how you need to read them; you can dip into the chapter that meets the needs of what you're working on or looking for at the moment.

Exercise

This element indicates an exercise. Exercises throughout the book put what you've just read in relation to the products and services that you work on or use on a regular basis. Use these exercises as check-in points or as a way to work through and define, check, or improve your product's experience.

Because no two projects are the same, this book won't offer a one-size-fits-all framework that you can follow from start to finish. Instead, the chapters cover some of the main steps that you usually find in a project and offer tools inspired by traditional storytelling that you can use as they are, or even better, adapt so they fit your specific project.

As a supplementary resource, I created a Storytelling in Design website at *storytellinguxdesign.com*. Here you can find case studies, examples, useful links, downloadable worksheets and templates, and more.

O'Reilly Online Learning

For almost 40 years, O'Reilly has provided technology and business training, knowledge, and insight to help companies succeed.

Our unique network of experts and innovators share their knowledge and expertise through books, articles, conferences, and our online learning platform. O'Reilly's online learning platform gives you on-demand access to live training courses, in-depth learning paths, interactive coding environments, and a vast collection of text and video from O'Reilly and 200+ other publishers. For more information, please visit *http://oreilly.com*.

How to Contact Us

Please address comments and questions concerning this book to the publisher:

> O'Reilly Media, Inc.
> 1005 Gravenstein Highway North
> Sebastopol, CA 95472
> 800-998-9938 (in the United States or Canada)
> 707-829-0515 (international or local)
> 707-829-0104 (fax)

We have a web page for this book, where we list errata, examples, and any additional information. You can access this page at *https://oreil.ly/storytelling-in-design*.

Email *bookquestions@oreilly.com* to comment or ask technical questions about this book.

For more information about our books, courses, conferences, and news, see our website at *http://www.oreilly.com*.

Find us on Facebook: *http://facebook.com/oreilly*

Follow us on Twitter: *http://twitter.com/oreillymedia*

Watch us on YouTube: *http://www.youtube.com/oreillymedia*

Acknowledgments

This book would not have existed were it not for my dad, who—ever since I was a little girl—inspired me to write. He also gave spark to the subject of this book and helped me see the connection between traditional storytelling and that of UX design.

A big thank you to everyone at O'Reilly and Nick Lombardi, who reached out to me and planted the idea of writing a book on the subject, something I at first brushed off with a *"Who me? Not a chance!"* Thank you, in particular, to my editor Angela Ruffino for believing in me and being patient. A big thank you also to Katherine Tozer, my production editor, Kim Cofer, my copyeditor, and Sharon Wilkey, my proofreader, who helped turn this into what you now hold in your hands. I'd also like to thank Jose Marzan, Jr. and the O'Reilly art department, whose drawings have really made this book come to life.

Because of various life events, this book took longer to complete than I'd envisioned. Without the support of my family and friends, and particularly my partner Dion (hereafter D), it wouldn't have been possible to make this book happen. From giving me the space and time to write, to the physical and mental support in various forms, from feeding me, listening to me, hugging me, and cheering me on, thank you. To my sister and her partner for lending us their Baby Björn, which immensely eased restructuring the book with a sleeping newborn.

To the first group of reviewers—Christian Manzella, Christian Desjardins, and Ellen DeVries—who took the time to read through the very early and not very good first-draft version and gave me their invaluable feedback, thank you. And to the second group—Ryan Harper, Christy Ennis Kloote, Frances Close, and Ellen Chisa—whose input helped me identify the final restructuring that was needed and provided invaluable input.

To everyone in the UX community who has helped me connect with people for case studies for the website, or spread the word about this book, be it through word of mouth or social media, thank you. Thanks to the organizers of SXSW Interactive, who had me do not just one but two "reading" sessions back in 2017, and to all of the conference attendees. And a big thank you to the organizers of the following conferences and meetups who have invited me to speak and run workshops, which both helped distill and put the tools and thoughts in this book into practice: UCD London (where I gave my first storytelling talk), Digital Pond, Design + Banter, UX Oxford, Digital Dumbo, Breaking Borders, Amuse, Bulgaria Web Summit, Funkas Tillgänglighetsdagar, UX London, Conversion Hotel, DXN Nottingham, SXSW, ConversionXL Live, Click Summit, UXLx, IIex Europe, CXL, Conversion World, NUX Camp, Conversion Elite, UX Insider, Digital Growth Unleashed, Agile Scotland, InOrbit, and Webbdagarna. Thank you to all of you who came to my talks and workshops and chatted with me afterward.

Last but not least, thanks to all of you who have bought this book and are now sitting with it in your hands, and to all of you who bought the early release and inquired about the book way back when it was originally supposed to be released. Thank you for your patience. I hope you like it and that it's been worth the wait. Now, once upon a time...

[1]

Why Storytelling Matters

How This All Started

EVERY GOOD STORY HAS a beginning, a middle, and an end, and the story of how I came to write this book follows that same structure. Back in 2013 I was invited to speak at a conference in London and proposed a talk about design and storytelling. My dad and I have had many chats about our respective lines of work, and during those talks I was often struck by the many similarities between writing books, as my dad does, and working on digital products and physical experiences, as I do. When it was time to put together my storytelling talk, I gave my dad a call to ask what he considered to be the key ingredients when he writes his books. It's said that "Good things come in threes," and my dad says that three elements should be present in a good story.

First of all, he said, a good story should *capture your imagination*. Just as the books dad would read to us when we were kids sent us to places we didn't know existed, a good story should be engaging and should get your imagination going by creating pictures in your mind. Brad Fulchuk, the co-creator of *American Horror Story*, says that "If you can imagine yourself in a situation, it's infinitely scarier."[1] Though you let your audience see some things, you leave the rest to the imagination. Whether it's a horror story or a fairy tale, one of the powers of a good story is its magic of making us see.

Second, according to my dad, is the *dynamic of the story*. Every single story has events and people that tie it together. The dynamic of the story is about how these develop, from the beginning to the end. Does the story start by looking back, or is it set in the present, or perhaps

---

1 Joe Berkowitz, "How To Tell Scary Stories," *Fast Company*, October 31, 2013, *https://oreil. ly/PY2Ng*.

the future? No matter how it begins, in a good story things happen for a reason. There are causal relationships, and a common thread or theme—or *röd tråd* as we call it in Swedish—runs through and connects them all. It is both the overarching theme of the story as well as the little details and how they make up the whole.

The last and third element of a good story, my dad identified, is the *element of surprise*. Fulchuk captures this perfectly:

> In general, there should be a basic idea of where the story is going, but not for every character. You don't know who's going to die and who's going to start becoming more important. Big picture-wise, there's a basic idea, but you need some surprises too. It's like driving from New York to LA: you know you're going to get to LA, but there's 10 different routes you could take.

This quote encapsulates all three elements of a good story. Just by reading it, you can imagine yourself sitting in a dark theater, watching the scary movie he is talking about. Your heart beats slightly faster than normal. The music is intense, and your hand is going back and forth between the popcorn bag and your mouth. You know something is about to happen and that someone most likely will die. Whether you like it or not, you start to imagine who it might be and how it might happen. You know the basic plot of the story, and as the story unfolds, the dynamic becomes clear. You start to identify the little details that shape the red thread. Piece by piece, your idea of how the story will unfold becomes stronger, but you don't want to know who will be killed, or who the killer is, at least not just yet.

As my dad and I continued talking about what makes a good story, I began to recognize the many parallels between what he does as an author and what I do as a UX designer. In our day-to-day jobs as UX designers, we need to capture the imagination and attention of the people we're working with and for, and the users we're designing for. Though we're not out to scare our users and customers, if they can imagine themselves using our products and services, and if they identify with the story we're telling them, then our products and services will be more successful.

Being able to capture the imagination is also key for creating empathy in the users for whom we're designing, as well as for getting buy-in from clients and internal stakeholders. This ability plays a role in everything from making them see what we see when it comes to the value we can offer and the vision we have, to the nitty-gritty of what we communicate verbally and "on paper."

As for the dynamic and that red thread, there needs to be a clear narrative and structure to what we're designing. Every piece of content and every feature should be there for a reason. As we'll look at in Chapter 11, "Theme and Story Development in Product Design," it should serve a purpose in asking the user to do something.

And last, with regard to the element of surprise, although that red thread and structure should run through everything, we shouldn't signpost every single call to action (CTA) or restrict the experience too much. Instead we should let the users find their way around. There's a great opportunity in including elements of surprise in the products and services that we work on, whether that's something that brings users back in and captures their attention as they scroll down a page, or something that turns a typically burdensome process like sign-up or checkout into a pleasant surprise.

These were just some of the thoughts that sprung to mind after the conversation with my dad. As I began to research traditional storytelling techniques, it became clear just how powerful of a tool storytelling really is. So many aspects of it—from the role that storytelling has, to the different ways to structure, tell, and bring a story to life—can be applied to various aspects of designing and working with digital products and experiences.

In this chapter we look at the role of storytelling throughout history, various storytelling mediums, and the role storytelling plays today. If you're familiar with the history of storytelling, feel free to jump to the end of this chapter, where I talk about storytelling today as well as its relevance to product design.

The Role of Stories Throughout History

When you look back through history, you can see that stories have always played an important part in our lives. In this section, we take a look at some of the roles of storytelling.

STORYTELLING AS A WAY TO CONNECT AND PASS ON INFORMATION

Long before the written word was invented in Mesopotamia around 3200 BC,[2] we'd tell stories about the moon and the stars, battles that'd been lost and won, and tales of the world out there that'd we'd not yet discovered. Telling stories was our way to pass along information across generations to make sure that history, facts, and customs like how to live off the land weren't lost. It was also a way for us to make sense of the world around us.

Storytelling helped us find a way to explain what we didn't understand, the things we feared, and that which we desired. Storytelling in various forms offered security in the explanations it provided. Stories helped make what we were going through more tangible and fostered and maintained a sense of community by connecting the past, the present, and the future. Through telling stories, we were able to give others a glimpse into what had happened and share our beliefs about the world we lived in.

STORYTELLING AS A WAY TO INSTILL MORAL VALUES

While storytelling in the early days was mainly used to explain and pass on information, *fables*—succinct fictional stories written in prose or verse that feature animals, plants, and mythical creatures that are given human qualities—are one example of how stories have been used throughout history to communicate moral values. Even to this day, *Aesop's Fables*, a collection of fables credited to the slave Aesop who lived in ancient Greece between 620 and 564 BCE, continue to teach us lessons about life. But fables have also been used for other purposes.

In medieval times, they were used as a way to make fun of and satirize tribal events without the risk of retribution, and in Ancient Greek and Roman times, fables formed the first of the *progymnasmata*–a training

---

2 Denise Schmandt-Besserat, "The Evolution of Writing," *Denise Schmandt-Besserat* (blog), *https://oreil.ly/a4adq*.

exercise focused on prose composition and public speaking. Students were asked to learn a variety of fables, expand upon them, make up their own, and then use them in persuasive arguments. This has a close connection to the role that storytelling can play today in design and the workplace overall, whether for delivering presentations, giving a talk, or simply presenting your work.

STORYTELLING AS A PROFESSION

Whether it's used for increasing sales or coming up with a best seller, mastering storytelling, in whichever form it takes, is a real art. During the Middle Ages, it was highly regarded, and being a storyteller was seen as one of the finest professions one could have. Troubadours, or bards, traveled from town to town and village to village and were in great demand as entertainers and educators. Storytellers from different tribes would even compete with one another to see who could come up with the most compelling and captivating tales to tell.

Just as students in ancient Greek and Roman times used fables to improve their prose composition and speaking skills, practicing the art of storytelling and presentation skills is something we see today in the globally run PechaKucha nights. In these events, presenters show 20 images, spending 20 seconds per image before it automatically moving to the next one. Now run in more than one thousand cities, PechaKucha was invented in 2003 by Astrid Klein and Mark Dytham of Klein Dytham architecture as a format for architects to show and share their work while not talking too much. Today it has expanded well beyond architects where anyone can present. Many companies run their own internal PechaKucha events to practice presentation skills in a fun and informal way that also brings the company or team together outside normal day-to-day responsibilities.

Though being a great storyteller doesn't take the same form as it did in the Middle Ages, the ability to present with impact or run a successful workshop with clients or internal stakeholders are skills that become ever more important the further up the career ladder you move. And these skills are closely related to being a good storyteller.

STORYTELLING AS AN EARLY FORM OF BRANDING

Storytelling has played a key role in fostering and maintaining a sense of community. It has also had a role in creating an identity that those in the inner circle could relate to and that outsiders would recognize, similar to how indigenous groups passed on customs and the prowess of their tribes.

Branding as we know it today started to take shape in the 1950s, when the images and characters that appeared on packages started to have personalities and backstories instead of just being decorative. The Marlboro Man is a good example. Clarence Hailey Long, an ordinary cowboy, became the face of the cigarettes and helped the Philip Morris cigarette company increase the sales of its cigarettes, originally aimed at women, by 300%.[3]

Today identity and values are key aspects of a brand. In *Tell to Win*, author and Hollywood producer Peter Guber says we're increasingly told that "without a compelling story, our product, idea, or personal brand is dead on arrival" and that "if you can't tell it, you can't sell it."[4] In a world so full of noise and competition, whatever your view on storytelling is, there's no denying that these quotes hold true. In the words of Linda Boff, CMO at General Electric, "Audiences are looking well beyond what you sell. They want to know who you are and what you stand for."[5] They want to be able to relate.

The Medium of Stories

Just as the role of storytelling has changed across the 200,000 years that human beings have been on this earth, how we've shared and told our stories has also evolved in a way that has shaped society.

---

3   Mustafa Kurtuldu, "Brand New: The History of Branding," *Design Today* (blog), November 29, 2012, *https://oreil.ly/1o-5B*.

4   Jonathan Gottschall, "Why Storytelling Is the Ultimate Weapon," *Fast Company*, May 2, 2012, *https://oreil.ly/wMbtW*.

5   Adam Fridman, "Fiction Isn't Just for Networks Anymore," *Inc.*, April 29, 2016, *https:// oreil.ly/v0ZJo*.

ORAL STORYTELLING

The earliest forms of storytelling were oral and combined gestures and expressions to communicate the narrative. It is believed that many oral stories were myths created to explain natural occurrences, from thunderstorms to solar eclipses, and that others were told as a way to express fears and beliefs as well as to share tales of one's heroism.

Oral storytelling would often take place with the audience seated in a circle, creating a close connection between the storyteller and people in the audience through the story they would share. Much of the power of the story would lie in the storyteller's ability to adapt the story to the needs of the audience and/or the location. Because each storyteller had a different personality, no single story would be the same. This still holds true to how we tend to tell stories today.[6]

ROCK ART

Other early forms of storytelling revolved around hunting practices and rituals and took the form of rock art. Rock art has played an important part in many ancient cultures.

The Aborigines in Australia used rock art not only as part of religious rituals, but also as a way to tell stories of now extinct megafauna such as Genyornis (a large flightless bird) and Thylacoleo (also called the marsupial lion). More recently, the rock art told of the arrivals of European ships. All of this helped bring meaning to various aspects of human existence.

While the Aborigines often told their stories through a combination of oral narrative, gestures, singing, dancing, and music, the pictures they painted on the stone walls were there to help the narrator remember the story. Similarly, the images we use in presentations today help us remember the points we are trying to get across.

PORTABLE MATERIALS

In addition to rock art, people used carvings, sand, and leaves to tell stories before developing a way to write. These materials allowed us to leave our stories behind and share them with others. As the written

---

6 Linda Crampton, "Oral Storytelling, Ancient Myths, and a Narrative Poem," *Owlcation*, July 2, 2019, *https://oreil.ly/f4_C5*.

word began to evolve around 3200 BC, stories could be transported and shared over larger geographical areas. We used whatever we had on hand and started painting and carving out our stories in wood, bamboo, leather, clay tablets, ivory, skins, bones, textiles, and more.

However, despite having a way to document our stories, oral storytelling retained an important role and ensured that the tales we were telling could travel even further and live on. *Aesop's Fables* is a good example of this tradition. His fables were kept alive through oral storytelling and written down only three hundred years after his death from the sixth century BC.[7]

The importance of stories being portable is something we've observed with the rise of the internet. Smartphones especially enable us to read, listen to, and watch stories almost no matter where we are.

MOVABLE TYPE AND THE PRINTING PRESS

Though there have been ways to reproduce a body of text with reusable characters since 3000 BC (through the punches used to make coins in ancient Sumer and later on stamps), the first known movable type system for printing paper books was made of porcelain and invented in China in 1040. The world's oldest extant book printed with metal movable type was *Jikji*, a Korean Buddhist document, during the Goryeo dynasty in 1377.

Around 1440, the printing press was invented by Johannes Gutenberg. The German inventor created a complete system that allowed for both rapid and precise creation of metal movable type. This system allowed prints to be made in large quantities, and over the next several decades, the printing press spread from a single print shop in Mainz, Germany, to around 270 cities across Europe. By 1500, it's believed that more than 20 million volumes had been printed. During the 16th century, the output increased tenfold. This gave birth to a completely new industry that took its name after the enterprise of printing itself, the press. Gutenberg's system was also the birth of the printed book, which is

---

7 "A Very Brief History Of Storytelling," Big Fish Presentations, February 28, 2012, *https:// oreil.ly/UQXKo*.

believed to have been in universal use from around 1480, and the rise of best-selling authors. This has some parallels to the growth of blogs and professional bloggers today.

THE RISE OF MASS COMMUNICATION

The introduction of mechanical movable type meant that the need for oral storytellers almost disappeared. This invention also led to an era of mass communication that altered society in Renaissance Europe. Think about how social media enabled movements like #MeToo (which encouraged women to speak out publicly about their experiences with sexual harassment and assault), to shake up not only the music and film industries, but also politics and academia. Similarly, the printing press enabled mass-produced information to circulate relatively unrestricted, and threatened the power of both political and religious authorities.

The printing press also made possible a rapid growth in literacy, which made learning and education something that no longer was limited to the elites, but instead bolstered an emerging middle class. The printing press also gave rise to a community of scientists who circulated their discoveries through scholarly journals. Authorship became both profitable and more important. Previously, authorship had not mattered as much; a copy of Aristotle's work made in Paris, for example, would be different from a copy made somewhere else. But now, all of a sudden, it was important who had said or written what and when. As a result the rule "One author, one work (title), one piece of information" was established.

In the 19th century, the hand-operated Gutenberg press was replaced with steam-operated rotary presses. Printing reached an industrial scale, allowing millions of copies of a page to be printed in one day. The mass production of printed works flourished and dominated the way we consumed and shared information, until the radio was introduced to our homes in 1910. Each medium of mass technology that was subsequently introduced, including the television and the internet, altered the way we told and experienced stories, as well as the role that stories played in our lives. While storytelling had previously been much more about passing on information and explaining the world around us, the introduction of the printing press, radio, and later TV and the internet, increasingly changed the focus to entertainment.

The Role of Personal Storytelling in Day-to-Day Lives

Over time, the way we tell stories and the role they play in our lives have changed. But what hasn't changed is the need for, and the art of, storytelling itself. Human beings are storytelling creatures by nature. In fact, storytelling is one of the many things that define us.

Every day we create stories of our own, from daydreams to actual dreams at night. Though they are easy to brush off as just "stuff," we can learn from them and even and draw from them in our professional life as well.

DREAMS

Dreams have always formed a big part of our personal day-to-day storytelling that we share with family, friends, and colleagues. The earliest record of documented dreams stems from Mesopotamia approximately five thousand years ago, when dreams were recorded on clay tablets so they could be interpreted.[8] Many people today have positive associations with dreams, from retelling the "you-wouldn't-believe-what-I-dreamt-last-night" dreams to fascinations around what it all might mean.

Back in the Middle Ages, however, dreams were seen as evil, with Martin Luther (among others) believing that dreams were the work of the devil. He wasn't the first to believe that dreams were messages from "someone" else. In ancient Greece and Rome, people believed that dreams were messages from deities and that they predicted the future. This led to some cultures practicing dream incubation in order to cultivate dreams that would reveal prophecies.

While there have been many theories and speculations about why we dream, many scientists now endorse the Freudian theory of dreams, which stipulates that they reveal hidden desires and emotions. Another well-regarded and prominent theory is that although some dreams are simply random creations by our brain's activity, in general dreams assist in problem-solving and memory formation.

---

8   Kristine Bruun-Andersen, "7 Reasons Why You Should Write Down Your Dreams" *Odyssey*, May 20, 2015, *https://oreil.ly/nSQzE*.

DAYDREAMS

For many years, *daydreaming* was associated with laziness and seen as something that could even be dangerous. This view primarily came into play when the work we did moved into assembly lines and was dictated by the motions of the tools that we were using. These tools left little room for zoning out, and the short-term detachment from the immediate surrounding that daydreaming inherently involves.

Today daydreaming is widely accepted as a way for the mind to ease boredom and consolidate learning. In fact, daydreaming is the default state of the mind, and we spend about half of our waking hours in fantasy land, the equivalent of a third of our lives. Whenever the mind isn't busy with something important or when it gets bored, it wanders, and this happens about two thousand times a day, lasting on average 14 seconds.[9]

For many, daydreams involve happy associations, hopes, and ambitions of things coming to pass. It's now commonly acknowledged that rather than being a sign of laziness, daydreaming can lead to constructive results, including the development of new ideas, both creatively and scientifically. In this sense, daydreaming is not too different from visualizations that are used to create mental images of what we want to happen or feel in real life.

VISUALIZATIONS

Visualizations are another form of powerful day-to-day story creation that is used by many professional athletes as part of their training process before big competitions and events. By going through and narrating in their minds how they would like an event to unfold or feel, the athlete is doing a mental rehearsal that is scientifically proven to cultivate a competitive edge and increase mental awareness as well as a heightened sense of well-being and confidence. Research has found that this mental rehearsal has positive effects on both mental and physical reactions, and it is as powerful in business as it is in sports. Through

---

9 Jonathan Gottschall, "The Science Of Storytelling," *Fast Company*, October 16, 2013, https://oreil.ly/yidOi.

visualizations that involve the visual, kinetic, or auditory senses, we step right into the story we're creating, which also positions us better for passing on and communicating our desired outcomes to others.[10]

THE POWER OF PERSONAL STORYTELLING

Dreams, daydreams, and visualizations all help us to put things into context, to process what we've experienced and learned, and to test ideas that are new or that we may fear. Just as the books dad would read to us took us to new places in our imaginations, the stories we create consciously and subconsciously in our minds take us on journeys too. They create emotional responses in our minds and bodies by making us see and feel things, not just in the moment, but for hours to come.

Igniting an emotional connection and sparking the imagination are both key desired outcomes for all great stories and storytellers. Whether we keep our dreams, daydreams, and visualizations to ourselves or retell them to friends, family, or colleagues, they are tools that help us process and learn. They also engage our imaginations and can help us practice retelling our experiences, which is something we can bring with us into our work.

Exercise: The Role of Personal Storytelling in Day-to-Day Lives

Think about the roles dreams, daydreams, and visualizations have for you:

- What role do dreams play for you personally? For example: Are they something you often share? Do you keep a diary of them? Or find that they often teach or tell you something? If you don't, how do you think doing so could benefit you?

- What role does daydreaming play for you? For example: Is it something you use actively as a way to create motivation, or perhaps simply to pass time or cope?

- What role does visualization play for you personally? For example: Have you ever practiced visualizations in any form? What was your experience? If you haven't tried, what area of your life—work and/or personal—could you see it being beneficial for?

---

10 Elizabeth Quinn, "Visualization Techniques for Athletes," *Verywell Fit*, September 17, 2019, *https://oreil.ly/nqNCE*.

Storytelling Today

In addition to the dreams we create ourselves, we're surrounded by stories created by others—from films and series that we watch on TV and on demand, to both shorter and longer narratives in the form of text, visuals, and audio. While stories back in the day traditionally were something we would observe or passively listen to, today's stories invite active participants.

We see it in traditional storytelling like films that have introduced interactivity. In the interactive film *Black Mirror: Bandersnatch*, for example, viewers make decisions for the main character (Figure 1-1).[11] We also see it in product or services campaigns that ask users to contribute with their own stories in the form of content, and that provide interactive mediums and platforms for the user or audience to influence the next turn of events in the narrative. With virtual reality (VR) and augmented reality (AR) still far from being mainstream, but gaining traction, we're at a point where we'll soon immerse ourselves right into the world of the stories that are being created.

THOMPSON TWINS   NOW 2

FIGURE 1-1

Screenshot from the film *Black Mirror: Bandersnatch* depicting one of the decisions the viewer has to make for the main character

---

11 Watch the interactive film *Black Mirror: Bandersnatch* on Netflix (*https://oreil.ly/mpnTt*).

Our exposure to storytelling isn't happening just through the more traditional platforms of TV screens, books, and magazines, however. We're increasingly seeing the art of storytelling being picked up by politicians on TV, CEOs and leaders in their speeches, and even in the restaurants, exhibitions, and open spaces we visit. We're living in a world that's increasingly being curated to help cut through the noise and wealth of information out there so that we can find what we're after more easily.

If you look at it from the seller's point of view, there's an increased need for a way to stand out from the competition. Whether it's a restaurant owner, an exhibition organizer, a CEO, or a store, they are all looking for interesting angles and different ways to get their story and their product and service offering across.

This shift toward curated experiences is not just something that is driven by brands. It's also reflected in consumer behavior and what we call the *experience economy*, people spending less money on clothes and food and more on holidays, cars, entertainment, and eating out.[12] This change in consumer spending behavior is partly what is driving the rise of curated experiences and content marketing and strategy overall. And it's all with good reason. Although immersive experiences are nothing new (nor content marketing or storytelling overall, for that matter), the need to excel at connecting with our audience has increased. This is where the importance of mastering the art of storytelling comes in, whether it's for us as individuals, as leaders, startup founders, brands, or as designers.

Exercise: Storytelling Today

What are the best innovative storytelling examples you've come across?

- In traditional storytelling? For example, a film, book, TV series or game.
- In relation to a product or service? For example, a campaign, or a website or app in the way it was executed or in the content it included.

---

12 Katie Allen and Sarah Butler, "The Way We Shop Now," *The Guardian*, May 6, 2016, *https://oreil.ly/5y8wP*.

Stories as a Persuasion Tool

For a long time, we were able to only speculate about the persuasive effect of stories. But over the last several decades, people have studied how stories in their various forms affect the human mind and how we process information.

These studies have revealed that when we read dry, factual arguments, we read with our guard up. In other words, we're skeptical and critical. When we're presented with a story, on the other hand, something happens to us. We lower our guard and are moved emotionally, and this somehow seems to leave us defenseless. In a Fast Company article from February 2012 titled "Why Storytelling Is The Ultimate Weapon,"[13] Jonathan Gottshall, the author of *The Storytelling Animal* writes:

> Results repeatedly show that our attitudes, fears, hopes, and values are strongly influenced by story. In fact, fiction seems to be more effective at changing beliefs than writing that is specifically designed to persuade through argument and evidence.

It's not surprising, then, that brands and organizations are increasingly paying attention to the importance of storytelling in relation to connecting and engaging with their customers. But how much truth is there, really, to the persuasive effects of stories? And to what extent can we use it in design?

STORIES AS A MEANS TO MOVE PEOPLE TO ACTION

In addition to serving as a communication tool and entertainment, stories have been used throughout history, from tribe wars to activists, to move people into action. Storytelling been used as a way to get behind a cause and to drive people forward, whether it's to move past enemy lines, fight for a cause, or go on a pilgrimage.

Peter Guber talks of purposeful stories and how they are essential for persuading others to support a vision or a cause. He defines a purposeful story as "a story you tell with a specific purpose in mind," and draws the parallel that it can be as simple as the laughter you want at the end

---

13 Gottschall, "Why Storytelling Is The Ultimate Weapon."

of a joke you tell.[14] Whether it's a laugh we're after or something else, every single story we tell, is driven by our a desire for an action and/or a response from the person or people on the other side. What many of us fail to do is be clear about what this action is, or even one step before that, to stop and identify the purpose of our story and determine how to best tell it to get the action or response we want.

PURPOSEFUL STORIES

While in any good story there tends to be a promise of something to come, inherent in purposeful stories is a goal that the story is leading up to and that the storyteller is trying to get people behind. Whatever purpose we might have with the story we tell, actions form a big part of how we tell that story, from the subtle actions that we ourselves take in how we tell and communicate our story, to the actions we ask the person on the receiving end to take.

Actions are particularly important when we talk about purposeful and persuasive stories in relation to design and business. Purposeful stories help us get internal team members, stakeholders, and clients to buy into UX, for example, and the other solutions we're proposing. These stories also play a key part in how we design experiences and the actual calls to action that we include and direct users to in our products, from the primary one to the secondary and supporting ones. These CTAs need to resonate and correspond to what matters to users, not just in terms of what they need and where they are in their journey and their own story, but also in how the language used on the CTA reflects that. Only when all these requirements have been met will the story be something that moves the user into action.

---

14 Mike Hofman, "Peter Guber on the Power of Effective Communicators," *Inc.*, March 1, 2011, *https://oreil.ly/jxvOC.*

Exercise: Stories as a Persuasion Tool

Knowing that purposeful stories provide a valuable way to move people into action, think about examples in the following three areas:

- What are some of the most purposeful forms of storytelling you have come across?
- How do you see purposeful storytelling benefiting you, personally?
- How do you see purposeful storytelling benefiting your product or service?

The Role of Storytelling in Product Design

A large part of what we do day to day at work is tell stories, whether we're aware of it or not. We might use a metaphor to explain something, for example, or talk about the experiences we're designing through the eyes of the persona or user journeys we've defined. As UX designers, we're used to using storytelling in various forms for defining and designing our work. At times our storytelling is more explicit, and other times it's something we're not really aware of but just do without giving it too much thought.

As the complexities of what we design for are increasing and users' interactions move beyond the paradigm of the screen, tangible and measurable benefits can be gained by applying storytelling principles in a more active and explicit way, from the start to the finish of a project. The rest of the book will cover this topic in more depth.

STORYTELLING AS A TOOL FOR THE PRODUCT DESIGN PROCESS

The most obvious way that storytelling can help us is in ensuring that we're designing a good experience narrative for our products and services. Learning from the traditional methods that are used when writing novels, plays, and scripts for TV and film can also offer many more tangible benefits to the process of a project. These benefits range from providing frameworks and tools that help us understand how things are and how they should be, to ensuring that we think through experiences holistically, addressing the increased challenges that we're facing with a growing number of devices, touch points (ways consumers interact with a business, e.g., via website, app, or other form of communication), and input methods, and, importantly, thinking through who we're designing for.

STORYTELLING AS A TOOL FOR GETTING BUY-IN

In addition to being a great tool for helping us understand, define, and design products and services, storytelling is a really effective tool for getting buy-in to user-centered design, agile ways of working, and our proposed solutions. As UX designers, strategists, marketers, and product owners, we're used to defining who our target audience is. To varying degrees, we develop personas, pen portraits, user journeys, flows, and other deliverables to help us, the rest of the team, and key stakeholders keep the users in mind. We define, among other things, what matters to them (needs), what they want to accomplish (goals), what may worry them (concerns), and any obstacles (barriers and risks) in the experience.

However, we often forget to apply these same principles and tools to the people we work with and, more importantly, the people we report to and present our work to. Whether it's a client or an internal stakeholder, the higher up the food chain you go, the more time-poor the person in question is and the more critical it will be to understand what really matters to them. Failing to do so will result in misalignments and miscommunication, and in really severe cases it can damage collaboration and relationships, be they internal or external. "Death by PowerPoint" is a(n almost) real thing, and more often than not we overdeliver in actual work deliverables, but underdeliver in the value that the work brings to our clients, and at times users. This is where the importance of storytelling comes in and where simple frameworks and principles can help ensure that you're telling a clear and well-structured story that is relevant and tailored to your audience.

STORYTELLING AS A WAY TO UNDERSTAND
THE PEOPLE WE DESIGN FOR

As for the customer on the other end, whether the user is just finding out about your product or service, or has been a loyal customer for a while, each and every user is different. Though users' journeys can be similar, each journey is also different, no matter how much we'd like to plan out the user's journey from A to B to C and so forth.

When you look at these journeys and break down what a user may think, feel, need, and worry about, and how they may have ended up right there, and where they may go next, then each and every journey also becomes a story. It's a story that the user is right in the middle of and a story that we, no matter how trite it might sound, are trying to control.

In order to achieve that control and to make sure that the user cares about the product story we're telling, we need to ensure that the two are compatible. Turning to traditional storytelling can help ensure that we both understand the people we're designing for better, and align the product story we're telling with the user's own story.

Exercise: The Role of Storytelling in Product Design

With the preceding areas in mind, think about your, your team's, or your company's use of storytelling:

- In what ways are you, your team, or company currently using storytelling?

    - In the product design process?

    - For getting buy-in?

    - For understanding the people you design for?

- In what areas could you, your team, or company improve how you use storytelling?

    - In the product design process?

    - For getting buy-in?

    - For understanding the people you design for?

Summary

Looking through the history of storytelling, we can see that the role and value that stories have had in the past remain relevant today. In the product design process, one of the key roles, no matter whether it's used in the design process, for buy-in, or for presenting, is for us to use storytelling in a purposeful way, focusing on an action or outcome. This isn't, however, about using storytelling as a marketing tool. It's about how we can better connect with the people on the other end.

Stories have a persuasive effect on us because they connect with us emotionally. They may tap into something that's already there, like an interest, passion, or subject that matters to us; or the story itself may convince us of something. Either way, the key to the persuasive effect lies in the connection the story and storyteller make with the person on the other side—just as oral storytellers always have done.

In traditional storytelling, the author has control over each turn of events. But when it comes to our users and customers' experiences today, we have very little control of how they get there and where they'll go next. That said, even if we can't completely dictate these parameters, it doesn't mean that we should leave them to chance. The more complex the experiences we work on become with regard to multiple entry and exit points and touch points overall, and the more sophisticated technology becomes, the more offline and online will connect. As much as we talk about digital products and experiences, nothing is purely digital anymore. Everything is connected. With the increased implementation of artificial intelligence (AI) and machine learning into products and services, the more curated our world will get. Therefore, it becomes even more important that we create products and services that not only resonate with and work for our individual users and customers, but also for the business. This is where learning from traditional storytelling comes in.

[2]

The Anatomy of a Great Story

The Architect Analogy of Explaining UX

THE FIRST BLOG POST I wrote and published was "An Information Architect vs. a Normal Architect."[1] It's from 2010. In it, I explain what I do for a living by drawing parallels between planning out a house and planning out online experiences and strategies. Ever since I was a little girl back in southern Sweden, I've been fond of analogies and metaphors that can capture the imagination and make you see something, whether it's actually there in front of you physically, or is just a mental image in your head.

Creating stories has always been my way of articulating and connecting things, from aspirations to drawing parallels between what's going on in my life and the people and experiences I encounter. I hold a love for piecing things together, and I've often talked about how being a UX designer is a bit like being a spider. Not in the sense of a creature that kills its prey and eats it, but one that carefully spins its intricate web, makes everything come together, and has an overview of everything that is going on—how it's all connected and how a change over on one end will affect everything else.

The spider analogy might not be that common. But the analogy between information architecture, or UX design, and building a house is, and I am in no way the first to come up with it. That said, it's been the way I've responded to and later preempted the blank stare that usually comes when I tell people that I'm a UX designer. Though the house analogy often leads to some follow-up questions about what I actually spend my time doing, the one thing I love about UX design is that there

---

1 Read my first ever blog post over on *https://oreil.ly/RzCgF*.

are so many parallels we can draw to our day-to-day lives, and to other professions. We can easily adapt our explanations of UX design based on who we're talking to. It's also an incredibly fascinating field, as there are so many other disciplines that we can learn and draw from, such as writing books like my dad, being an architect, or a landscape architect like my brother Johan, or an actor like my partner D.

We all work with experiences in different ways, but each of us is a storyteller dealing with how the stories we're working with will take shape and be acted out. Whether it's my dad putting it down in words, my partner acting out the script he's been given, my brother planning out a physical space, or me defining what the story means in the form of an online and offline experience, each of us works with character development, the actual narrative, and where it will all lead to. For my dad it's about structuring a story from the first page to the last. For D, it's about the first part of his performance—a line, a movement, or a gesture—to the last. For my brother, it's about the physical experience and the role it will play in people's lives, and for me it's about where it all begins and the actions I want the user to (be able to) take throughout and at the end.

In each of our professions, we're working with a promise of what's to come. In one way or another we want to inspire the people on the other side, whether they are the readers of dad's books, D's audience, the people who will visit the spaces my brother designs, or the users who will use the product experiences I've worked on. My dad and I, in particular, are responsible for putting all the little pieces together and planning out, to lesser or greater detail, where the story begins and where it will end. At times we create simpler, more linear stories and journeys. Other times they jump back and forth between this, that, and the other. The process may seem chaotic or arbitrary, but it's all choreographed, from the high-level picture it paints to the little details that make all the difference to the story as a whole.

It's dad's fascination with and passion for making all the pieces come together when he writes books and the similarities this has with the work of a UX designer that first sparked the idea for the talk that later became this book. Just as there are tried and tested principles, tools, and processes for delivering great work and projects in UX and product design, there's more to writing a good story than just putting pen to paper. In this chapter, we'll look at what makes a great story, including how to structure it, and the elements it should contain, starting with Aristotle's seven golden rules of storytelling.

Aristotle's Seven Golden Rules of Storytelling

Aristotle was the first to point out the interrelation between the way we tell stories and the raw human experience of the same. Back in 300 BC, he wrote a work called *Poetics* that examines the relationships between character, action, and speech, and the reactions a play evokes in the audience. Through his work, he concludes that these seven golden rules of great storytelling exist:

1. *Plot*

   The arrangement of the incidents (actions) that take place

2. *Character*

   The moral or ethical character of the play

3. *Theme/thought/idea*

   The reasoning that explains the characters or story background

4. *Diction/speech*

   The conversation between the characters but also the narrator

5. *Song/chorus*

   The chorus and sound that supports the story

6. *Decor*

   The design of the place in which the story takes place

7. *Spectacle*

   Something that makes a real impact on the listener and that they'll remember

Even though reading Aristotle's *Poetic* won't give you a Buzzfeed-style how-to guide to writing a great story, many interpretations of his work have made the seven golden rules easier to understand. Based on the industry they're applied to, the seven golden rules have been given slightly different names. Table 2-1 gives two examples of how the names of the seven rules have been adapted to be more appropriate for the subject in question.

TABLE 2-1. Aristotle's seven rules adapted to the film and UX industry (source: Jeroen Vaan Geel[2,3])

ORIGINAL	FILM INTERPRETATION	UX INTERPRETATION
1. Plot	Plot	Plot
2. Character	Character *or* stars	Character
3. Theme/thought/idea	Idea	Theme
4. Speech	Dialogue	Diction
5. Chorus	Song/music	Melody
6. Decor	Production design/art direction	Decor
7. Spectacle	Special effects	Spectacle

While Aristotle's principles were aimed at Greek theater, they remain relevant to this day and are even considered essential for writing good film screenplays. Though Aristotle considered plot to be the most important element, above character, most screenwriters today would argue that plot and character are two sides of the same coin.[4]

Throughout this book, we'll come back to Aristotle's seven golden rules of storytelling in reference to product and UX design. Before that, however, we'll take a look at what else should be present in a good story.

The Three Parts to a Story

In addition to the seven golden rules of storytelling, Aristotle discusses the whole of a story and defines it as "that which has a beginning, a middle, and an end." He further goes on to define a beginning, a middle, and an end as follows:

> A beginning is that which does not itself follow anything by causal necessity, but after which something naturally is or comes to be...An end, on the contrary, is that which itself naturally follows some other thing, either by necessity, or as a rule, but has nothing following it...A middle is that which follows something as some other thing follows it.

---

2 From notes by Jalal Jonroy used while coaching graduates for their final thesis films at Film & Television: Tisch School of the Arts at New York University, *https://oreil.ly/sHFiU*.

3 Read the full Johnny Holland interpretation on *https://oreil.ly/_nxiG*.

4 "Character-Driven Vs. Plot Driven: Which is Best," NY Book Editors (blog), *https://oreil.ly/ZD5JU*.

His overall conclusion is that "a well-constructed plot, therefore, must neither begin nor end at haphazard, but conform to these principles," meaning that the events should follow each other by probability and have a causal chain. Jean-Luc Godard, a French writer/director and one of the pioneers of the French Nouvelle Vague argues, "A film should have a beginning, a middle and an ending, but not necessarily in that order!"[5] As we'll cover later in this chapter and throughout the book, when it comes to storytelling for digital products that have to work across multiple devices and touch points, elements aren't necessarily linear, but the three parts still hold true.

Though Aristotle never said that there should be three acts in a drama, the three parts—a beginning, a middle, and an end—have given rise to the three-act structure used in much of traditional storytelling.

The Art of Dramaturgy

The process of applying structure to a story is called *dramaturgy*. Merriam-Webster defines it as "the art or technique of dramatic composition and theatrical representation." In its broader definition, dramaturgy deals with how to shape a story into a form that can be acted by giving the work a structure.

Dramaturgy was invented by Gotthold Ephraim Lessing in the 18th century and is a practice-based as well as practice-led discipline that looks at the context of the play in a comprehensive way. This context can include anything from the environment (physical, social, economic, and political) in which the action takes place, to the psychological underpinnings of the characters, to how the play is written (structure, rhythm, flow, and choice of words).

The person who is the expert on this is called the *dramaturg*, or *production dramaturg* in the United States. This person is often involved throughout the many phases of a production, influencing casting and providing input on the in-progress state of the play in order to help shape the performance and story in the right direction by working with the director and the cast.

---

5 For more Jean-Luc Goddard quotes, see IMDb (*https://oreil.ly/9u8xu*).

The overseeing role of the dramaturg is not too different from that of a *lead*. The responsibilities of a lead can vary between organizations. When I worked at the digital agency Dare, the *experience leads* to looked after a client account from a UX point of view, by ensuring consistency across projects and providing a clear understanding of user and business needs among all team members. Experience leads were also responsible for understanding the bigger picture, in terms of where a specific project would sit, so that all things related to the user experience and the business side were considered. Those of us who were experience leads were part of resourcing, most UX, design, and technical reviews, and worked closely with those respective leads to make sure everything came together.

In addition to the similarities between the role of a dramaturg and a lead, the art of dramaturgy is something that greatly benefits product design, as it's focused on giving the work a structure. Two of the most famous works of dramatic theory are Aristotle's three-act structure and Freytag's pyramid.

ARISTOTLE'S THREE-ACT STRUCTURE

Aristotle's three-act structure consists of a beginning, where the plot is set up; a middle, where the plot reaches its climax; and an end, where the plot is resolved. To this day, the three-act structure is a model used in screenwriting, divide the narrative into three parts.

The parts, or *acts*, are connected by two *plot points*—key events that spin the story in a new direction. The first plot point occurs at the end of Act 1 and the second one at the end of Act 2, as seen in Figure 2-1.

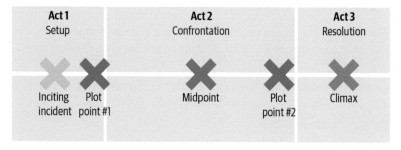

FIGURE 2-1
The three-act structure

Act 1

The first act, the *setup*, is usually used for exposition. Act 1 the main characters, their relationships, and the world they live in are developed. A bit later in the first act, the *inciting incident* occurs: the main character, also known as the *protagonist*, is confronted with something to solve, leading to a more dramatic situation known as the *turning point*. The first plot point signals the end of the first act and is where the dramatic question is asked—for example, will they live happily ever after—ensuring that life will never be the same for the protagonist.

Act 2

In the second act, the *confrontation*, or rising action, the protagonist attempts to solve the problem initiated by the first turning point. In this act, the protagonist often lands in a worse situation than before due to not yet having the skills required, or not knowing how to deal with the antagonism with which they are confronted.

The second act is where the character development, or the *character arc*, takes place. The protagonist not only has to learn new skills, but also come to a higher awareness of who they are as a person and what they are capable of doing, which often in turn changes who they are. More often than not, this challenge requires the help of a mentor or co-protagonist.

Act 3

In the third act, the *resolution*, the main story and all the substories come together in the *climax*—the most intense scene or sequence, where the dramatic question is answered. Here, we find out whether the boy and the girl will live happily ever after, as well as where the protagonist and the other characters are often left with a new sense of self.[6]

FREYTAG'S PYRAMID AND CRITICISM OF THE THREE-ACT STRUCTURE

There is some criticism of the traditional three-act structure, including that it's too focused on plot points rather than character, and that it was made for theater. As an extension of that, the three acts are arbitrary

---

6 "How to Write a Novel Using the Three Act Structure," Reedsy (blog), June 15, 2018, https://oreil.ly/KOGoQ.

and don't, for example, fit with commercial breaks for TV series and films. As we'll look at in Chapter 5, "Defining and Structuring Experiences with Dramaturgy," there are also a number of interpretations and further work done on the acts and their plot points. One of the most important alternatives is the work of Gustav Freytag (Figure 2-2). In the late 19th century, he published *The Technique of the Drama*, which is considered the blueprint for the first Hollywood screenwriting manual. Contrary to Aristotle's three acts, Freytag saw five parts to a story—the exposition, the rising action, the climax, the falling action, and the denouement (also known as the resolution).

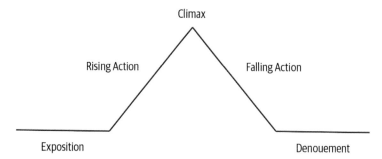

FIGURE 2-2
Freytag's pyramid

Exposition

This part of the story introduces important background information, including the setting, the characters' backstories, and events that have taken place before the main plot. This information can be conveyed through background details, flashbacks, the narrator telling a backstory, or through dialogue or the characters' thoughts.

Rising action

During the rising action, a series of events take place that build toward the point of greatest interest—the climax. These events begin immediately after the exposition and are often the most important part of the story because the entire plot depends on them.

Climax

The climax is the turning point in the story that changes the fate of the protagonist. Here the plot begins to unfold in favor of the protagonist or the antagonist, and the protagonist is often required to draw on hidden strengths.

Falling action

During the falling action, the conflict between the protagonist and the antagonist unravels, and the protagonist either wins or loses.

Denouement

Similarly to how the rising action builds up to the climax, in the denouement the final events take place, from the falling action to the ending scene. The conflict is resolved, and a sense of normality is created for the characters as the complexities of the plot are "untied."

What Dramaturgy Teaches Us About Product Design

What both Aristotle's three-act structure and Freytag's pyramid teach us is that there are certain acts to a story: it begins, something happens, and then some, and then it ends. When it comes to product design, we're often too focused on the details and forget that the overall narrative structure needs to be defined. As Aristotle pointed out, the way we tell a story has an impact on the raw human experience of the same. The way we structure the experiences of the products and services we work on will shape what the user on the other end thinks, feels, and does.

The Circular Nature of Digital Product Experiences

Although Aristotle's seven principles for good storytelling, the three-act structure, and Freytag's five acts, were meant for linear and finite stories, most of our experiences online are interlinked and have no universal beginning or end. In fact, when it comes to product design, applying storytelling principles is a matter of circular narratives: each circle links up with other circles, forming a chain of substories, some independent and some more closely linked. This applies both to the various parts of an experience as well as to the overall process in which each part—be it strategy, UX design, visual design, or development—overlaps and depends on the others as well as their own unique area of work.

As for how the parts of a product experience make up a chain of substories, just think of the journey a user might take in making a purchase. This type of end-to-end experience often consists of multiple smaller experience circles that are linked. It may start with the user spotting a product on social media, clicking the link, and ending up on the blog of the influencer whose post they'd seen the product in. As users warm more to the product, they enter a more active research phase: they visit the website where the product is sold, and potentially go off to look for the best price on other websites or see how it compares to competitor products, or both. The higher the price point, and depending on the type of product, the research (and eventually the consideration phase, where options are narrowed down), may be longer. This phase also may involve more touch points, including offline ones, such as speaking to friends and family and/or visiting a physical store before going back online again. The user might make a final check of the original blog post where they learned about the product for validation and then repeat their research one final time before deciding on buying the product. In essence, interdependencies and overlaps exist, and very few journeys happen in one go, but instead include breaks between the first and the final step.

MULTIPLE BEGINNINGS, MIDDLES, AND ENDS

When I was a child, I at one point got this idea in my head that the world was flat and existed at the bottom of a milk carton. I think it stemmed from a kids' album we used to listen to that described the world as being flat as a pancake. In my imagined view of how our flat-bottom-of-the-milk-carton world worked, the milk carton belonged to giants, and these giants would sometimes shake the carton, which, I figured, must be what made waves and earthquakes and the like.

If we imagine that a giant shakes our milk carton filled with overlapping and intricately linked circles of stories, then as these circles shuffle around, some will suddenly overlap and connect with new or different substories. While I now know, for sure, that we don't live at the bottom of a milk carton, and that giants shaking us around doesn't cause natural disasters, our online experiences are constantly shaken and stirred, in a way that throws us off our path and onto a new one, where a new substory begins. At times we choose whether we continue our journey on a different site or through a chat with friends (Figure 2-3). Other times these shifts are more haphazard—caused by things we spot while casually browsing, or by notifications that pop up, or by things that we see that our friends and acquaintances or peers have also seen.

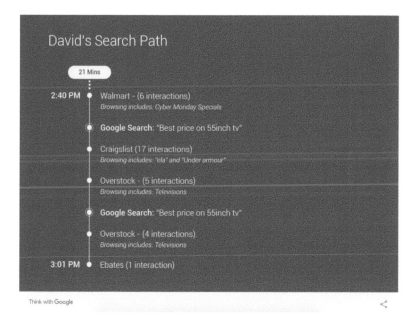

FIGURE 2-3
An example of the complexity of users' online paths to purchase with multiple interactions on different websites[7]

NARRATING THE CHAOS

The chaos of the user's journey—as well as our lack of control over how users arrive and experience our products and services, and on what medium—is what makes the role of storytelling so important. Regardless of where the user's journey starts and ends, and however interlinked or haphazard it is, the user is still going on a journey. Wherever they are in that journey and whatever page or view they are

---

7 "How supershoppers use search to tackle the holiday season," Think with Google, October 2016, *https://oreil.ly/Ndxa_.*

on, as UX designers, product owners, marketers, and startup founders, we need to make sure that we meet their needs right then and there, and on the next leg of their journey as well.

Even if the ending won't ever be as finite as Aristotle defined it, but instead will spark the next part of the story, we should still aim to make the user's journey more structured. Though the experience will differ among users, each user's journey will still have a beginning, a middle, and an end.

ADAPTING TO HOW THE JOURNEY BEGINS

There's a nice parallel to the Arabic alphabet here. Arabic is written from right to left; each letter in the alphabet has a slightly different form, depending on whether the letter comes in the beginning, middle, or end of a word. Not all letters can join to the following letter (to the left), but all letters can join to the preceding one (to the right).[8]

Similarly, we won't always be able to control how the journey *ends* for the products and services that we design, but we can always ensure that we do our best to join up with the *start* of a user's journey. This is true no matter what and where that is. We can design for multiple entry points and plan out what the experiences should look like from the start to the end of what we can control. In Chapter 7, "Defining the Setting and Context of Your Product Story," we'll look at how the context impacts the user's experience and what we as UX designers should consider and adjust according to that context. Next we'll look at what we can learn from other forms of storytelling.

Five Key Storytelling Lessons

The power of a good story lies in the emotional connection that it creates with its audience. Without this emotional connection, there really isn't a story to speak of. But what else sets a great story apart from an average, or even good one? What is it that makes films like *Toy Story*, *Monster's Inc.*, and *The Lion King* box office hits and books like *Harry Potter*, the *Twilight* series, and the *Millennium* trilogy into best sellers?

---

8 "Arabic alphabet table," The Guardian, Febraury 6, 2010, *https://oreil.ly/DcLuK*.

When you search for the world's best storytellers, a range of professions and people pop up. Some are historical people, leaders, or activists, as we've covered before. Others are storytellers in a more literal sense, like authors, playwrights, filmmakers, songwriters, and photographers. Every profession uses aspects of storytelling in slightly different ways, and we can learn something from all of them.

TRADITIONAL STORYTELLING AND THE DRAMATIC QUESTION

The *dramatic question* focuses on the protagonist's central conflict and is at the center of traditional storytelling. It's the job of the writer to pose the dramatic question in such a way that the reader wants the answer to be a resounding "yes." The writer must then create suspense by posing obstacles in the narrative that makes the reader want to read on, or keep on watching, or keep listening. It's the dramatic question together with the suspense that makes the likes of *Twilight* into best sellers rather than your average novels. Even if the rest of the writing is mediocre, if the dramatic question is used effectively and the right kind of suspense is created, people will generally still read what's been written.

A story often has more than one dramatic question, but the major, or central, dramatic question is the one that keeps us reading or watching. It concerns the protagonist's main goal and, rather than being a reactive and internal one, it's active and external. The question of whether the protagonist achieves this goal has to be answered with a yes or a no, and when it is, the story comes to an end. Similar to the red thread I mentioned in the previous chapter, the major dramatic question is the through line that we follow from the first act until the climax.

Here are some examples of dramatic questions:

- Will Romeo and Juliet ever be together? (*Romeo and Juliet*)
- Is Odysseus going to make it home from Troy? (*The Odyssey*)
- Will Scarlet win Ashley? (*Gone With the Wind*)
- Will Indy obtain the legendary Ark of the Covenant? (*Raiders of the Lost Ark*)
- Who/what is Rosebud? (*Citizen Kane*)
- Will Marlin find his son? (*Finding Nemo*)

In some cases, like in *Schindler's List*, the major dramatic question isn't 100% clear. Yet even in those circumstances, you still want to know what will happen next and how things are going to end. This desire to know how a story is going to end also applies when you are pretty sure from the start what the answer to the dramatic question will be, and that the boy and the girl will most likely live happily ever after.

Applying it to product design

Most products and services that we work on have both major and minor dramatic questions. Just think of the overarching goal of a user, buying a new TV, for example. As part of completing that goal, the user will have to carry out several smaller tasks, such as researching different brands, finding the best price, and locating a store that sells that particular TV or that can ship it to the user's home. And then additional aspects might arise if the user needs help and turns to others for recommendations or even chats with the personnel in store.

By being clear on what the major and minor dramatic questions are, we help ensure that we keep the core of the product experience in focus. At the same time, we can remain aware of all the smaller aspects in the overall end-to-end experience.

Exercise: Traditional Storytelling and the Dramatic Question

Pick out one of your favorite novels or movies and analyze the following:

- What are the dramatic questions?
- What is the major dramatic question?
- What are the three main obstacles related to the major dramatic question that creates suspense?

This simple exercise makes you focus on the key aspect of the main events that take place in relation to any novel or movie that create suspense and move the story forward. According to the Gotham Writers Workshop, the largest adult-education writing school in the United States, the way to find your major dramatic question (MDQ) is by thinking through your protagonist's main goal and the obstacles that present a conflict in achieving it.

Working with goals is something we're very used to in UX design, and adapting the exercise slightly provides a simple yet effective framework for thinking through the product experiences that we design. Pick out a typical online experience to analyze:

- What are the goals of the experience? For example, find a holiday, book the trip, save my trip, send it to my travel partner.
- What is the main goal of the experience? For example, book the trip.
- What are the three main obstacles or events that can impact accomplishing the goal? For example, not finding the type of holiday you're after, wanting to know that it's a good hotel, not being able to choose the right kind of package.

DISNEY'S MAGICAL ATTENTION TO DETAIL

Disney is often mentioned in conversations about great storytelling. The Walt Disney Company has created iconic films and the worlds, from the actual Disney theme parks to the vibrant worlds in movies like *The Lion King*, *The Little Mermaid*, and *Beauty and the Beast*. Everything in Disney's creations, whether in the Walt Disney World experience or a film, is there for a reason. It's one reason Walt Disney is hailed as a great storyteller. He had a fantastic ability to focus on the minute details and understand how all those nuances contributed to the big picture and the story that the audience experiences.

We often talk about this in design, and famous blogs like "Little big details" offer examples of lovingly created and thought-through details of an experience. These details are often referred to as *delights*, and although they are equally as often left out because of budget or time limitations, they can make a big difference to specific points in a journey for a user, and for the overarching experience as a whole.

Walt Disney's attention to detail and desire to continuously make things even better—something he called *plussing*—transcends into the physical experience of the Disney theme parks. Walt Disney didn't stop at just creating a theme park. Just as with his movies, he wanted to create a memorable experience that customers wouldn't get anywhere else.

In 2008 work began on a major initiative that looked at every single aspect of the Disney World experience, from when visitors first enter the park to when they leave, with the aim of removing friction points.

This work included looking at experiences like waiting in line for a ride, finding a place to eat, and then waiting to be seated in a restaurant. The solution was the Disney MagicBand.[9]

Together with the website and app that you as a visitor can use to explore the attractions, restaurants, and entertainment and make your itinerary and wish list, this wristband becomes the key to the magical kingdom. Through the use of RFID chips and triangulation technology, the wristband lets you skip queues, walk into a restaurant, and automatically have your food order placed and delivered to the table you've chosen. The system is based on preplanning; visitors reserve their rides and make restaurant and food choices in advance. But the end result is one that feels almost magical, down to the little things including that the staff knows your name as you walk through the door.

Applying it to product design

The drive to always do better and to pay attention to every single aspect of an experience is becoming increasingly critical for product design. As we'll talk about in Chapter 3, "Storytelling for Product Design," technological developments and user expectations are increasingly moving toward more tailored and personalized experiences that result in making users feel like the product or service knows them.

No matter what type of product or service we're working on, we would do well to have Disney's attention to detail combined with a deep understanding and care for how it all fits together. Everything is connected, and though our product may be only digital, the user's overall end-to-end experience with it includes offline aspects, too. In Chapter 5, we'll also touch on friction in product design.

---

9 Cliff Kuang, "Disney's $1 Billion Bet on a Magical Wristband," *Wired*, March 10, 2015, *https://oreil.ly/_ThwX*.

Exercise: Disney's Magical Attention to Detail

Think about your product or service, or one you use on a regular basis. Without considering the practical or physical limitations of your solutions, think about the following:

- What are the main friction points in its current state? For example: registration, payment, being overwhelmed by choices.

- What would remove these friction points? For example: using existing social accounts for login, one-click payment, ability to narrow down choice.

- How could you make the experience more magical and seamless? For example: facial recognition for login, touch to pay, three carefully recommended options based on preferences and behavior.

PIXAR'S STORYTELLING LESSONS

Since releasing *Toy Story* in 1995, Pixar has developed a wealth of wisdom around storytelling, from a basic structure from which to start, to the simple advice of finishing your story, even if it isn't perfect. Back in 2011, story artist Emma Coats tweeted 22 story basics guidelines that she'd learned from more senior people she was working with:[10]

1. You admire a character for trying, more than for their successes.

2. You gotta keep in mind what's interesting to you as an audience, not what's fun to do as a writer. They can be very different.

3. Trying for theme is important, but you won't see what the story is actually about, til you're at the end of it. Now rewrite.

4. Once upon a time there was . Every day, ____. One day ____. Because of that, ____. Because of that, ____. Until finally ____.

5. Simplify. Focus. Combine characters. Hop over detours. You'll feel like you're losing valuable stuff, but it sets you free.

6. What is your character good at, comfortable with? Throw the polar opposite at them. Challenge them. How do they deal?

---

10 "Pixar Story Rules," The Pixar Touch (blog), May 15, 2011, *https://oreil.ly/jDea9.*

7. Come up with your ending before you figure out your middle. Seriously. Endings are hard; get yours working up front.

8. Finish your story; let go even if it's not perfect. In an ideal world you have both, but move on. Do better next time.

9. When you're stuck, make a list of what *wouldn't* happen next. Lots of times the material to get you unstuck will show up.

10. Pull apart the stories you like. What you like in them is a part of you; you've got to recognize it before you can use it.

11. Putting it on paper lets you start fixing it. If it stays in your head, a perfect idea, you'll never share it with anyone.

12. Discount the first thing that comes to mind. And the second, third, fourth, fifth—get the obvious out of the way. Surprise yourself.

13. Give your characters opinions. Passive/malleable might seem likable to you as you write, but it's poison to the audience.

14. Why must you tell *this* story? What's the belief burning within you that your story feeds off of? That's the heart of it.

15. If you were your character, in this situation, how would you feel? Honesty lends credibility to unbelievable situations.

16. What are the stakes? Give us reason to root for the character. What happens if they don't succeed? Stack the odds against.

17. No work is ever wasted. If it's not working, let go and move on—it'll come back around to be useful later.

18. You have to know yourself: the difference between doing your best and fussing. Story is testing, not refining.

19. Coincidences to get characters into trouble are great; coincidences to get them out of it are cheating.

20. Exercise: take the building blocks of a movie you dislike. How'd you rearrange them into what you *do* like?

21. You gotta identify with your situation/characters, can't just write "cool." What would make *you* act that way?

22. What's the essence of your story? Most economical telling of it? If you know that, you can build out from there.

Applying it to product design

Some of these lessons provide practical references for exercises you can work through. Others provide guidance and food for thought, and others, yet again, like lesson 4, resemble what we already use in product design; in this case, user stories. These lessons teach us to get our ideas down on paper, focus on what's most important, structure both the narrative and the way you work, and understand the importance of being able to identify with the characters of your story. All of which also applies to product design.

Exercise: Pixar's Storytelling Lessons

Many of Pixar's storytelling lessons could just as well have been written for UX and design projects. The following are of particular relevance for the products and services we work on and, rewritten slightly, they can help guide and focus the experiences we create:

- Lesson 2: You have to keep in mind what's needed and relevant to the actual users, not what you as the designer would like. These can be very different.

- Lesson 4: Once upon a time, there was [*description of user*] who wanted to [*goal*]. Every day [*their backstory*]. One day [*what they came across/ realized they needed*]. So they [*what they did/thought*]. And then they, [*what they did/thought*]. And then they, [*what they did/thought*]. Until finally they [*the action they took*] and ever since then [*how it made them feel*].

- Lesson 5: Start by embracing the complexity of what you're designing for. Write, draw, and scribble down all your thoughts, ideas, and questions. Then simplify. Focus. Pull out the key parts.

- Lesson 6: What do your users like, what do they need, and what are they comfortable with? Look at the opposites. How would they react? What would they do or not do?

- Lesson 7: Come up with the end goal of the experience before you start working on the rest. Keep this at the front of your mind throughout everything you do. It will help you remember the "why."

- Lesson 11: Work with pen and paper as the first thing you do. Write, sketch, scribble, and get all your thoughts, ideas, and questions down.

- Lesson 14: Why do you have to create this particular product/experience/feature? What is the main problem it is solving? That is the heart of it.

- Lesson 15: If you were your character, in this situation, how would you feel and what would you think and do? Empathy helps create better experiences and products.

- Lesson 20: Write down the steps of a journey for a product or service you think can be improved. How would you change it so that it works better?

- Lesson 22: What's the essence of your product or service? Most economical telling of it? If you know that, you can build out from there.

VIDEO GAMES AND IMMERSIVE STORYTELLING

Just as VR and AR place the user in the middle of an experience, what is so distinct in video games is that the player is part of an immersive world. As UX designer Joanna Ngai writes, "From start to finish, the player is dropped into a fully fleshed out world with a unique aesthetic that touches the interface, voice, and interactions the player has within the world."[11] Every aspect of this world has been designed, and the user is made into the main protagonist. The rules are what govern everything about the world, from what the user can and can't do, to what touch points are available.

Applying it to product design

As the products and services we work on move from just being apps or websites that users interact with to experiences of intricately linked touch points, including but not limited to that app and/or website, every aspect of the experiences we work on will need to be fleshed out, too, just as in games. Users' interactions no longer involve just clicks with a mouse, but often a mixture of clicks, touch, conversations with bots, gestures, and the use of their own voice, all aspects that we as designers need to define.

While users of the products and services we design have their own goals in mind, one of the defining characteristics of games is that the players have to learn what their goals are and how the world they've been immersed in works. Sometimes the goal is taught through the narrative of the game, as in *The Legend of Zelda*, the playable character

---

11 Joanna Ngai, "What UX Designers Can Learn From Video Games," *Medium*, September 22, 2016, *https://oreil.ly/n-_E-*.

Link is given the task of rescuing Princess Zelda and the kingdom of Hyrule from Ganon, the main antagonist, through dialog boxes. Other times it's learn by play, or no dictated goal at all, as in *Second Life*.

Our interactions with technology increasingly involve touch interfaces, where the interactivity of certain elements isn't always clear, as well as natural user interfaces (NUIs) and voice user interfaces (VUIs), where a user quickly has to go from novice to expert in order to be able to use them. As a result, we can draw a lot from the way games approach easy learning of goals and rules and the world in which users have been immersed—from making learning part of the experience rather than a separate tutorial, to providing feedback loops and visual cues.

Exercise: Video Games and Immersive Storytelling

Think about one of your favorite video games and consider the following:

- What is the goal of the game?
- What rules are established early on in the game?
- How do the rules teach you about the world that you've been immersed in?

We often think we know or can articulate aspects of what we're working on. However, actually doing so is a different matter and often highlights that putting things into words is hard.

Being explicit about what it is that we're designing and going through the exercise of articulating our design decisions is great for helping us make sense of and think through our offering and what should govern the same. It's also great for ensuring that everyone—clients and the team—are on the same page.

Using a project that you're working on, or a website and app that you use on a regular basis, think through these questions:

- What is the goal of the website or app?
- What rules exist, or should be established, as you use the website or app?
- How should you teach the user (or how are you taught) about the world of the website or app?

PUBLIC SPEAKING AND THE PULL OF
POSSIBILITY IN STORYTELLING

When you think about a great talk that you've seen and what it was that made it great, it's often the motivated feeling that you were left with afterward. Johnson Kee, the founder and editor of 100 Naked Words, writes about the *pull of possibility* and quotes Tom Asacker's *The Business of Belief* (CreateSpace Independent Publishing):[12]

> We hunger for direction and inspiration. We want what's important to us to get better—our bodies, work, home, and relationships. We want to imagine ourselves transforming our lives, and the lives of others. We want to feel good about our evolving narratives. It's why we read books, scan the internet and flip through magazines. We're looking for the before and after stories. We want to feel the pull of possibility; of moving beyond our existing reality.

Nancy Duarte, an American writer, speaker, and CEO talks about the pull of possibility and its importance in storytelling.[13] Each and every one of us has the power to change the world, she says, and that it all starts with an idea. What separates one idea from another is the way it's being communicated. If the idea resonates, she says, then it has the power to change the world, but it has to come out of us and be shared in order to do so—and the most effective way to achieve that resonance is through story.

When we hear a good story, Duarte says, our bodies react. We get chills down our spines, feel it in our stomachs, and get goosebumps. Our eyes dilate and our hearts beat faster. But when a presentation is given, she says, at times it flatlines.

Duarte decided to look at other disciplines in order to see how they structure their stories. She researched Aristotle's three-act structure and Freytag's pyramid with its five acts and strong shape. This triangular shape sparked a question: what if great talks have a shape? By examining two of the most famous speeches of two men whose ideas

---

12 Johnson Kee, "The Secret Structure of Steve Jobs' Stories," *Medium*, April 30, 2016, *https:// oreil.ly/hvip-*.

13 Nancy Duarte, "The Secret Structure of Great Talks," *TEDxEast* Video, November 2011, *https://oreil.ly/qZGSV*.

have changed the world, Martin Luther King Jr. and Steve Jobs, she found that there was indeed a shape that could be overlaid on all great speeches. Just as in the three-act structure and any good or bad story, the shape she found in great talks has a beginning, a middle, and an end. It looks like in Figure 2-4.

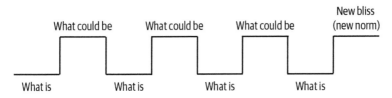

FIGURE 2-4
The shape of great talks according to Nancy Duarte

The beginning of all great talks, according to Duarte, starts out with a flat status quo that rises to the loftiness of the future. This beginning is similar to the first plot point and the inciting incident in Aristotle's three-act structure, where the dramatic question is asked. The gap between the status quo and the promise of the future needs to be big, she says, in order to plant the idea of the possibility in audience's minds.

In the middle, the shape of a great talk shifts between what is and what could be, and this, she explains, is because you'll encounter some resistance. People may love their world the way it is, and just as you have to move a boat back and forth in order to capture the wind and move forward so you pick up speed, you also need to move your presentation back and forth between status quo and the promise of what could be until you get to the end. The end includes the strong call to action, which she, just like Peter Guber, says that every good story or presentation should have.

Applying it to product design

When it comes to presenting our work, we're often told that we shouldn't tell, but show instead. While that often holds true, we need to plan out what it is that we're going to tell, even if we mainly end up showing it. In Chapter 14, "Presenting and Sharing Your Story," we'll look at the role of storytelling and its importance when it comes to getting buy-in. We'll also look at adapting the way we tell our stories, just as Steve Jobs did, to get the desired outcome no matter who the audience might be.

Using the structure of What Is—What Could Be—What Is...New Bliss, work
through how you'd organize and give your next presentation, or alternatively,
how you might reorganize a presentation you've just given:

- What is the main thing about the current What Is that you need to pull
out?

- What's the New Bliss that you're working toward?

- What are the key What Could Be elements in relation to what you're
presenting?

- What is their corresponding What Is elements?

Summary

Although we might not be able to change the whole world, Duarte says
that we all can change our own world by the way we tell our stories and
include a strong call to action. What Aristotle and traditional storytelling teach us, in its simplest form, is that a good product design experience should have a beginning, a middle, and an end. As previously
mentioned, at times we're too quick to jump straight into the details,
whether that's a page or the requirements that we're defining. By doing
so, we lose out on taking a step back and actually defining and designing the overall story that our product should be telling, as well as how
best to bring the small details to life.

What I hope to show you through the rest of this book is how you can
help change the world of the people you design for by applying traditional storytelling principles and tools to the way you define, design,
and sell in your product design projects. No matter what type of story
you're telling, you want to avoid that flatline and instead connect emotionally with your audience. And the way to do that is through truly
shaping the story that you tell.

[3]

Storytelling for Product Design

When Any Device, Used Anywhere and at Any Time, Is Your Starting Point

BACK IN 2011 LUKE Wroblewski, an internationally recognized digital product leader tweeted: "So how do you do anything if everything, anybody, anywhere, & anytime are your use cases?" (@lukew, May 12, 2011). Though I didn't have a clear answer, the topic of his tweet got me excited and kept my mind buzzing for the rest of the week. So much so, that I ended up submitting a proposal for a talk to a conference, which resulted in my first public speaking appearance and, as an extension of that, why you're reading this book today.

A lot has happened since that day in 2011, and it's even more fascinating to think about just how much our lives have changed since Apple released the first iPhone in 2007. Before then, we were limited to going online at work or at home, or to using a Wireless Application Protocol (WAP) browser—a web browser for mobile devices—on our phones. WAP was introduced in 1999, but what we experienced when browsing using WAP didn't look anything like those websites we'd visit on our laptops or desktops (Figure 3-1).

By 2010 WAP had been replaced by more modern standards, and today most internet browsers of modern handsets fully support HTML, allowing us to experience the web the way it's intended to look and work. This development has drastically changed things. In 2009, only 0.7% of all global web pages were served on a mobile phone. In 2018 that number rose to 52.2%.

FIGURE 3-1

A page viewed in a
WAP browser (source:
Norbert Huffschmid,
https://oreil.ly/NJW1Q)

We now go online absolutely everywhere and anywhere—the average smartphone user in the US checks their phone 150 times a day–from the first thing we do in the morning (including bringing our smartphone along to our morning visit to the little boys or girls room), to the last thing we do at night. Our addiction to smartphones has become such an issue that both Android and Apple have started releasing updates to help us monitor our usage and take a break from them and the apps we've installed.

Tasks like buying online, which we previously considered ludicrous to do on anything but a desktop or laptop, are now second nature to do on a smartphone. More than a fifth of online spending in the United Kingdom takes place on a commuter journey.[1] Mobile-optimized websites that only a few years ago were still considered a nice option are now an across-the-board essential for business-to-consumer (B2C) and increasingly so for business-to-business (B2B), as more and more of the workforce is becoming flexible. In 2015, Google's "Mobilegeddon" famously came into action, and websites that aren't mobile friendly now get penalized in search rankings by the updated Google algorithm.

---

1 Lynsey Barber Barber, "We're Spending Billions Shopping Online While Commuting," *City A.M.*, July 2, 2015, *https://oreil.ly/MieZG.*

All of this has happened in just a few years. There's no denying that the introduction of the iPhone and the other smartphones that followed have changed our world. This technology has changed how and where we go online, how we as human beings now communicate (or don't, for that matter), the products and services we use, and how we go about our day-to-day lives with everything accessible at the tap of a button.

We're now at a point where advances in AI, machine learning, Internet of Things (IoT), smart home devices, and VUIs are yet again changing everything. Though VR has yet to kick off as predicted, both VR and AR are making progress in the devices that are available and afford-able as well as in the offerings for both. As for IoT, a growing num-ber of devices are becoming connected via Bluetooth and the internet, from pregnancy tests, to fridges that scan food, to smart speakers like Amazon Echo and Google Home that enable us to control an increas-ing number of other devices and appliances in our homes with voice commands.

Soon pretty much everything will be connected in one way or another. The question Wroblewski asked is increasingly not a "What if," but the new norm. Everything, anybody, anywhere, and anytime is what we're dealing with, and we're only at the beginning.

How Traditional Storytelling Is Changing

Technology and the other mediums that we've used have always shaped the way we tell and interact with stories as well as how people come across them. The latest developments in technology have contributed to the creation of new types of stories, from the introduction of photog-raphy, motion pictures, radio, TV, and later on internet with mobile as well as social media. These developments have not only influenced the creative ways that stories are brought to life, but also altered the struc-ture of the stories themselves.

The immediate structure that comes to mind when we think of a story is the one we're used to in books, film, and TV: a beginning, a middle, and an end, just as Aristotle defined it. But with recent developments in technology, new platforms and devices, and a growing on-demand culture, storytelling is changing. Next we'll look closer at changes in eight areas, how they impact storytelling, and their relevance for prod-uct design.

THE SHIFT TO ON-DEMAND

One of the most obvious ways we experience stories is the increasing shift from linear TV to on-demand viewing. I remember as a child sitting in front of the TV with the test screen showing, which meant that there was nothing airing at that time (Figure 3-2).

Most TV programs would start around 3 p.m., and in total we had around five channels. Fast-forward a few years, and a more consistent broadcast schedule offered something to watch 24/7, albeit in some instances just the TV shopping channel. Still, we had to wait a week for the next episode of most shows. This wait was frustrating, but it built anticipation and made us look forward to certain shows, days, and times, in a way that most of the things we watch nowadays never come close to.

Today that wait for the next episode is almost nonexistent, and has been replaced in many cases by the wait for the next series. Netflix and other subscription video on demand (SVoD) services like Now TV, Amazon Prime Video, Hulu, and TVPlayer have changed the way we watch TV and films. We now watch when and where we want instead of at predefined broadcast times. And even more growth is expected to come in this area. In 2018, there were 283 million SVoD subscribers worldwide, and the number is expected to rise to 411 million by 2022.[2]

The shift to on-demand isn't restricted to just TV and films. It also applies to novels and audio-based storytelling, as well as to games and applications. Back when I was a child, we went to the library in Lund, my hometown, every Saturday morning. We'd sit in the cafeteria and bring books along with us to read and used our library card to bring some of them home when we left. While this was a type of on-demand experience, and one that is still very possible, ebooks now account for about a quarter of global book sales,[3] and digital audio book apps like Audible allow you to listen to almost any book in English if you subscribe and pay a monthly fee.

2 Amy Watson, "Subscription Video On Demand," Statista, October 10, 2018, *https://oreil.ly/ RB51N*.

3 Amy Watson, "E-books - Statistics & Facts," Statista, December 18, 2018, *https://oreil.ly/ wDqhe*.

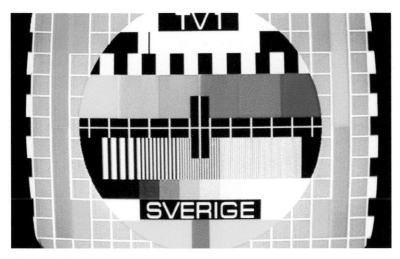

FIGURE 3-2
Swedish State Television screen used when nothing was on air

What this means for product design

The on-demand trend is an example of a general shift in consumer expectations. The rise of tap-of-a-button expectations increasingly means that users can get a growing number of products and services at the tap or click of a button. Users choose to view, read, listen, and interact on their terms, when it fits them, on the device and in the place that they prefer. We are no longer confined to watching the latest episode of a much-hyped TV series like *Stranger Things* in our living rooms; we can watch it anywhere with a good 3G, 4G, 5G, or WiFi signal, whether during the commute to work, in the airport, or sitting on a park bench.

We may have a particular device and viewing experience that we think is ideal for our users—for example, watching on the TV at home. But what users prefer is up to them, and "on my terms" is increasingly becoming a need rather than a "nice to have." Where appropriate, we have to make sure that the content we're creating can be experienced anywhere and anytime, and that goes for our products and services overall as well.

Exercise: The Shift to On-Demand

Think about your own product or service, or one that you have used on a regular basis over the last few years:

- Has the way it's used changed?
- Are there any new expectations from users that you can trace back to a shift to the on-demand culture?
- What aspects of your product or service are most attractive for an on-demand audience?
- What could make your product or service more attractive for an on-demand audience?

THE AUDIENCE AS STORYTELLERS

Thanks to smartphones, we now consume more media than ever before, but how and what we consume has evolved. In 2017, we spent a billion hours on YouTube every single day. While the time we spend watching TV has been in a steady decline, YouTube is steadily on the rise and has surpassed both Netflix and Facebook video in terms of the number of hours we spend on the respective platform. As Cristos Goodrow, VP of engineering at YouTube said:

> Around the world, people are spending a billion hours every day rewarding their curiosity, discovering great music, keeping up with the news, connecting with their favorite personalities, or catching up with the latest trend.[4]

This is a new type of storytelling, one that is less scripted, created by the masses rather than a specialist team, and is turned around in a very short period of time in comparison to other types of video content.

---

4 Sirena Bergman, "We Spend a Billion Hours a Day on YouTube, More Than Netflix and Facebook Video Combined," *Forbes*, February 28, 2017, *https://oreil.ly/UsdVP*.

Every single hour, four hundred hours of content are uploaded to YouTube by what's called *YouTube creators*. This creator trend isn't just limited to YouTube, or to the more grown-up among us. At the end of 2018, YouTube revealed that its highest-earning creator was a seven-year-old boy named Ryan who reviews toys.[5]

As Lance Weiler, co-founder of Connected Sparks—a next-generation media and connected toy company—writes about his son and his friends, "The reality is, they are not watching TV but instead have become their own little media companies."[6] Weiler's son and his friends are being inspired by creators that they watch, and then they themselves create their own Let's Play (LP) videos, which document the play-through of a video game, usually involving commentary from the gamer. To some, these kinds of videos may seem pointless, and many would, if asked, have dismissed it as a terrible idea: "Who'd want to watch that?!" Turns out, a lot of people, to the extent that dedicated platforms have sprung up. The live-streaming video platform Twitch, for example, in 2019 boasted 3.7 million monthly broadcasters and active daily users who tune in to view both live and on-demand content on the platform.

What this means for product design

Increasingly, anyone can be a storyteller. From the updates, pictures, and captions we share on social media, to the videos we create, platforms like YouTube, Twitch, Snapchat, Facebook, and Instagram have made it easy for anyone to publish and reach an audience. And based on users' needs, these platforms are constantly evolving.

In 2018, Instagram launched IGTV, a new app for watching long-form, vertical video content that can also be experienced within the Instagram app. In IGTV, your videos can be up to an hour long instead of being restricted to 15 seconds as Instagram Stories are, and the format is full-screen vertical video that automatically starts playing. And IGTV has channels just like TV, only the channels are the creators.

5   Caitlin O'Kane, "The 10 Highest-Paid YouTube Stars of 2018, According to Forbes," *CBS News*, December 4, 2018, *https://oreil.ly/qrYup*.

6   Lance Weiler, "How Storytelling Has Changed in the Digital Age," *World Economic Forum*, January 23, 2015, *https://oreil.ly/oTAuD*.

The new formats of storytelling combined with the audience as story-tellers is putting changing requirements on brands, products, and services. While a piece of long-form video content previously would take months and a considerable budget to produce, brands and products and services owners increasingly need to be nimble and fast on their feet to keep up with how quickly their users and customers are producing content; and as an extension of that, how fast and frequently they expect others to be doing the same.

As we'll cover in Chapter 4, "The Emotional Aspect of Product Design," people are increasingly looking for ways to connect. That connection is usually not a polished piece of video when it comes to branded content, but a real story that moves the user—like the tweet series that Rosey Blair shared in July 2018. Blair's tweet about a simple seat switch turned into a romantic story that was aired live as the events unfolded on the plane (Figure 3-3). The tweet has since been deleted, but at the time of this writing, over nine hundred thousand people had liked her tweet. Media across the globe, from the BBC to Buzzfeed, picked up and wrote about the story.

FIGURE 3-3

The first tweet in Rosey Blair's tweet saga about #planbae and mystery woman Helen

Exercise: The Audience as Storytellers

With your own product or service in mind, think about the following:

- How has the audience as storytellers impacted your product or service?
- What actual implications has this had?
- How do you foresee the audience as storytellers developing in the next few years?

THE AUDIENCE AS THE PROTAGONIST

One of the main characters in the preceding real-life saga was Euan Holden, otherwise referred to as #planebae by the public. While the woman of the story chose to remain anonymous, he went public. People from across the globe were checking in and following along the classic will-the-boy-get-the-girl kind of saga, and Holden found himself the focus of attention, with everyone wanting to know what would happen next.

One of the reasons film is said to make more of an impact on its audience than a play is that when watching a film, you can be more up close and personal with the characters than when sitting back in a theater watching a play. Though Euan didn't deliberately place himself in the middle of the story, until he got involved, a possible reason for the attention this story got is how relatable it was. Many of us travel on some kind of public transport on a regular basis, and the "it-could-happen-to-anyone," or even more so, "it-could-happen-to-me" aspect created a close connection to the story, plus, of course, the fact that we're all drawn to a great love story.

The desire to experience things has been on the rise in the last few years. Interactive plays and experiences have sprung up, inviting the audience to be part of the story. One such example is Punchdrunk's *Sleep No More*, which is an immersive and interactive version of *Hamlet*: the audience wears masks and experiences the play by wandering through the rooms of a hotel. Each room has actors playing out a scene, and the audience can engage with them and stay for however long, or short, they want. In some productions, the audience becomes the protagonist, and sometimes even antagonists and villains as well.

While not all of these types of interactive storytelling make the audience the main protagonist, they do make the audience one of the characters. This potential to offer something different and attract people has spread to other areas, too, like museums. Advances in technology are revolutionizing everything from how we experience art to how we learn about a subject, resulting in many museums seeing the best attendance they've ever had. The people who always tend to visit museums will visit either way, but for those who use museums as family time, or to fulfill a trend, the inclusion of tech like VR makes visiting a museum an easier choice[7] As an example, Figure 3-4 shows a screenshot from *The Night Cafe: A VR Tribute to Van Gogh*, in which the audience can explore the world of Vincent Van Gogh first hand, from his iconic sunflowers in 3D to walking around and seeing the chair he painted in his bedroom from every angle.

FIGURE 3-4
The Night Cafe: A VR Tribute to Van Gogh[8]

What this means for product design

People are increasingly looking for new ways to connect, and to experience things. With the development of AR and VR, actually placing the user in the middle of the experience has become a reality. Though

7 Kelly Song, "Virtual Reality and Van Gogh Collide," *CNBC*, September 24, 2017, *https://oreil.ly/QPGIK*.

8 "The Night Cafe: A VR Tribute to Van Gogh," Oculus, *https://oreil.ly/n_hkO*.

these types of experiences, otherwise referred to as *immersive storytelling*, have so far had a fairly small audience, there is a growing appetite for it. In the AOL 2017 State of the Video industry study, 31% of Australian consumers expect to watch more movies in VR, and 22% already engage with AR at least once a week.[9]

From a creative and a data point of view, VR and AR are part of a fantastically exciting field. A staggering amount of data is available to gather from these types of experiences through heat maps that track eye movement, "gaze through rate" (the percent of people who trigger an event using their gaze), and motion-based interactivity. Creatively, AR and VR offer a new type of experience with no frame, and the ability to create a lot of empathy and participation from the audience. And it has the ability to do immense good for the user too.

While not all products and services lend themselves, or should, to offering immersive experiences in the form of 360° VR or AR, we should still aim to make the user the main protagonist of the products and services that we design. The way we talked about our products and services back in the early days of "digital" was much more about us than our users and customers. Today, the focus of the most effective and successful products, services, and marketing campaigns is on the users and customers rather than the company or the brand. We've come to realize, not the least through data, that what users and (prospective) customers respond to the most is messaging that's indirectly about them, and we do this by creating pictures in their heads about what using the product or service will enable them to do.

Exercise: The Audience as the Protagonist

Imagine that you add a 360° VR or AR capability to your product or service, or one that you use on a regular basis:

- What purpose would this serve?
- How could it benefit users in a way that a plain web experience can't?

---

9 What Is Immersive Storytelling?" *The CMO Show*, *https://oreil.ly/ZTcKl*.

PARTICIPATIVE AND INTERACTIVE STORYTELLING

In interactive experiences like Punchdrunk's *Sleep No More*, audiences are invited to participate and explore the space individually, hereby influencing what to watch and where to go. This is in line with how audiences in general aren't shying away from wanting to have a say. In a Latitude study about what audiences want, 79% suggested wanting interactions that would allow them to influence the characters' decisions and thereby the way the story developed, or for them to become characters themselves. The ability to influence the story is something that became popular with the choose-your-own-adventure (CYOA) genre for books back in the 1980s and 1990s. However, for film and TV, though there have been a couple of examples, it has not taken off. At least not yet.

Over the last few years, movies have been losing potential viewers to games, a problem that is likely to only increase in the years to come.[10] Young audiences in particular are less keen on being passive viewers, and broadcasters are looking for better ways to engage viewers and create loyalty.[11] One example is *Mosaic*, a murder mystery by Steven Soderbergh that was released as an iOS/Android app in 2017 and then in 2018 as a TV series. The app worked like an interactive movie where the user could choose which viewpoint to see the movie: as well as explore different facets of it. The TV series didn't have any interactivity and was slightly shorter than what could be experienced in the app. Both the app and the TV series got mixed reviews, some praising it and some saying that the storyline got a bit confusing and you risked missing crucial bits in the plot.

What this means for product design

When audiences are involved in helping shape what happens next through co-creation, or even if they're only choosing the way in which they experience the different parts of the product or service, it places bigger emphasis on creating a flexible and adaptable product experience—one that can be viewed or engaged with in whichever order the user chooses. A few years ago, I was watching an interview on *BBC*

---

10 Scott Meslow, "Are Choose-Your-Own-Adventure Movies Finally About to Become a Thing?" *GQ*, June 21, 2017, *https://oreil.ly/kCgT5*.

11 Owen Gibson, "What Happens Next?" *The Guardian*, September 26, 2005, *https://oreil.ly/qCNtj*.

Breakfast with part of the cast of the British "Nordic" Noir TV show *Marcella*. During the interview, the cast told how they didn't know what would happen in the next episode until they got the script for it. In real co-creation, this will always be the case for the people involved. Though co-creation can often shorten the production process, in instances like the AXE Anarchy campaign, it can also take longer. In this case the men's fragrance company created a campaign in which users created a narrative out of their own choices, and the agency Razorfish then transformed into a comic book that engaged thousands.[12]

Exercise: Participative and Interactive Storytelling

Think about your product or service, or one you use on a regular basis:

- Would it benefit from some element of participative storytelling, and if so, why and how?
- If it already includes participative elements, what role do these play? How do they benefit both the users and the product?

DATA-DRIVEN STORYTELLING

Beyond participative and interactive storytelling, we're increasingly seeing examples of data influencing what we see, as well as when and how we see it. One of the main examples of data driving what we watch can be found in the way Netflix uses data to, among other things, identify which shows to commission and then what the ideal combination of factors (actor, duration of the film, setting, etc.), will be before making a decision about the same.

One of the most talked about examples here is how *House of Cards* came to be. The team at Netflix analyzed the organic viewing behaviors of its users to understand what they were already paying the most attention to. Netflix identified that the people who watched the original BBC

---

12 PSFK Originals, "Participatory Storytelling in Advertising," YouTube Video, March 22, 2013, *https://oreil.ly/r-Qh6*.

version of the series also watched movies that were directed by David Fincher and starred Kevin Spacey. This led to the new version of *House of Cards* starring Spacey and directed by Fincher.[13]

In a TED talk analyzing the then difference between Amazon's and Netflix's approach to data for making hit TV shows, data scientist Dr. Sebastian Wernicke talks of how Amazon looked at data in relation to a controlled subset of pilot episodes when it commissioned *Alpha House*, whereas Netflix analyzed the consumption across its entire platform when it came to *House of Cards*. What Wernicke identified over the course of his career as a data scientist is that data in itself is good only for dissecting a problem and for understanding the multivariables of the same. Additionally, he's identified that to be successful and to apply the data and the insight in the right way, you need to combine industry expertise in the process. With *House of Cards*, the data didn't specifically direct Netflix to license it, but it pointed the company in the right direction.[14]

What this means for product design

Just as Netflix did when it came to investing in and making decisions around *House of Cards*, when it comes to the products and services we work on and the decisions that guide what we do and don't do, we have to look at data holistically, across the whole system, rather than fall down the trap of looking at just reactionary data in relation to a subset of what we're testing. As Wernicke pointed out, we should also include industry expertise to help get to the right insight and ensure we make the right strategic decisions.

With the right insight and the right decision making around it, data has the potential to improve both the bottom line for the business and the experience for users by providing more of what the user is interested in and less of what they'd prefer not to see.

---

13 Kristin Westcott Grant, "Netflix's Data-Driven Strategy Strengthens Claim for 'Best Original Content' in 2018," *Forbes*, May 28, 2018, *https://oreil.ly/YhqCW*.

14 Sebastian Wernicke, "How to Use Data to Make a Hit TV Show," TEDxCambridge Video, June 2015, *https://oreil.ly/S9ME2*.

Exercise: Data-Driven Storytelling

With your product or service in mind, or one that you've worked with:

- What role does, did, or could data play?

- How is, was, or could data be analyzed to make sure it was viewed holistically?

- How is, was, or could the insight of the data influence the product direction?

NEW STORYTELLING FORMATS

Lance Weiler, co-founder of Connected Sparks, describes how storytelling has changed in the digital age, that while motivations are at the heart of storytelling, our desire to commercialize storytelling is what has driven and given birth to new storytelling formats. When theater owners realized that their audiences looked at the length of the films as a measure of quality, short form was replaced with longer-form film. Feature films also meant that a higher price could be charged, and various distribution channels were established to make the most of the opportunity. However, as Alfred Hitchcock famously said later, "The length of a film should be directly related to the endurance of the human bladder," and theaters went from previously having intermittent breaks to account for the audience's physical needs to the more bladder-friendly running times that we have today.[15]

The commercialization drive and the advances in technology have also evolved the types of stories that we are engaging with. When Snapchat launched in 2011, it was the first to introduce disappearing pictures. Brands that had previously created horizontal and mainly long-form video content for their users and customers had to adapt and create vertical video and image-based content as well as adapt to the original 10-second restriction that Snapchat had for snaps. After Instagram followed in Snapchat's footsteps with 15-second videos called "Stories" that also disappeared after 24 hours, both platforms adapted— Snapchat allowed users to save snaps as "Memories," which Instagram

---

15 Lance Weiler, "How Storytelling Has Changed in the Digital Age," *World Economic Forum*, January 23, 2015, *https://oreil.ly/R6MFc.*

called "Highlights." Snapchat's original 10-second limitation was also removed in 2017 in favor of sending snaps with unlimited viewing time.

What this means for product design

The rise of new platforms like Snapchat and the accompanying new formats impact businesses as, for example, print and TV budgets are being replaced by Snapchat and Instagram stories. Rather than just push purchases, these stories often give a behind-the-scenes look at the brand in question for the purpose of entertainment and connecting with the brand, and that's increasingly what audiences are after.

By listening to what our users want, and those who create content for our products and services, we are able to follow along with and adapt to their changing wishes and needs, and to the new formats out there. But, as we'll cover next, we also have an opportunity to push how we tell our stories. Creativity, technology, and the idea of the kind of story we'd love to tell are leading the way.

Exercise: New Storytelling Formats

With your own product or service in mind, one you've worked on previously or just come across, think about the following:

- In which ways have the way we present content and messages changed over the last few years?
- Are there any particular design trends that have stood out as a new way of bringing the content to life?

TRANSMEDIA STORYTELLING

As the previous examples of Snapchat and Instagram show, new formats for storytelling are closely linked to new platforms and players in the technology market. A form of storytelling that is increasingly being talked about in relation to (new) platforms is transmedia storytelling.

Transmedia storytelling is a technique that is used to tell stories across multiple platforms—TV, radio, novels, games, online social media, a website, or any platform where a story can be told.[16] In transmedia storytelling, the story itself unfolds in different ways; the audience can not only enter the story through different entry points, but also continue exploring the story through the various platforms. The idea behind it is that by telling (part of) the story across different platforms, you can give the audience more of what they want but also make sure you reach audiences that you may not otherwise have attracted (e.g., through social media).

A show that's been widely acclaimed for its approach to transmedia storytelling, as well as the storyline and subjects it covered, is the Norwegian show *Skam* ("Shame" in English), which follows a group of teenagers at the Hartvig Nissen School in Oslo. *Skam* is a fairly traditionally produced TV show with four seasons, each one following a different central character. What makes it unique is how it aired in real time and evolved, transmedia, between each episode.

At the start of each week a clip, conversation, or social media post was published on the *Skam* website at the same time that it would happen in the world of the characters; for example, if two of the characters, Eva and Noora, are discussing something on Tuesday morning at 9:30 a.m., then the clip would go up on Tuesday morning at 9:30 a.m. New material was added daily before all of it was put together into an episode that aired on Friday each week. Between the updates, the audience could also read text messages that the characters would send each other via the *Skam* website and follow their Instagram accounts, where the audience was also encouraged to interact with the characters (Figure 3-5).[17]

---

16 "Transmedia Storytelling," *BBC Academy,* September 19, 2017, *https://oreil.ly/GsblO.*

17 Kayti Burt, "What Is Skam and Why Is It Taking Over the Internet?" *Den of Geek,* April 9, 2017, *https://oreil.ly/9c0CE.*

FIGURE 3-5

The Skam website (*www.skam.p3.no*) showing an Instagram update by one of the characters as well as text conversations

What this means for product design

Transmedia storytelling requires a deliberate choice to tell the respective story across platforms instead of just on a select few. When it comes to product design, we not only have to ensure that we tell our story across platforms, but also need to consider how and what we deliver in that context. Our users are on multiple platforms, and, as we'll be covering later, we can't always control how they start their journey with us. When it comes to transmedia storytelling, 82% want complementary apps instead of duplicated content, and this is something we have to keep in mind for products and service experiences too.[18] While the general guideline is that the same website content should be present on the mobile view as on a desktop or tablet, opportunities exist to adapt to the specific platform, and also, where appropriate, to provide an additional offering in, for example, an app.

Exercise: Transmedia Storytelling

With your own product or service in mind, identify the following:

- Which platforms are used to communicate the product message in one way or another?

- How does the role of each platform differ in terms of the message or the experience that it provides?

---

18 KC Ifeanyi, "The Future of Storytelling," *Fast Company,* August 17, 2012, *https://oreil.ly/baLgf.*

EXPANDED VERSUS ADOPTED UNIVERSE

Closely linked to transmedia storytelling is the concept of the expanded versus adopted universe. The *expanded universe* includes any official content that essentially expands the existing fictional universe beyond what we already know; for example, *The Walking Dead* video game that's part of the franchise and that introduces new characters and storylines. The *adopted universe*, on the other hand, can have either official or unofficial content that reimagines or reinterprets parts of the fictional universe, but what happens here doesn't affect the original fictional world. *The Walking Dead* TV show is an example of an adopted universe, as what happens there doesn't impact the original comics.

Before the internet, some quite obvious factors restricted how much the expanded or adopted universe of a fictional world could grow. These restrictions were physical in terms of awareness and accessibility—a book or comic book may not exist in your location, for instance. The internet changed that, and with social media and a growing on-demand culture, both expanded and adopted universe content is readily available, and it's relatively easy to reach a large audience base.

Creators, fans, and investors benefit from the expanded and adopted universe of content. As with transmedia storytelling, this expansion provides an opportunity for us as brands, and for our products and services, in terms of what story we tell where. And it has the potential to turn what is otherwise a risk or threat into a new opportunity. This was the case with the role-playing game series original *Mass Effect* game, which was a huge success. In order to keep fans happy while waiting for the game's sequel (which would take a long time to make), publisher EA Games began to release new downloadable content that expanded the stories and kept the audience engaged.

What this means for product design

The more we understand our users and what they are after, or would respond well to, the better positioned we are to fully cater to and look after them. We can then tell a story with our product or service that offers opportunities for expanded and adopted universe content as well as works across platforms and devices.

Next we'll be looking in more detail at how the multidevice, multiplatform, multi-input method landscape that we now design for is evolving and the challenges these pose for us in product design, as well as why storytelling is so suitable to our field.

How the Landscape of Product Design Is Changing

The preceding sections cover a few ways in which traditional storytelling is changing and the way it's impacting product design and marketing. Throughout history, traditional storytelling has influenced and driven innovation in technology and science. One example is Arthur Conan Doyle's stories about Sherlock Holmes, which have had a lasting impact on the way crimes are solved. In the books, Sherlock Holmes is obsessed with protecting crime scenes from contamination. He is an avid user of chemistry, ballistics, bloodstains, and fingerprints to solve his crimes, all of which has helped shape what we now consider to be the foundation of forensic investigation.[19]

Of course, many fictional works have visions of the then future, now current day, that haven't come to pass, yet. When Marty McFly warps from 1985 to 2015 with his girlfriend Jennifer and Dr. Emmet Brown,

---

19 Weiler, "How Storytelling Has Changed."

otherwise known as "Doc," flying cars and hoverboards are widely used—neither of which are quite here yet. We also have a few years left until we'll find out whether what we see in the movie *Minority Report*, which is set in 2054, will hold true.

However, as reported in *Bloomberg*: "It's not hard to predict what the world will be like in 20 years. The hard thing is actually predicting or figuring out how to get there."[20] Be it those flying cars, intelligent humanoids like those in the film *Ex Machina*, or operating systems that we talk to and even fall in love with as in the movie *Her*, the one thing we know is that how and where we'll be experiencing content and in what way we'll interact with it is changing. In a not-so-distant future, we'll look back at those pictures of people bending their heads down to look at their phones while walking on the pavement and smile saying, "Can you believe we actually did that?" just as we today chuckle sentimentally about how we used to use pens and pencils to rewind and fast-forward cassette tapes to save our Walkman's battery.

THE FUTURE STARTS NOW

The thing about "the future," however, is that it isn't just about futuristic things like flying cars or talking humanoids. The future is very much about what's happening, and starting to happen, right now—from the small to the big things. In its simplest form "the future" increasingly involves AI-powered products and services, multiple touch points, connected devices, apps and experiences, as well as a mixture of interfaces we touch, interfaces we talk and chat to, interfaces we cannot see, and interfaces that we are an actual part of through sensory data or AR and VR. We'll increasingly be served with more tailored content and experiences based on preferences and what we've done or haven't done. And we'll come to expect more from technology. In fact, we already do. Google reported at the start of 2018 that people are increasingly using search as a personal advisor, with the qualifiers "me" and "I" in mobile searches up by 60% over the two previous years.[21]

---

20 Bryant Urstadt and Sarah Frier, "Welcome to Zuckerworld," *Bloomberg Businessweek*, July 27, 2016, *https://oreil.ly/qOgRU*.

21 Lisa Gevelber, "It's All About 'Me'," *Think with Google*, January 2018, *https://oreil.ly/SIw3m*.

With a growing number of moving parts (as we'll look at in Chapter 7), making sure we know what story we're telling with our products and services, along with why and how, is increasingly fundamental to making sure we deliver against users' ever moving and more sophisticated expectations. It's also critical in order to ensure that we not just keep up with, but also stand out from, the competition.

Next we'll be looking at eight key areas, related to product design, the developments therein, and the challenges that we're faced with in product design.

FREE-FLOWING CONTENT AND UBIQUITOUS EXPERIENCES

For many of us, when we think about the future of interfaces, what we've seen in *Minority Report* comes to mind—interfaces that are controlled by gestures and that we can manipulate with ease. There are no restrictions on how we can move information around, or on what we can do. We simply "touch" the bits we want to interact with and manipulate them in any way we want, with the interface responding accordingly.

John Underkoffler, founder and chief scientist of Oblong, was part of the team that worked on the technology ideas for *Minority Report*. One of the principles behind what they developed was that the camera could go anywhere, and as a result, what they proposed had to be able to follow that and adapt. The technology concepts they worked on were originally based on setting *Minority Report* in 2080, but that was downgraded to 2044 and then at the very last minute upgraded again to 2054. Many of the ideas, like self-driving cars, didn't make it into the movie, but the gestural interface, called *g-speak*, did, and it's one of the things that *Minority Report* has become famous for. It's also what became the foundation of what Oblong is working on today.

One of the underlying principles of how Underkoffler and his team see the future is that it shouldn't stop at the boundaries of the device. If you're near other pixels, and what you're experiencing on one device can fit on that pixel, then what you experience should also be able to flow onto that other nearby pixel. This will require more systems and apps to talk to each other and for us to be able to map experiences in physical space rather than just a relative position on one screen.[22]

Minority Report isn't the only example of where we've seen touch UIs and other NUIs be a key part of how people interact with technology. Though attempts have been made at larger touch interfaces, none have so far taken off, mainly because of cost.

In concept videos like materials science innovator Corning's "A Day Made of Glass" vision for the future video series, we see what our future might look like when we have large surfaces in the kitchen, bathroom, and home office where we can be presented with information and interact with various apps. These range from watching the news and seeing the weather forecast while looking in the mirror and brushing our teeth, to following along with the recipe we're cooking on the interactive kitchen counter.

What this means for product design

All of this is without a doubt a very exciting evolution of technology and user interfaces. But until it becomes a reality, the flow from one screen to another and having large interactive surfaces in our homes are but a good metaphor for, and reminder of, how we should think about product and service experiences overall. Our content will increasingly have to be able to go anywhere, and the way users experience it will be even more nonlinear than what it already is today.

We're all well accustomed to touch being an input method. With voice input on the rise, we are starting to take a more natural approach to the ways we interact with technology. For product design teams this means that we have to think beyond touch and the mouse as a way for users to interact with the products and services that we work on. Though we're far from Underkoffler's vision, we are increasingly seeing apps that can talk to each other—something that, with the user's permission, will enable us to deliver more value and take away the user frustration of having to repeat information between product and service providers.

---

22 Zoe Mutter, "Why We Need Critical Dialogue Around the User Interface," *AV Magazine*, November 2, 2018, *https://oreil.ly/p0WKB*.

For designers, however, it means that we increasingly need to consider other apps and systems as players as well as providing input to our product experiences.

How Storytelling Can Help

- Creating a vision for the future product experience by visualizing what could be (through, for example, a storyboard).

- Bringing this vision to life by storyboarding a key part of the experience story

- Identifying what input method is used when by mapping out how the experience may play out in every key scene

- Identifying key needs for each input method by narrating experiences for each touch point

MULTIDEVICE DESIGN

Consider Cliff Kuang's assertion that "If you want to imagine how the world will look in just a few years, [...] skip Silicon Valley. Go to Disney World."[23] In this magical wristband world, the restaurants we visit will know we're on our way before we've stepped into their venue. They'll know our names, where we've been, where we're going next, what we like, and they'll adapt the service we receive accordingly.

It's a much more scaled-back future than the one Underkoffler talks of, but it's one where everything is connected. While we're still some way away from it being everyday life, it reflects the development we're seeing in both user expectations and technology trends around our multidevice experiences.

Increasingly, when it comes to thinking through and designing multidevice experiences, it's not going to be as much about what the user does as it is about preempting what the user wants to do so that we can deliver the right content to the right device, at the right time. According to a Google study, 90% of users switch devices multiple times a day. With the growing number of devices that we use on a daily basis, users

---

23 Cliff Kuang, "Disney's $1 Billion Bet on a Magical Wristband," *Wired*, March 18, 2015, *https://oreil.ly/SzDnI.*

are expecting to be able to continue where they left off, irrespective of the device they are using. This means being able to do not only the same thing and have access to the same functionality, but also see the same content.

What this means for product design

A few years back, a big debate arose online on bespoke mobile websites versus responsive websites. Back then, the prejudice around what users do and don't do on smartphones in particular, but also on tablets, was more prevalent than it is today, and part of the industry was arguing for cut-down versions of mobile experiences as a result. There will always be differences between devices, from the role they play to which device users prefer to use for certain things, as well as what's a more optimal experience on one type compared to another. Today, however, it's more widely accepted that users carry out more or less the same tasks, particularly on smartphones, as they do on laptops, though not necessarily in the same way.

For everyone involved in product design, this means that the starting point should always be to provide an equal experience on all devices so people's interactions with them are similar (i.e., laptops, tablets, and smartphones). But we also need to look at the context of use and the strength/weakness of each type of device and adjust the what and then how accordingly. As we'll cover further on in this book, devices also play a role in the experiences that we design, and defining that role is an important factor to consider.

How Storytelling Can Help

- Identifying all the device actors through mapping the characters
- Identifying how best to deliver the experience by defining what role the devices play and when and where
- Identifying how to deliver the content to varying screen sizes by choreographing the content and messaging between device sizes

MACHINE LEARNING AND AI

Film and literature are filled with examples of AI, both the good and the bad. One of the most famous AI movies is *2001: A Space Odyssey,* in which the spaceship's sentient computer, a HAL 9000, is the most reliable computer there is, at least according to itself. It controls most of the spaceship's (called Discovery One) operations, but soon starts killing off the crew. A less terrifying but still thought-provoking movie is *Ex Machina,* in which the protagonist Caleb, a programmer, wins a visit to his CEO Nathan's home. Nathan asks him to look into whether Nathan's humanoid robot Ava is capable of thought and consciousness as well as if Caleb is able to relate to her even though she's artificial. It's a captivating movie about the potential challenges we'll have in the future around controlling AI as it becomes more sophisticated, as well as what it would do if it is set free. Though we are still some way from either of these scenarios becoming a reality, machine learning and AI are increasingly part of the products that we design.

What this means for product design

Taking advantage of machine learning and AI doesn't have to go all out, but can include small integrations to provide an uplift to the product experience for users and the bottom line for the business. Examples include recommendations (sorting the data we have and prioritizing it so it adds more value and relevance to the user), predictions (looking at what's next based on what you're doing now), classifications (organizing things based on classes or categories), and clustering (looking at unsupervised categories and getting the machine to figure out how the things are organized).[24]

When it comes to implementing machine learning and AI, business requirements and goals will always be pushed. For example, as we've seen from former employees of Facebook, hard conversations increasingly need to be had around the use of data capture and interaction patterns. Those of us involved in product design that uses any kind of data to influence the product experience must be prepared to question and push back, if what's asked by the business is not in the best interest of users. We all have a responsibility to make sure that we're not creating

---

24 Josh Clark, "The New Design Material," *beyond tellerrand*, November 5, 2018, *https://oreil. ly/AoyK-.*

a dystopian future in which the machines take over, and silently kill us off while they still consider themselves the most reliable "computers" there are, just like HAL.

Though this is a very pessimistic look at machine learning and AI, it is important to remember that AI and machine learning needs to be taught everything. What we put in impacts the end result, and if we put in biased or narrow data, then that is the world that the machine will evolve in. That becomes apparent in what we'll cover nex: bots and conversational interfaces.

How Storytelling Can Help

- Defining the personality and behavior of AI by using methods from character development

- Defining the vision by drawing inspiration from film and TV

- Accounting for all eventualities by mapping out the narrative flow of different scenarios

BOTS AND CONVERSATIONAL INTERFACES

As the previous section covers, many movies feature AI. Some movies have even given rise to real-life AIs and bots:, for example, *Iron Man's* Jarvis is the inspiration for Mark Zuckerberg's personal smart home with the same name.

In 2017, talk of bots and conversational interfaces was everywhere. It was looked at as the next big thing, and briefs for bots as part of interfaces were appearing everywhere. Then the chat around bots got a little quieter. Even if bots didn't live up to the hype, partly because of bad implementations, in some cases bots may offer real value—not only to the business, but also to the customer. Customer service is one such area.

The average customer service response time is 20 minutes, yet studies show that if that response time is cut to less than 3 or 4 minutes, a fivefold increase occurs in customer spending.[25] But the use of bots and chat is not just for improving conversions. It's a very appropriate medium when there are barriers to talking to other real people (e.g., picking up the phone in the work place).

What this means for product design

While a chatbot might seem like a straightforward "feature" to add, it comes with many considerations. It may be novel, but using chat is not always the best way for users to navigate their way around a product or service. When to use a bot should always be viewed in light of the context of the rest of the product and that of its users. And as we covered in the previous section, the machine learning and AI that powers it needs to be taught how to behave and respond, as well as how not to behave and respond in certain situations.

Additional considerations should be taken in how the bot is personified, if it is. What might be appealing to some might feel whimsical or too formal to others. Based on the role of the bot, finding the right balance between how it talks and behaves and how it looks is often critical to its success.

How Storytelling Can Help

- Knowing if a bot is right by helping define the role of the bot, including when and where it should be used
- Developing the bot character by drawing on character development principles
- Finding the right tone of voice (TOV) by developing the character and drawing on natural language principles
- Identifying the narrative by mapping out the conversation flow

---

25 Eleanor Kahn, "Bots Are Still in their Infancy," *Campaign*, June 21, 2017, *https://oreil.ly/ QEMpA*.

VOICE UI

Though we are a long way away from the situation we see in the movie *Her*, voice has become more mainstream over the last couple of years. Millions of homes worldwide now have Alexa, Cortana, or Google Home present. By 2020, it's estimated that 30% of all web browsing sessions will be carried out without a screen.[26]

While designing VUIs is new to most, it's a kind of interaction that's very natural for people. Just think of how we'd ask the questions in Google compared to how we would if we spoke to a person. Conversations are natural for us, though there is some first-use awkwardness to get past when it comes to VUIs. Most of us will speak in a somewhat oversimplified manner, slower and clearer than we normally do, to increase our chances of receiving an accurate answer.

The frustrations VUIs can cause when they don't work (i.e., misunderstand you, hear you inaccurately, or do something different than what you asked), should not be taken too lightly, and the context of use is incredibly important for VUIs.

What this means for product design

Even if more devices on the market now, like Amazon Echo Show and the Google Home hub, provide visual results as well as spoken ones, when it comes to VUIs, there is less room for the product design team to provide multiple results to the user. As UX and product designers, we have to think of intuitive ways to deliver results that encourage a natural follow-up answer by the user. And we have to think about all the possible answers and questions the VUI will be subject to, and what to respond for each. While many UX designers have previously been able to "get away with" not accounting for every possible outcome or scenario and focus on the ideal and a couple of alternatives, VUIs require work that's a lot more detailed. All the possible outcomes need to be identified and accounted for, and even if there is no result for a user's query, there still needs to be an answer.

---

26 Raffaela Rein, "UX Design Trends for 2018," *Invision*, January 4, 2018, *https://oreil.ly/_LIne.*

This brings up a different skill that's also needed by the UX designer. There won't always be a specific VUI copywriting team in place, and the role of writing out the initial VUI will often land on the VUI/UX designer.

How Storytelling Can Help

- Defining the personality of the VUI by drawing on character development techniques
- Defining the TOV by identifying what's appropriate in possible situations
- Writing the VUI by drawing on traditional writing skills
- Accounting for all possible situations by looking at branched narratives and mapping out main plots and subplots
- Creating shared understanding of the context by identifying the different scenarios of use

IOT AND THE SMART HOME

Disney released the movie *Smart Home* back in 1999. In it, an ever-present AI called PAT takes care of all your needs, from displaying menus on wall displays in the kitchen, to controlling the lights and the temperature in the house, to absorbing spilled milk on the floor and preparing food. Since then, numerous other movies have featured smart home aspects. There's Stark Mansion in *Iron Man* with, among other things, see-through screens that cover the windows, displaying the weather and other essential information when you wake up. Then we have Nathan's lab in *Ex Machina* with smart lighting. The movie *Her* features, besides the iMac-style laptop, a very apparent lack of screens in the apartment of the main character, Theodore Twombly. Everything is controlled through voice interactions and gestures, including when he plays a VR/AR game that is projected over his furniture.

Though there is a very close connection between AI-based voice assistants and the smart home, there is more to it than that. Many of us will start with a smart home speaker that lets us control music, set a timer, perhaps turn on and off the lights. Or by simply having smart meters, thermostats, and fire alarms. Though many of us are still skeptical about letting technology take over our homes, 68% of Americans are confident that smart homes will be just as commonplace as smart-phones within 10 years.[27] My prediction is that it will happen a lot quicker than that, but we have some hurdles to overcome before that happens.

We're at a turning point; we're sharing more and more data with the devices and technology services that we use. With the smart home, we're going to be able to track everything, from what we do, to various aspects of the house itself. There's a great deal of opportunity here for delivering value and easing everyday life, from being able to check whether the front door is locked and the stove turned off from afar, to automatically ordering food when our smart fridge notices that we're out of groceries. But all of it involves data. We need to ensure that we not only gain users' trust in how we handle this data—and of course, actually handle the data securely and ethically—but also avoid bombarding them with it and all the potentially accompanying notifications that could follow.

For the smart home to be adopted and become mainstream, we need to provide value, be reliable, and make the experience effortless. And there's a great likelihood that we will do just that. Inherent in IoT and its definition is that it's a network of objects that can communicate with each other by sending and receiving data, without the involvement of humans. Many of you who read this will be technology enthusiasts and early adopters, just like myself. But all new technology faces some resistance after the initial excitement wears off, just as there was back when Thomas Edison invented the electric lightbulb. At first people marveled at his creation when it started to light up the streets of New York in 1880, but later they started to mistrust the electric light and considered it unsafe for their homes when stories started to spread of horses being electrocuted from traveling over lanes where transmission cables had been laid.

What this means for product design

While severe accidents like that are not likely to happen, nor the skepticism to be as profound, the value in IoT, smart homes, and increasingly connected experiences across all of our devices lies in the data

---

27 Chris Klein, "2016 Predictions for IoT and Smart Homes," *The Next Web*, December 23, 2015, *https://oreil.ly/rljG8*.

that we'll share with technology, and technology providers, as well as between different touch points, like apps and operating systems. The aim should be to create devices and experiences that work seamlessly together, regardless of the kind or brand of device. This is where the true potential lies in connected experiences, and it's not too far from what Underkoffler is talking about.

But until we reach that point, and in preparation of the same, there is plenty we can do to ensure that the experiences we design tell the right story, to the right user, at the right time, and on the right device. And there is plenty that we, the people behind these products and services, *should do*, in the best interest of everyone. In addition to taking an ethical approach overall, handling data, and not spamming users with notifications, we must also consider how our products and services can be misused, even if that is never the intention. As John Naughton, an author and professor of public understanding of technology at The Open University, writes: "The newest conveniences are now also being used as a means for harassment, monitoring, revenge and control."[28]

How Storytelling Can Help

- Connecting experiences by identifying all the actors that the user as well as our product or service can connect with

- Avoiding cases of misuse by identifying the antagonist in the experience narrative of our products and services

- Identifying the unhappy story by mapping not just the happy journey, but what the opposite, unhappy journey would be and how to avoid/address it, should it happen

AR AND VR

In the movie *Ready Player One*, which is based on the novel of the same name, much of humanity uses virtual reality to escape the grim surroundings of the real world, or as the main character, Wade Watts, puts it: "there's nowhere left to go, except the OASIS." In the OASIS, which

---

28 John Naughton, "The Internet of Things Has Opened Up a New Frontier of Domestic Abuse," *The Guardian*, July 1, 2018., *https://oreil.ly/pksjf.*

is the name of the VR software, people can be whoever they want to be; the only limit is your imagination. The movie takes place in Columbus, Ohio, in 2045 and is a fascinating, yet somewhat chilling, example of how we're able to create worlds online that draw us in and away from the "real" world.

AR, however, has the ability to bridge this gap. According to a study carried out by Latitude, a Boston-based research firm, the real world is also increasingly becoming a platform: 52% of respondents said that they consider it another platform, where they expect the likes of 3D technology and AR to link the digital and physical.[29] Though the hype around Pokemon Go died down not too long after it started, for many this was the first time they got to experience the "overlay" added to the world, where character and additional information was shown.

What this means for product design

Designing for VR and AR draws a lot from film and game design. As product designers, we need to evolve our skills beyond traditional product design as factors like depth, touch, sound, and emotion are all integral parts to the experience. There are additional considerations to keep in mind, such as that the player or user will assume that any object that is made part of the experience will have a role to play and an action or event associated with it, similar to the case with movies.

One of the biggest differences in designing for AR and VR is that the player or user is not just a passive observer but an actual part of the product experience story. Additionally, you're designing for an immersive, 360° space rather than a fixed desktop, tablet, or mobile screen. There are a lot of specifics to keep in mind when it comes to AR and VR. To really understand what we're designing for, we need to immerse ourselves in both VR and AR and experience it first hand.

---

29 Ifeanyi, "The Future of Storytelling."

How Storytelling Can Help

- Placing the user in the center of the experience by making the user the protagonist, putting a first-person's perspective on the experience

- Defining the scenes in the AR and VR products by drawing on principles and methods from game design and cinematography

- Planning out the sequence of events by drawing from traditional storytelling methods

OMNICHANNEL EXPERIENCES

In a well-told story, everything from big to small details comes together. Today, we're seeing how online and offline experiences are increasingly merging and influencing one another. For a few years now, we've been talking about omnichannel experiences. *Omnichannel experiences* are defined as cross-channel experiences, which include channels like social media, physical locations, ecommerce, mobile apps, desktops, and more. All of these channels are increasingly providing input and output for each other. Just as companies that optimized their mobile experience had an advantage a few years ago over those that didn't, today companies that optimize so that the user can move seamlessly across channels will have a competitive advantage over those that don't. Advantages will include higher conversion and increased brand loyalty as ease and equal experiences become ever more important.[30]

What this means for product design

The line between digital and physical environments is increasingly blurring. As they essentially become one and the same, product design teams will have to learn, relearn, and learn again to keep up with the changes in technology. This also means that everything is increasingly an experience and that team members beyond those with "UX" in their titles will benefit from at least a basic understanding of user experience design.

---

30 Kim Flaherty, "Seamlessness in the Omnichannel User Experience," *Nielsen Norman Group*, March 19, 2017, *https://oreil.ly/YWIrz*.

As for the actual UX designers, they will have to understand the digital aspect, device, and hardware capabilities, how the products they work on live outside the screen, the role and influence of context, and also the possibilities these provide.

How Storytelling Can Help

- Identifying how our designs will live outside screens, by bringing the experience narrative to life through storyboards

- Creating a shared understanding, by getting teams and departments to work through the experience narrative together

- Creating a coherent story across all touch points, by identifying all the actors and characters that play a part in the experience

Changes in Consumer Expectations

There are also changes in consumer expectations connected to the ways storytelling and product design are changing. Next we'll look at three such areas that span both storytelling and product design.

IMMEDIACY AND TAP-OF-A-BUTTON EXPECTATIONS

One of the main impacts of the iPhone when it first came out, and all smartphones thereafter, has been a shift in user expectations. Everything is now available at our fingertips by reaching into our bags and pockets. We can hardly remember what is was like when we had to plan in advance or even go to the library to get answers. Instead we've come to expect an answer the moment we want to go somewhere, do something, or buy something.[31]

This immediacy is an increasing expectation from users and customers, from health providers that offer appointments 24/7, the tap-of-a-button expectations, to brands and governments being expected to respond and address matters on social media the minute they happen, and be transparent about it.

---

31 Natalie Zmuda, "The New Customer Behaviors That Defined Google's Year in Search," *Think with Google*, December 2017, *https://oreil.ly/yrUsK*; Lisa Gevelbier, "Micro-Moments Now," *Think with Google*, July2017, *https://oreil.ly/vAshk*.

What this means for product design

What users have gotten used to in social media, they start to expect elsewhere for the products and services that they use. It's increasingly important for brands and companies to know how to act and respond. With more bots and AI-driven interfaces, knowing when to hand off to a human being is crucial or it can have a negative impact on a brand and business.[32]

The "right here and now" immediacy also places an interesting aspect on content and context. As we'll cover shortly, there is a growing expectation around "for me" and a growing emphasis on search as a shortcut straight into the most relevant thing that users are looking for. For anyone involved in product design, it means that we should be able to deliver our lines—that is, our content—in the blink of an eye, no matter where the user has come from.

How Storytelling Can Help

- Determining how to behave when and where by defining and developing all the actors in a potential experience

- Narrating the experience by taking a step back and looking at how and where we can be relevant

- Removing friction, by exploring the "what if…" of doing things differently

- Accounting for all eventualities by mapping out both the happy and the unhappy journeys

---

PERSONALIZATION AND TAILORED EXPERIENCES

An Ericsson Trend report captured personalization well: "Today you have to know all the devices. But tomorrow all the devices will have to know you."[33] The more we can tell about our users, and the more sophisticated machine learning and programmatic anything will become, the more tailored all our experiences will be. There will no longer be "one website" or one experience, but just as the results in

---

32 The State of UX in 2019, *https://trends.uxdesign.cc/*.

33 "10 Hot Consumer Trends 2018," ericsson.com, *https://oreil.ly/N6B9v*.

our Google searches are already tailored to us specifically based on our previous searches and online behavior, so will all of our online experiences be.

What this means for product design

Personalization and tailored experiences don't just have to do with content. There is a big opportunity in adapting users' actual needs (e.g., larger or smaller font sizes, location, history, actions they've taken or not taken). To truly do so, however, we really need to understand their needs in the different contexts and situations they are in, and responsibly leverage the power of data.

How Storytelling Can Help

- Understanding user needs by developing and creating empathy for the user

- Designing for specific users by making the user the main hero of the product experience

- Knowing how to personalize by identifying what would turn the happy story into an unhappy one

---

USE OF SEARCH AND HOW WE ACCESS INFORMATION

Many of us, myself included, have stopped memorizing certain things, like phone numbers—even our partner's. Instead, we memorize where we can find that information. We're becoming experts at searching, but even more so, we're expecting to be able to find almost anything by searching, and our expectations of what we will find are growing.

Over the past year, Google in particular has reported about searches using the qualifiers "the best" and "should I." This shows a shift in both trust and expectation. Users are increasingly turning to search in an advisory way, just as you would a friend. They're asking for specific things, for them, and they expect a relevant answer.

In addition to this, users are increasingly using search as a way to navigate websites and apps, skipping the main navigation and jumping straight in. It's at times quicker, and if the result they get back is any good, they get just what they need in that moment.

What this means for product design

When we define and design the pages/views and the overall experience of the products and services we work on, we increasingly need to do that with a key consideration in mind: users will most likely not arrive on the home page first. In fact, the "home page" of our products or services is often search.

This has implications for the way we think about content and page design. The background context that users otherwise would have gotten if they'd navigated through our website or app in the way we usually so carefully plan it out is often not there. Instead, a user should be able to grasp that context, or at least part of it, regardless of what page they first land on.

How Storytelling Can Help

- Identifying the content by defining the narrative structure of pages and views
- Optimizing for search by ensuring not only accurate search results but also context around them

Summary

Over the years, storytelling has influenced and driven innovation in both science and technology, from Sherlock Holmes and how crimes are solved, to *Star Trek* providing inspiration for Amazon's Alexa. Storytelling has also played a critical part in communication and connecting with audiences, and that's something we're increasingly struggling to do with the products and services that we're working on today.

The context in which they are used is becoming more complex by the day. At the same time, users are increasingly expecting products and services to work for them, specifically, no matter where they are, what device and input methods they are using, and in whichever way they want to use them.

Designers require new skills, as what we're designing increasingly involves AI and machine learning, multiple touch points, connected devices and apps, as well as a mixture of interfaces we touch, interfaces we talk to, interfaces we cannot see, and those that we are an actual part of through sensory data or AR and VR. As designers, we need to master Walt Disney's skill of being be able to get the bigger picture right in addition to the small details. We also need to account for a growing number of eventualities and moving parts that need to be defined and designed, so that they all come together. Just like a good story.

[4]

The Emotional Aspect
of Product Design

Shouting at the Voice Assistant

Back in 2016 I was working with the full-service advertising agency 72andSunny in Amsterdam and helping out on the launch campaign of Google Home in, among other countries, the UK. Fast-forward to 2019, and Google Home is now an integrated part of my own family's home life. Even our daughter, who was born in the summer of 2017, knows what Google Home is because of the voice command "Hey Google."

Many of the scenarios and use cases that we identified as part of the launch campaign apply to my family. Our primary use of Google Home right now is for simple things, like asking it to play music on Spotify, or to make various animal and vehicle sounds, to our daughter's delight. But life can get complicated, and at times Google Home adds to that. Sometimes the really simple things don't work, like Google Home misunderstanding "Turn up the volume" for "Turn *off* the volume," or failing to hear when we ask it to turn off the music or turn down the volume. That causes the emotions in us to rise, particularly when things are already a bit hectic, or we're tired.

During the launch campaign work, we kept the scenarios fairly high-level, as that's all that was needed. Had we worked on the actual software for Google Home, it would have been a different matter. When you're working with technologies that use sound as the primary UI for both input and output, you need to go into detail to understand scenarios. For our daughter's first Christmas, we stayed with friends in Malmö, Sweden. Their whole apartment was hooked up to Amazon Echo, and the easiest way to turn on and off the lights was simply to ask Alexa to do so. In 2017, when you asked Alexa to turn off the lights, she responded "OK" and then turned off the lights. At first this wasn't a problem, but when it came to turning off the bedroom lights when my partner and the baby were asleep, Alexa's verbal response wasn't ideal. Not knowing the volume level of Alexa added another dimension to the problem.

Turning off the lights in your kid's bedroom when it's time to go to sleep, or changing the lights to a different color, was one of the scenarios that we'd identified for the Google Home launch campaign. It's one of those things that when it's new, it's quite magical, and from a practical point of view, not having to get up can be really handy, especially when you have young kids. How that feature is implemented, however, needs careful consideration, and in my opinion, there is no need for a voice assistant to confirm using voice that it has turned off the light. The act of doing so is evidence enough.

There is some talk about how VR and AR will influence both the experience of users and storytelling overall, but also how we as designers can experience what we design. Traditionally, whether we're designing, watching a movie, or listening to a concert, we're used to being the observer looking in. The fourth wall is there between us and what goes on behind the screen or on stage. With AR and VR in particular, we're placing ourselves in the middle of the story and the experience, and increasingly it will feel like we're there and part of it. Studies have shown that our bodies can't tell the difference between a thought and an actual experience in the way it responds. Our senses are easily fooled, and if we feel joy and happiness, our bloodstream is flooded with endorphins; if we feel fear, adrenaline is released into our bodies.

At every single point of the experience with your product, even if it doesn't include AR or VR, users go through emotions—from frustration (like that most of us have around passwords, or when we can't find what we're after, or something simply doesn't work), to happiness (when it just works seamlessly, without any problems, as if the website or app we were using knew exactly what we wanted). Whether it's a user using our products and services, an internal team member going through our work, or a client listening to us presenting it, in every kind of experience, emotions are involved and play a big part. Just as they do in stories.

The Role of Emotion in Storytelling

All the way back to ancient times, when storytelling was used to explain everything from natural phenomena to the adventures of a tribe, stories were told with a purpose. They might aim to calm and reassure people that after rain comes sunshine, or to help the rest of the tribe that wasn't there to relive a battle and make sure they never forgot about important events. Each novel, movie, TV series, or play has a story to tell and a desired emotional response that it wants to evoke in its audience, and it's the storyteller's job to do so.

In the words of Daniel Dercksen of the Writing Studio, "The storyteller is the puppet master of emotion." He writes:

> As a writer you have the power to make your audience laugh whenever it pleases you, cause grown men to cry shamelessly, keep millions on the edge of reason, prevent couch junkies to switch channels, and grip people with fear.[1]

Evoking the audience's emotions lies at the heart of storytelling, and without that emotional connection, there wouldn't be a story to talk of. Writers and storytellers have numerous ways to capture the audience's attention and pull them to the edge of their seats; for example, through the way the story is told, or by it including suspense, tension, and conflict. But the most powerful way to create an emotional connection is through the characters themselves. Just think back to some of the movies, books, or plays that have left a long-lasting impression on you; it's the characters and their destiny that engaged you.

Emotion also plays a role in making that story come to life for the storyteller(s). Meg LeFauve, an American screenwriter, talks of how in the making of Pixar's movie *Inside Out*, the personification of the emotions (Joy, Anger, Sadness, Fear, and Disgust) were already designed when she came on, which meant that she could see Riley, the girl who the emotions belonged to. The fact that the voice artist of Joy had also already been cast as Amy Poehler added another layer to the character

---

1 Daniel Dercksen, "The Art of Manipulating Emotions in Storytelling," *The Writing Studio*, February 22, 2016, *https://oreil.ly/K1bxJ*.

that in LeFauve's case, meant that she could really write to Poehler.[2] Writers are often advised to draw from their own, or at least real, experiences when it comes to finding inspiration and giving the story depth. Being able to relate themselves is an important aspect in making sure that the story they're writing will create an emotional connection with its audience.

As for product design, having empathy for the users we're designing and building our products and services for is an important aspect, and we'll touch more on that in Chapter 6, "Using Character Development in Product Design." In this chapter, however, we're going to focus on why striving to elicit certain emotions in design, otherwise known as *emotional design*, is so important in order to create a better experience for users.

The Role of Emotion in Product Design

In the early days of personal computing and human-computer interaction, the focus was on usability, functionality, and improving processes. More recently, there has been a shift toward also considering the emotional side. This change is to a large extent thanks to the thought leadership of Don Norman, a researcher, professor, and author of *Emotional Design* (Basic Books, 2004) (Figure 4-1), and Aaron Walter, author of *Designing for Emotion* (A Book Apart, 2011).

Emotional Design was in part a response to critics who argued that if they followed his advice in his earlier book, *The Design of Everyday Things*, products would be functional but ugly. Norman didn't mention emotion in the first edition of *The Design of Everyday Things*. Instead, he focused on utility and usability, function and form in a logical, and in his own words, dispassionate way. In *Emotional Design,* he explores the profound influence that feelings and emotions have on us and how these are evoked through everyday objects.

---

2 Joe Berkowitz, "7 Tips on Emotional Storytelling," *Fast Company,* December 1, 2015, *https://oreil.ly/yBG-l.*

FIGURE 4-1

Norman's *Emotional Design* with the infamous Juicy Salif citrus squeezer on the front cover

A big theme of the book is that much of human behavior is subconscious and that consciousness comes later. If you look at how we react to a situation, he writes, we usually react emotionally before we assess the situation cognitively, and when most of us are asked why we decided on something, we often don't know why. We just "felt like it" or "it felt good."

Let's explore the role of emotions in design and how storytelling can assist.

THE EFFECT OF EMOTIONS ON DECISION MAKING

The role of emotions in decision making is well researched in marketing as well as in psychology. Antonio Damasio, professor of neuroscience at the University of Southern California, writes in *Descartes' Error* that emotion is a necessary ingredient for almost all decisions. When we need to make a decision, our emotions from previous related experiences affect how we perceive our options, eventually leading us to create preferences.[3] This is similar to the positive feedback mechanism and Freud's pleasure principle, which states that we instinctively

---

3 Peter Noel Murray, "How Emotions Influence What We Buy," *Psychology Today*, February 26, 2013, *https://oreil.ly/Hsfp4*.

seek out pleasure and try to avoid pain by re-creating previously pleasurable experiences and avoiding situations that we consider likely to cause pain.

Many of us believe that the decisions we make are carefully considered and rational. We also often assume this approach when thinking through the actions a user might take in the experiences that we design. While this may sometimes be the case, often what sways us one way or the other in our decision making is our emotional response to what we're experiencing. Take, for example, why we sometimes choose a specific, more expensive brand over another, or even the more generic and cheaper store brands. This is where our emotions come into play. A brand "is nothing more than a mental representation of a product in the consumer's mind." We create our own stories around everything that we experience, and when it comes to us evaluating brands, we primarily base it on our personal feelings and experiences rather than on information, features, and facts.

Positive emotions are also what influences brand loyalty to a larger extent than, for example, trust. As was the case with both the first iPod and the latest version of the iPhone, positive emotions are also what makes us buy certain products over others, even if they aren't always the most practical ones, like Philip Starck's iconic Juicy Salif that's on the cover of *Emotional Design*.

Without emotions, our decision-making ability would be impaired and we wouldn't be able to decide between alternatives, especially choices that appear equally valid.

The role of affect and cognition on decision making

When it comes to our everyday decision making, emotion and affect are crucial. Affect and cognition are both information processing systems, but with different functions. The *affective system* responds quickly by making judgments on whether things in the environment are dangerous or safe, good or bad. It's our lizard brain, and the responses can be either conscious or subconscious. The *cognitive system*, on the other hand, interprets and makes sense of the world. Where emotion comes in is in the conscious experience of affect combined with the attribution of its cause and the identification of its object.

Both affect and cognition influence one another. In some situations, the affective state is driven by cognition, but most of the time cognition is impacted by affect. The example Norman uses to illustrate this relationship is that of a plank. If I place a plank on the ground and ask if you can walk on it, the answer will be a resounding "Of course I can!" If, however, I place it a hundred meters up in the air and ask the same question, the answer will be very different. What this example illustrates is that the affective system works independently of conscious thought. The visceral level, what we feel deep down in our gut, of looking one hundred meters down wins. Fear dominates our response rather than the reflective part of our brain that may try to rationalize that it's the same 10-meter-long, 1-meter-wide plank, so of course you can walk it.

This is similar to the way we react when we watch a scary movie, or the way we feel after having watched one. Our cognitive system can rationalize and tell us that there's a 99.9% certainty that no one is hiding in the darkness of the room, but what we've just seen and the emotions that are evoked in us may at times stop us from walking into that room without the lights on.

Exercise: The Role of Affect and Cognition on Decision Making

Think of two situations that you've experienced in your life:

- How did your affective system respond?
- How did your cognitive system respond?

While the gut-feel response to the experiences we have with products and services seldom are as strong as in the example with the plank 100 meters up in the air, sometimes the affective system dominates our response. Now, think about the product or service you work on:

- How is the user's affective system likely to respond?
- How is the user's cognitive system likely to respond?

The coupling between our emotional and behavioral systems

Our emotional system is so tightly coupled with behavior and preparing our bodies to respond, Norman says, that the reactions we feel to any given situation are real manifestations of the way our emotions control our muscles and, for example, our digestive system. We have these same reactions when we're subject to a story. Whether it's in response to a story or an online experience, be it good or bad, something that makes us tense or relaxed, our emotions pass judgment and prepare our bodies accordingly, and the conscious, cognitive self observes these changes.

In response to our emotions, neurochemicals are sent to particular parts of our brain, changing our parameters of thought. What scientists now know is that affect changes our operating parameters of cognition, with positive affect enhancing creative, breadth-first thinking, and negative affect focusing our cognition as well as enhancing depth-first processing while minimizing distractions. This means that stress has a negative impact on people's ability to cope with difficulties and to be flexible in how they approach problem-solving and that, to the contrary, positive affect makes people more tolerant.

Evidence also shows that aesthetically pleasing products work better and that when people are in a relaxed situation, pleasurable aspects of a design can make them more tolerant of difficulties and problems. Although poor design is, in Norman's words, "never excusable," good human-centered design practice becomes more essential for tasks or situations that may be stressful and where distractions, bottlenecks, and irritants in general need to be minimized.

Exercise: The Coupling Between Our Emotional and Behavioral Systems

Think of your product or service, or a product or service that you are familiar with, and identify the following:

- Where and how might stress be related to the use of the product or service? The stress could be caused by part of the task the user has to do, external factors in the user's environment, or simply bad design.

- Where is there, or should there be, positive affect in the experience journey of that product or service?

THE INFLUENCE OF EMOTIONS ON TAKING ACTION

One of the most interesting things about emotions is that they push us to action. We might have a fight-or-flight response if we feel afraid in a physical confrontation. Daily social situations that elicit desire or insecurity may lead us to buy the latest iPhone. Or our emotional responses might simply determine how we click or tap our way through a website or app. As we covered in Chapter 1, storytelling has been used throughout history to move people to action, from sparking our imagination to getting behind a cause. And that's all caused by the emotions they evoke in us.

When you look at what influences purchase decisions, research shows that the emotional response to the content is more influential than the content itself. What this means for brands is that you need to ensure that you hit the right level of emotional resonance, at the right time. In other words, you connect with your potential customers on the right emotional level.[4]

However, understanding the impact of our emotions on our actions is just as much about understanding why we decide not to take action. Alessandro Suraci, a visual designer at Google, writes about how commitment is hard and that when it comes to setting goals and working toward achieving them, actually doing so is often further afield than the excuse for not doing what you've set out to do.[5] As UX designers, we need to know the typical situation narrative and what users are feeling in order to understand how to move them into action, including what's holding them back from following through.

[TIP]

This exercise is particularly useful in relation to mapping out plot points and visualizing the shape of an experience, as we'll cover in Chapters 5 and 9, respectively.

---

4 Andrea Lehr, "The Role of Emotions in Shareable Content," *HubSpot* (blog), *https://oreil.ly/ImfOe*.

5 Alessandro Suraci, "Picture a Better You," *Medium*, April 13, 2016, *https://oreil.ly/c3T9J*.

The Influence of Emotion on Brand and Product Perception

Emotions also play a critical role in our long-term memory and our ability to understand and learn about the world. It's one of the reasons storytelling has become such a buzzword, not the least in marketing. Marketing that includes the kind of storytelling that tugs on your heartstrings is more effective than any other type of marketing.

The reason for this increase in efficacy is that emotional storytelling is memorable. It creates deep connections that makes it harder to forget the message. Emotional storytelling also creates positive associations with the brand in question by linking positive images with the objective behind your marketing campaign. And last, marketing that involves emotional storytelling appeals to emotions instead of reason and gives the user an experience.

When you think about it, it's a given. Very few of us will remember an OK movie or book, but we remember the really good or bad one. It's the same when it comes to the products and services that we use. We remember the ones that caused us massive frustrations and the ones that brought us joy. More often than not, the ones on either side of the spectrum are the ones we talk to others about and the ones we tend to write a good, or a bad, review of.

The next time you talk to a (prospective) user or customer, ask these
questions:

- What's the one thing you remember about [the name of your product,
  or a marketing campaign]?

- Why do you remember this particular [aspect of your product]?

Emotions and Our Different Levels of Needs

Aaron Walter, the author of *Designing for Emotion*, defines emotions
as the "lingua franca of humanity," the native tongue that all human
beings are born with, and says that emotional experiences are critical to our long-term memory. When it comes to design, an emotional
response makes the experience feel like there's a human being on the
other side rather than just a machine.[6]

In his book, Walter has developed a pyramid of user needs that draws
on Maslow's pyramid of needs. The latter was developed in 1943 and
included in his paper "A Theory of Human Motivation" (Figure 4-2).
Maslow posed that, as human beings, we have basic needs (like phys-
iological ones), that have to be met before more advanced needs (like
self-actualization), can be addressed.

FIGURE 4-2
Maslow's pyramid of
needs

---

6 Aaron Walter, "Emotional Interface Design," Treehouse, August 7, 2012, *https://oreil.ly/
PBC5y.*

If the four most basic needs, which Maslow calls *deficiency needs*, or *d-needs*, aren't met, the individual will feel anxious and tense even if there is no physical sign. This has some interesting parallels with design. If we map this insight from Maslow's pyramid over to interface design, Walter says, we can "get a better understanding of the way our audience works."

Just as with Maslow's pyramid of needs, the four basic layers have to be met in Walter's pyramid of user needs before the user can appreciate the pleasure layer (Figure 4-3).

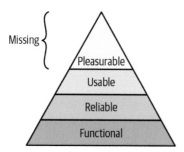

FIGURE 4-3

Walter's hierarchy of user needs states that basic user needs must be fulfilled by the interface first before more advanced needs can be met

Walter's theory suggests that the first thing we have to do with our products and services is to address the functional layer and ensure that we solve a problem for our users. After that, we have to make sure that what we design and build is reliable and usable, meaning easy to learn, easy to use, and easy to remember. What we often overlook, however, according to Walter, is the pleasure layer that comes next.[7]

PLEASURE IN DESIGN

The *pleasure layer* is where we have an opportunity to take the user experience to the next level. What we normally talk about in design as *delights* aren't just the gimmicky things that will get you a mention in the press, but the small touches that help make the user connect on an emotional level. Delightful details can be as simple as an animation or the illustrations that accompany many of the Install Application dialog boxes on a Mac.

---

7 Walter, "Emotional Interface Design."

Delights, however, are so much more than that. They are also in the overall feel of an experience, or how you move seamlessly without any delays from one screen to the next, the animations and transitions that are being used, as well as the use of micro copy and iconography throughout, to mention a few examples.

Walter refers to these delights as *pleasures*, and draws a great parallel to eating out. We go to a fancy restaurant, we don't just hope for an edible meal. We hope for much more. We hope that the food will be amazing, that the ambiance and service will be great, and that the whole experience will be memorable. Walter argues that we shouldn't settle for just *usable* in design when we can create designs that are both *usable and pleasurable.*

Walter defines two types of delights within the pleasure layer:

Surface delights
> These delights are local and contextual and often derived from isolated interface features like animations, gestural commands, micro copy, high-resolution imagery, or sound interactions.

Deep delights
> These delights are holistic and are achieved only when all the user needs are met and the user has reached a state of flow with little distraction from the main task.

Deep delights are much harder to accomplish than surface delights. Even if users have a poor overall experience, they may still experience some surface delight. Deep delights, on the other hand, are experienced only when things work just the way they should and deliver everything as expected without getting in the way; a bit like the magic of a good story, where everything just comes together.

It's when users experience deep delights that they are most likely to recommend a product or service to their friends, families, and colleagues. While they might be less sexy from a design point of view than surface delights, deep delights are the ones to get right first and foremost, after the lower-level user needs are met, just as with Maslow's pyramid of needs.[8]

---

8 Therese Fessenden, "A Theory of User Delight," *Nielsen Norman Group*, March 5, 2017, *https://oreil.ly/X7xwX*.

Exercise: Pleasure in Design

Come up with two examples of websites or apps that have surface delights and deep delights:

- What are the surface delights, and where can you find them?
- What are the deep delights?

Now think of your own product or service:

- What could an appropriate example of a surface delight be; where would you include it, and why?
- What could an example of a deeper delight be, and how would it manifest itself?

ADDRESSING THE LOWER-LEVEL NEEDS FIRST

As Norman points out, positive affect makes people more tolerant of difficulties or problems. While many of the emotions we're hoping to ignite with our users would fall under the pleasure layer, plenty of emotions can be evoked on the lower levels, many of them negative if we fail to deliver on the most basic level. John Maeda, an American executive, designer, and technologist, talks about complexity and simplicity and suggests that the latter is "about living life with more enjoyment and less pain."[9] *New York Times* columnist David Pogue started out a TED talk by singing out his frustrations around technology and being on hold with customer service before going on to talk about software rage.[10]

We've all been there and know that when technology doesn't work, or when websites make it difficult to do what we want, or when voice assistants add to the chaos as mentioned at the beginning of the chapter, it can send emotions as strong as rage through our bodies. But even if it's not rage we feel, everyday frustrations caused by technology are more than enough. The passwords of a family member are a funny tribute to the frustrations of using technology. Hardly any of them are what you'd

---

9 John Maeda, "Designing for Simplicity," TED2007 Video, March 2007, *https://oreil.ly/O074K*.

10 David Pogue, "Simplicity Sells," TED2006 Video, February 2006, *https://oreil.ly/ExNFa*.

expect. Instead they might include swear words and any other imaginative words along the same lines. The passwords say more than a little about what that person thought of passwords.

As much as we might be excited to work on areas and experiences of the product that fall under the pleasure level, we have to make sure, as Walter points out, that we have first addressed the most basic levels of needs. It doesn't matter how beautiful a website or app is if it isn't functional or doesn't have a purpose. And if it's functional but not reliable, it will leave users frustrated. Equally, if a product requires a lot of effort to use, or to learn how to use, it won't be considered very usable. It's only when a product is functional, reliable, and usable that users can appreciate the delightful and pleasurable aspects of the product. We need to get the basics right, and what constitutes "basic" is constantly evolving.

THE STRIVE FOR CONSTANT BETTERMENT AND THE NEW NORMAL

One of the other things Maslow posed in his theory of human motivation is that we strive for constant betterment and seek to go beyond the scope of the basic needs. *Metamotivation*, as he calls it, is something we should keep in mind in design. When the first iPhone came out, we didn't think much about how websites appeared as they were on a desktop, but smaller, in our phones. However, when we started developing mobile sites, we became more accustomed to mobile-optimized solutions, and these gradually became the norm and something we expected.

What this "new normal" illustrates is that when it comes to development in technology and the products and services that run on them, the goal post for what constitutes *functional, usable, reliable,* and *pleasurable* moves as our devices become more advanced and user behavior changes. Being able to do the same things on our phones as we can do on our desktops is no longer something that we'd say would fall in the pleasure layer, as it did in the early days of the mobile web. Instead, it's the new normal and part of the functional layer of the product. This constant need to adapt to technological advances and strive for betterment is why understanding user expectations and emotions are so closely tied and important in product design.

Understanding Emotions

Just as a good story, whether it's a film, book, or play, connects with us on more than the visual level, the appeal of products is about more than how they look. Steve Jobs famously said, "Design is not just what it looks and feels like, it's how it works."[11] Author Cindy Alvarez says that she'd like to go one step further and say, "Design is how you work. [It's] how you feel when you are using things or having experiences."[12] While products and services, like those of Craigslist or Amazon, for sure can and do work, design and the UX of the same are increasingly becoming competitive factors, and emotional design plays a key part. Design thinking and experience design as well as customer experience, otherwise known as CX, have increasingly become well known, and for good reason.[13]

When the first iPod came out in 2001, it made a big impact. That wasn't just because of the enormous number of songs it could hold, but also because of its design with the iconic white headphones and scroll wheel. Bruce Claxton, then president of the Industrial Designers Society of America, has said, "People are seeking out products that are not just simple to use but a joy to use."[14] The iPod was both seductive and simple to use, and it connected with users on an emotional level.

THREE LEVELS OF EMOTIONS IN RELATION TO PRODUCT DESIGN

According to Norman, when it comes to objects, we form connections on three levels:

The visceral level
> This deals with aesthetics and the perceived quality of the product from its look and feel to the way it engages our senses. This level is closely related to our initial reaction (more precisely, that gut feeling) when we encounter a product.

---

11 Rob Walker, "The Guts of a New Machine," *New York Times*, November 30, 2003, *https://oreil.ly/Z8Qyk*.

12 Mary Treseler, "Design Is How Users Feel when Experiencing Products," *O'Reilly Design Podcast*, August 20, 2015, *https://oreil.ly/Z3SMH*.

13 Manita Dosanjh, "Building Magic Moments," *The Drum*, August 5, 2016, *https://oreil.ly/Bdb37*.

14 Walker, "The Guts of a New Machine."

The behavioral level

This refers to the usability of the product and our assessment of whether it performs the desired functions, as well as how easily we can learn to use it. At this level, we'll have formed a more informed opinion about the product.

The reflective level

This concerns the impact we perceive the product to have on our lives. This level is about "after" usage; for example, how we feel after we've held a product and the values we attach to it in retrospect. This is where we'll want to create as much desire as possible when it comes to product design.

Each of these three levels plays a role in shaping our experience of a product, but each level also requires a different approach by the designer. In order to provide and design for a positive experience, we should address the user's cognitive ability on each level and put it into the context of the experience.

TYPES OF EMOTIONS

Norman's three levels provide a great framework for thinking about emotions in relation to product design. But at times we need to go deeper than that and look at the types of emotions users experience when using our products in order to really help define the experience of the same.

A good place to start is with *Plutchik's wheel of emotions* (Figure 4-4). Psychologist, professor, and author Robert Plutchik devised one of the most influential classifications of general emotional responses in his psychoevolutionary theory of emotion, which categorizes primary and secondary emotions.[15]

---

15 For more on Plutchik's wheel of emotion in relation to putting emotions into your designs, visit the Interaction Design Foundation (*https://oreil.ly/-gJtl*).

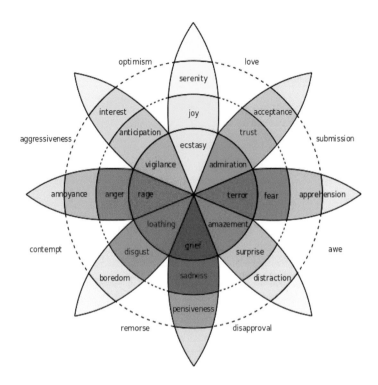

FIGURE 4-4
Plutchik's wheel of emotions

Primary emotions

Plutchik considered there to be eight primary emotions:

- Anger
- Disgust
- Fear
- Sadness
- Anticipation
- Joy
- Surprise
- Trust

He considered these "basic" emotions to be the ones that have evolved in order to increase the chance of survival.

Secondary emotions

As part of his psychoevolutionary theory, Plutchik also defined 10 postulates, one of which is, "All other emotions are mixed or derivative states; that is, they occur as combinations, mixtures, or compounds of the primary emotions" (Figure 4-5).

The secondary emotions are as follows:

- Anticipation + Joy = Optimism (its opposite being Disapproval)

- Joy + Trust = Love (its opposite being Remorse)

- Trust + Fear = Submission (its opposite being Contempt)

- Fear + Surprise = Awe (its opposite being Aggression)

- Surprise + Sadness = Disapproval (its opposite being Optimism)

- Sadness + Disgust = Remorse (its opposite being Love)

- Disgust + Anger = Contempt (its opposite being Submission)

- Anger + Anticipation = Aggressiveness (its opposite being Awe)

Understanding the nuances of emotions, their opposites, and the makeup of each emotion is useful when going into detail on what emotional responses we are evoking, and which ones we would like to evoke in the products and services that we design. As with all stories, if we're clear on the outcome we're after, it's easier to identify the right principle, tool, or method to make it happen.

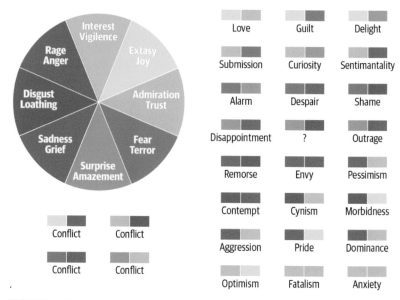

FIGURE 4-5

Plutchik's mixture of primary emotions into combinations and opposites[16]

Exercise: Types of Emotions

Think about a website, app, or product you use on a regular basis. Which emotions would you assign to key steps, pages, or views in the experience of the same?

Now think about the product or service you work on/have worked on:

- What emotions are you trying to evoke at each step in the journey?
- Why are you trying to evoke those emotions?
- How are you doing it?
- Does it reflect what users and customers are actually feeling?

WHAT MAKES US SHARE

As Plutchik's wheel of emotions demonstrates, emotional responses aren't always positive feelings. Although most of the experiences we design seek to evoke positive feelings, at times the opposite drives our

---

16 Interactive Design Foundation, *https://oreil.ly/yGGjL*.

behavior. Viral content, for example, can thrive on negative emotions. For instance, on YouTube, a lot of funny videos go viral, but so do also a lot of angry political rants. Whether they're funny, heartfelt, or angry rants, what these videos have in common is that they contain triggers that get people talking.

Andrea Lehr, a Promotions Supervisor at Frac.tl, wrote about the role of emotions in shareable content and referenced a study carried out on one hundred viral Reddit images. "The dress" of 2015 that had the internet going mad about whether it was gold or blue is one of her examples of something seemingly pointless that influenced behavior. The seller of the dress saw its organic traffic increase by 420% and sales of the dress increase by 560%, all because an image of it went viral. So what is it, then, that makes people share it?[17]

Lehr's research found that virality is a combination of emotional connection paired with additional dimensions of arousal and dominance. The top emotional responses to viral images are as follows:

1. Happiness

2. Surprise

3. Admiration

4. Satisfaction

5. Hope

6. Love

7. Happiness for

8. Concentration

9. Pride

10. Gratitude

While negative emotions like hate, reproach, and resentment were far less common in viral content, they can still play a role as long as they hit the right combination of arousal and dominance. Lehr refers to additional research carried out on the roles that valence, arousal, and dominance play on generating viral content and defines them as follows:

---

17 Andrea Lehr, "The Role of Emotions in Shareable Content," HubSpot (blog), July 20, 2016, https://oreil.ly/t_Ehr.

Valence

The positivity or negativity of an emotion

Arousal

Ranges from excitement to relaxation, with anger being a high-arousal emotion and sadness low-arousal

Dominance

Ranges from submission to feeling in control, with fear being low-dominance and admiration high-dominance

When the research team mapped arousal and dominance levels against the one hundred viral Reddit images that they analyzed, they found that the three combinations shown in Figure 4-6 are more successful in generating shareable and viral content.[18]

COMMON EMOTIONAL COMBINATIONS **IN VIRAL IMAGES**

LEVELS OF AROUSAL AND DOMINANCE		EMOTIONAL SENTIMENT
AROUSAL	DOMINANCE	ACCOMPANYING EMOTIONS
High	High	All Positive **OR** Positive + Surprise
High	Low	Surprise + Negative + Positive **OR** Positive + Surprise
Low	Low	Surprise + Negative + Positive **OR** Surprise + Negative **OR** Surprise + Positive

FIGURE 4-6

Lehr's identified common emotional combinations in viral images

Creating a viral marketing campaign, or content in any form, is the dream of many brands, startups, marketers, and aspiring influencers. Understanding the underlying emotional sentiments and the

---

18 Lehr, "The Role of Emotions."

combinations that are most likely to produce the desired effect is a powerful tool to apply to both marketing campaigns and product design in general. By being clear on what we're trying to evoke, and why, we have a better chance of accomplishing our objective. Next we'll take a look at some situations where emotions play a particularly important role.

Exercise: What Makes Us Share

Using an example related to a past campaign, initiative, or content related to your product or service, identify how you would define the following:

- What was the emotional sentiment of the content?
- What was the arousal level?
- What was the dominance level?

Using the same example, identify what could you have changed and how, in order to achieve one of the three levels of arousal and dominance that Lehr identified as generating the most shareable and viral content.

Situations Where Emotion in Design Can Play a Key Role

As we covered earlier in this chapter, good design practices are particularly important in parts of any experience that may be deemed stressful or more complicated. In these situations, aesthetically pleasing design alone won't be enough for us to forget the stress we might feel concerning the task at hand, whether that's filling out a form, finding critical information, or placing an order. As both Norman and Walter point out, design needs to be usable as well.

Understanding how emotions play a particular role in the experience with a product or service is an important step in helping define and design the right experience of and around that product. In Chapter 5, we'll look at narrative structures and key points in an experience. However, as background for that, we'll take a look at some particular situations and moments where emotion in product design matters.

CATEGORIZING PRODUCT EXPERIENCE MOMENTS AS HAPPY, UNHAPPY, NEUTRAL, OR REFLECTIVE

When looking at the various situations and moments in product design where emotions can play a key part, I group them into four categories: unhappy, happy, neutral, and reflective.

Unhappy moments

Unhappy moments are those that a user would rather be without, skip, or avoid altogether (Figure 4-7). They're often the hygiene features and steps in a journey that have to be completed when users carry out a task, and the moments when things don't go the way they expect.

FIGURE 4-7
Unhappy moments in product design

Examples of unhappy moments are as follows:

Barriers

Creating an account, logging in, making a payment, filling out long forms, making a selection

Unclear CTA, unclear usage, confusing information architecture (IA), wrong use of language

Errors

404 pages, error messages

Referring back to Plutchik's wheel of emotions, some of the emotions that the user may experience here are anger, annoyance, apprehension, disapproval or even rage, loathing, sadness, remorse, and fear.

With regard to Norman's three levels of emotions, unhappy moments primarily fall under the behavioral level. The visceral level and the reflective level also come into play in terms of our first impression and the overall feeling it leaves us with.

Happy moments

Happy moments, on the contrary, are moments that should either be positive (e.g., after a user has completed a task), or moments in which the user is pleasantly surprised (Figure 4-8). They can also be moments where you've identified that, compared to your competitors, you want to stand out and create a memorable experience for the user through added delights.

Happy moments can range from a little happy to very happy. Here are some examples of moments that can or should be happy:

First impressions

Onboarding, landing pages

Task completions

Confirmation pages and messages

Physical deliveries

Unboxing experiences

Delights

Explicit use of personality, animations, imagery

These happy moments often evoke the following emotions in the user: amazement, interest, anticipation, joy, love, optimism, and surprise. They primarily concern Norman's visceral and reflective levels.

FIGURE 4-8
Happy moments in
product design

Neutral moments

Though we want to avoid unhappy moments, as we'll cover in Chapter 9, not every moment in an experience can, or should be, a happy one. Some moments need to be neutral and not ask anything of the users, but instead let them go through the experience with very little cognitive load (Figure 4-9). *Neutral moments* aren't just important to help minimize the cognitive load for the user. They are also essential in creating contrast to happy and reflective moments.

Though the circumstances and context surrounding the following listed examples can change them from neutral to unhappy, happy, or reflective moments, these are some examples of neutral moments:

Day-to-day tasks
Answering emails, checking Slack

Researching
Noncomplicated searches, such as for opening times or menus

Carrying out a task
Form completion (unless barriers are encountered)

Trust, acceptance, as well as more moderate levels of optimism, interest, and joy are examples of emotions that a user may experience in relation to neutral moments.

As for Norman's levels of emotions, neutral moments primarily deal with the behavioral level with regard to ease of use and usability.

FIGURE 4-9
Neutral moments in product design

Reflective moments

Reflective moments are moments that should intentionally be designed to add friction in design, according to Per Axbom, a coach, designer, and writer (Figure 4-10). In contrast, neutral and happy moments should encourage flow and action in the user's task completion or experience of the product. This friction is not necessarily meant to stop users, but instead look after them by ensuring that the decisions they make and actions they take are decisions and actions they want to take, and will be happy to have taken afterward.

FIGURE 4-10
Reflective moments in product design

Here are some examples of reflective moments:

Parting with data
    Permissions

Parting with monetary value
    One-off payments, subscriptions, selecting payment options

Termination

Canceling a service or subscription

Contributing

Commenting, uploading, submitting

Confirming

Choosing delivery address or date/time

With regard to Norman's three levels of emotions, reflective moments are a bit of an outlier in that, though they concern the behavioral and visceral levels of emotions, they should also activate the reflective "after" usage level while in the moment.

As with Walter's pyramid of user needs, there is little point in focusing on the happy moments—for instance, adding pleasures and delights to add to the experience—before the other categories of moments have been identified.

Though the preceding categorization is a generalization, in some instances, depending on the specifics of a product or service, a moment that I've categorized as neutral should have more focus as a happy moment, or vice versa. An example of this is an Amazon confirmation page after purchase, which does very little to evoke happiness, but instead functions more as utility. Another example is Typeform, an online form and survey builder tool. Typeform focuses on adding more delight and ease of use into the user experience of completing and creating its forms and surveys (Figure 4-11).

Which category situations and moments will fall in, and what type of emotions certain parts of the experience should evoke in your users and customers, will always come down to the specifics of that product or service as well as the objectives and goals you have with it.

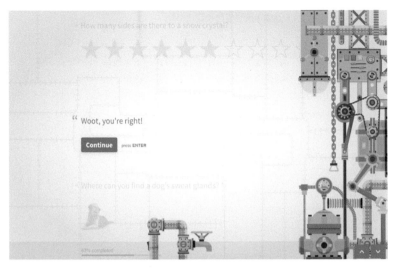

FIGURE 4-11

The Impossible Quiz, one of the featured examples of the kind of form you can create with Typeform

Exercise: Categorizing Product Experience Moments as Happy, Unhappy, Neutral, or Reflective

With your own product or service in mind, or one of that you use on a regular basis, identify the following:

- What moments would you define as currently being, or potentially being, unhappy moments in your product or service?

- What moments would you define as being, or should be, happy moments in your product or service?

- What moments would you define as being, or should be, neutral moments in your product or service?

- What moments would you define as being, or should be, reflective moments in your product or service?

- What emotions would you say that each of these moments evoke in the user?

DESIGNING FOR POSITIVE EMOTIONS

Simon Schmid of *Smashing Magazine* says that we shouldn't be afraid to show our personality in design, as long as it's geared toward the right people.[19] He outlines a nonexhaustive list of eight psychological factors, based on his own personal observations, that can help evoke positive emotions in design:

Positivity
> Focus on the positive

Surprise
> Do something unexpected or new

Uniqueness
> Be different from other products and services in an interesting way

Attention
> Offer incentives, or to help, even if you're not obliged to

Attraction
> Build an attractive product

Anticipation
> Leak something ahead of launch

Exclusivity
> Offer something exclusive to a select group

Responsiveness
> Show the audience a reaction, especially when they don't expect it

When it comes to applying these factors to design, or examples in design, there are often overlaps between them. How users will respond to them, he says, will vary based on who they are, their background, cultural factors, and more.

---

19 Simon Schmid, "The Personality Layer," *Smashing Magazine,* July 18, 2012, *https://oreil.ly/ dvEcV.*

What Storytelling Can Teach Us About Evoking Emotions in Product Design

Just as certain techniques are used to evoke certain emotions in films, books, plays, and the design of physical experiences like exhibitions, there are methods and principles we can use to evoke specific emotions in design. In this section, we'll take a look at five ways inspired by traditional storytelling that can help create an emotional connection with the end user.

SPARK THE IMAGINATION

I came across an article by Joe Berkowitz, a writer and staff editor at *Fast Company*, that talks about how to tell scary stories. According to Berkowitz, "If you can imagine yourself in a situation," he says, "it's infinitely scarier."[20]

Most of us have at some point watched a movie or TV show where the plot and how it's brought to life did something to us—something made our heart beat faster; perhaps we pulled up our legs toward our chest, or covered our ears or our eyes. It's those moments that Berkowitz is talking about where the movie or TV show has captured our imagination to the point where the storyline holds us in its grip. By the way the music changes, or the light goes slightly dimmer and darker, we can tell that something bad is about to happen. It's usually not something

---

20 Joe Berkowitz, "How to Tell Scary Stories," *Fast Company*, October 31, 2013, *https://oreil.ly/ GupTC*.

we can put our finger on, but somehow we just know. Our anticipation grows and we're on the edge of our seat, as any minute now, the killer may strike.

What makes something scary is, according to Berkowitz, often the *not* seeing. In the movie *The Blair Witch Project*, for example, you never see the force that is involved in the attacks. In the movie *Jaws*, you don't see the shark until the Fourth of July weekend, which is more than halfway through the movie. Steven Spielberg had originally included the shark in the first scene of his script but because of mechanical errors was forced to use the shark very sparingly.[21] What makes us relate isn't just in what we can see. It lies in the overall emotional response.

This is something to keep in mind when it comes to the work we do. While we're not out to scare our users or audiences, we are out to capture their imagination and their attention (Figure 4-12). We want to evoke emotional responses through the work and experiences we're presenting, no matter what platform or technology we're using. We want to place our users and audience in the middle and, not too different from the job of a writer, to present our version of the dramatic question in such a way that our audience and our users want the answer to be "yes." We want our products and services to benefit and help users accomplish their goals and improve their lives, no matter how small the impact might be. Or, we want the idea or solution we're presenting to internal stakeholders or clients to be just what they need.

FIGURE 4-12
Spark the imagination

---

21 Watch "The Making of Jaws–The Inside Story" and hear Spielberg tell more about the use of the shark (*https://oreil.ly/S-aPa*).

Whether it's our clients, colleagues, or users who are our audience, we want them to be able to imagine themselves in the picture we're painting. But as UX designers, we too should be able to imagine ourselves in their situation.

Exercise: Spark the Imagination

Think about a recent project, or a project you're currently working on, and give an example of the following:

- How does the product or service that you work on spark the imagination with its intended users? Or, if it doesn't, how could it spark the imagination?

- How have you or another member of your team sparked the imagination of clients or internal stakeholders in a recent presentation or meeting?

- What is something you've done or used during the project to help you imagine yourself in the user's situation?

ADD PERSONALITY IN PRODUCT DESIGN

One of the ways we can evoke emotion in design is through the personality of the products and services we create (Figure 4-13). Walter argues that "personality is the platform for emotion." It's what we use to both empathize and connect with other humans, whether through laughter or tears. Similarly to the way babies learn to trust that their parents will come and soothe them when they need it, a feedback loop exists in interface design. Positive emotional stimuli can build trust and engagement with users over time, and this positive affect, as Norman pointed out, can make users more forgiving of shortcomings, or when things go wrong.[22] Personality, however, is also an increasingly important element when it comes to the experience in general, the brand, and the overall narrative that it tells.

---

22 Walter, "Emotional Interface Design."

FIGURE 4-13
Add personality in product design

Some of the ways we can add personality in product design and evoke emotions are through the images, iconography, and animations that we use. These can convey literal emotions, such as people smiling in the images that are used, or a shopping cart icon smiling after you've added items to it, as on threadless's website. Other ways are through copy and micro copy and the TOV that is used in them. As we'll cover in Chapter 6, it's becoming increasingly important to develop the character of the product or service that we're designing and know how this behaves across different touch points and devices, and in different situations.

Exercise: Add Personality in Product Design

With your product or service in mind, or one you use on a regular basis:

- What are some examples of where its personality comes through?
- What impact, desired or undesired, do you think this has on the user's experience with it?

FOCUS ON OUTCOMES INSTEAD OF FEATURES

A great article by Hoa Loranger of the Nielsen Norman Group says that instead of focusing on features, we should focus on outcomes.[23] At times there's a tendency to focus a bit too much on the product we're

---

23 Hoa Loranger, "Minimize Design Risk by Focusing on Outcomes Not Features," *Nielsen Norman Group*, August 14, 2016, *https://oreil.ly/aYRiU*.

creating or specific features without thinking thoroughly about the problem we're trying to solve. This, the problem, is the outcome, and the product or feature is the *output*. This distinction, the article argues, is related to the classic difference between a feature and a benefit. A *feature* is something that is offered by the product and service. The *benefit* is the value it offers to the user and what the user is actually after (Figure 4-14).

This benefit, if presented well, is closely related to story and, as we talked about in Chapter 1, the human mind processes facts differently when they are embedded in story. One of the oldest tricks in marketing is that you sell more if you focus on the benefits rather than the features. Similarly, when it comes to the products and services we design, Loranger argues, if we focus on the benefits we offer and how they solve users' pain points, those users are more likely to pay attention than if we simply present a list of features.

FIGURE 4-14
Focus on outcomes instead of features

MAKE THE MESSAGE ABOUT THE USER

In addition to focusing on features, we should focus our messaging on the user. However, "what companies know best will always be their products and services." So starts an article by consultant Melanie Deziel about why brands need to branch out from product-focused content.[24] Consumers and users generally trust companies to educate them on topics that are within their expertise, but as soon as that company includes a product-focused message, the credibility drops from 74% to 29%.[25]

Over the last few years, we've started to see more and more brands and companies moving away from self-promotional content and instead shift toward messaging that focuses on use of the product and service and the emotional aspect of how these make the consumer/user feel. Dove's "Real Beauty" is one such example. Team America's "Gold in the US" is another one.

As we talked about in Chapter 3, technology products and services are increasingly becoming about the needs and experience of the individual user rather than broader target audiences as a whole. Deziel talks about a ring of the personal, internal, and emotional reasons someone might use your product, and that the motivation for using it is driven increasingly by the feeling users get (or the lack thereof, for that matter). Squarespace, an all-in-one website-builder platform, is a good example, Deziel says. At the most basic level, Squarespace helps people share information about their business. But on a more emotional level,

---

24 Melanie Deziel, "Why Brands Need to Branch Out From Product-Focused Content," Contently, November 30, 2015, *https://oreil.ly/6Yo_a*.

25 "Kentico Digital Experience Survey," Kentico, June 2, 2014, *https://oreil.ly/tJlek*.

it empowers people to build something themselves, which in turn can help dreams come true (Figure 4-15). That's the story the product-related messaging should be focused on.

Exercise: Make the Message About the User

With your product or service in mind, or one you use on a regular basis:

- Give two examples of your current message being focused on the product rather than the user.

- How could you change these messages to be more about the user?

FIGURE 4-15
Make the message about the user

IDENTIFY THE "WHAT IF" OF YOUR PRODUCTS AND SERVICES

All good stories spark the imagination. The really good ones tap into the dreams and desires of their audience by raising the "What if...?" question that makes them feel that those dreams are actually attainable. Raising the "What if...?" question is something we can and should do in product design as well—but to do that, we need to start at where things are. When it comes to product design, we can't focus only on the emotions we want users to feel. It's equally important to consider what they might be feeling right now and what they felt before coming to us.

If you think back to Duarte's TED talk, she says that listeners (or in this case, the users), might be fairly happy with the way things are right now. Perhaps they tend to use a competitor site of yours that isn't perfect, but it works. Perhaps they've come to expect that forms or registration processes are a pain and expect nothing else. We need to take them to the elevated "What if" scenario. This scenario isn't always posed as a question or call to action, but can be done through simply showing how it, and life as we know it, can be different (Figure 4-16).

FIGURE 4-16
Identify the "What if" of your products and services

I remember unpacking my first mobile phone in the late '90s and having to charge it before it could be used. That was the norm. But, then Apple came along and delivered partly charged products that could be used straight out of the box. This was a simple we're-going-to-show-you-how-it-can-be-done "what if" that soon had the other players in the market following suit.

The change was simple, yet it significantly changed the experience of the people who unpacked their products for the first time. As we covered earlier in this chapter, what we consider *functional, usable,* and *pleasurable* with regard to product design constantly moves. When new becomes the norm, as with Apple's partly charged phone, and as more companies followed suit, consumer expectations shifted such that buyers now assume that the battery will be partly charged.

In order to innovate and to ensure that we deliver against the ever-moving goal post of what's considered a *functional*, *reliable*, and *usable* need versus "pleasurable," we need to identify what the partly charged battery is for our products and services. We need to dare to dream big and then figure out how to make that come true.

Exercise: Identifying the "What if" of Your Products and Services

Think about a situation where your product or service is being used. What would a "What if...?" question and possible solution be, similar to that of the partly charged battery?

Try to think about where you could change the product experience for the better. For example:

- Where and how could unwanted friction be removed?

- What would complete this sentence related to your product or service: "Wouldn't it be great if..."?

- What would be a completely different way of doing things that would make you stand out from the competition?

- What are some assumptions of how the product works that haven't been challenged for a while?

Don't limit your imagination to what is possible, but try instead to identify the lofty "what could be" if anything was possible, just as in the movies. How to get there, if it's at all possible and actually the right solution to a problem, is part of the next step.

[TIP]

This exercise is useful to do as a full end-to-end review of your experience/ service design that uses a customer experience map, \ or a customer journey map. Work through the "What if...?" for each relevant step of the experience.

Summary

As with everything we plan, design, and build, there are no guarantees that users will have the experience we hope they will have, or that they will feel the emotions we're trying to evoke. In fact, we can almost be sure that it won't happen exactly the way we planned. This chapter, however, has provided a deeper understanding of the emotional responses users will have throughout their experience with our product or service. By understanding the role of emotions as well as the types of emotions, and being clear on which ones we want to evoke at which points in the product experience and why, we're one step closer to achieving both our goals and those of our users.

In addition to ensuring that the fundamental levels of Walter's pyramid of user needs are met, we should also strive to identify where adding to the pleasure layer will benefit the user in the product experience. More often than not, designers are encouraged to add surface delights like animations, micro copy, or other visual elements. Though they can help with branding and creating personality in design, we should increasingly try to achieve holistic deep delights that help the user achieve flow—something that is closely linked to identifying the story we should tell with our product or service, which is what we'll be looking at next.

[5]

Defining and Structuring Experiences with Dramaturgy

Understanding and Defining Your Product Life Cycle

AT THE SAME TIME that I started freelancing back in 2011, my partner and I decided to completely refurbish our apartment and build a loft conversion. It was terrible timing in hindsight, but it taught us a lot. Neither of us had any previous experience with renovations, and we had no idea about all the decisions we'd have to make. We soon found out, though.

The company that was doing the work for us kept asking us to make decisions about this, that, and everything in between. It happened on an almost daily basis and was usually accompanied by a, "We need it by tomorrow morning." Most of the questions were about aspects we'd never thought about before, such as where to place sockets and light switches. Some of the questions were about things we didn't even know about, and we often didn't know what we ought to consider before making a decision. It was a painful process that involved a lot of research online, which in turn was made even more painful as none of the websites we visited catered to our needs or to the stage we were at in our journey.

This is how a typical "Alright, let's just figure out what type of bath (or insert any other renovation-related item) we should get" experience would go. We'd do a search on Google for "types of baths," and 99% of those searches took us to websites with a landing page containing zero "what-you-need-to-know" information. Instead, the websites presented us with decisions to make before any more information was given, such as selecting what type of bath we were after. How should we know?! At this point in our journey, we didn't even know that there were so many kinds of baths, let alone what made them different, or which the really good ones were and the ones we should avoid. It was the perfect example of the kind of siloed experience that we, as designers, should avoid. Forcing the user into a niche section without enabling them to view all options results only in a lot of back and forth because there isn't one page that provides an overview of everything that's on offer. In addition, it makes it much harder for the user to assess how the different products compare or relate to one another.

As we gradually learned more about the types of baths and what features to consider, and to identify what was right for us, this siloed experience worked better. But the experience certainly didn't work right at the beginning of our journey. At that point, it caused frustration and forced us to do additional Google searches to find a site that would meet our needs and give us some background information about what we needed to know and should consider. The websites we originally visited could easily have provided this information, which would also have helped turn us into customers rather than send us to their competitors.

When we think through and plan our websites and apps, we need to take a step back and consider where our user is in their journey. We often talk about a first-time visitor and a returning visitor, but the difference between, for example, two first-time visitors or two returning visitors can be like night and day. It all depends on their backstory: where and at what stage they are in their journey, and how much they know already.

One of the key points of this book is that every user's journey and story is different. Though that doesn't mean we need to design and build a custom experience for each user, it does mean that we need to have a framework that can help us deliver this kind of tailored experience and to think through what matters when, and why. In this chapter, we'll look at how traditional storytelling can help us do just that and the connection it has with product life cycles.

The Role of Dramaturgy in Storytelling

As discussed in Chapter 2, dramaturgy, which Merriam-Webster defines as "the art or technique of dramatic composition and theatrical representation," helps provide a structure and understanding of the context in which the story resides so that it can be acted. No matter how many acts a story has, whether it's three acts as per Aristotle or five as defined by Freytag, story structure is, in the words of Pixar story artist Kristen Lester, "the answer to the question, What do you want your audience to know and when?"[1]

As Aristotle points out, the way we tell and structure a story impacts the way the audience experiences it and responds. There's a great example in Pixar in a Box, which is a behind-the-scenes look at how Pixar artists do their jobs on the online learning platform Khan Academy. The example walks through how the initial story structure of *Finding Nemo* differed from the final version.

In the original story structure, the director wanted to have flashbacks throughout the film. This meant the audience wouldn't learn that Marlin's wife, Coral, and all her eggs were killed by a barracuda until the end of the film. When Pixar showed the movie with this structure, the audience didn't understand why Nemo's dad Marlin acted the way he did toward Nemo, and consequently, they didn't really like him. So Pixar re-edited the movie, removing almost all of the flashbacks except the scenes where Coral and Marlin's home was being attacked by the barracuda, and moved them to the beginning. This change didn't just alter the story. It affected the audience's perception of Marlin: now they loved him for his bravery in going after Nemo.

As one of the comments and related answers to this episode of Pixar in a Box stated, the story could have worked with the original structure—just as Snape's feelings weren't revealed until the end of *Harry Potter,* and the audience hated him for the majority of the movie but then came around. The way you structure your story has to do with the desired outcome. In *Finding Nemo,* the writers wanted the audience to empathize with Marlin, so understanding the reasons for his behavior

---

1 "Introduction to Structure," *Khan Academy,* https://oreil.ly/1Bvih.

up front was necessary. In *Harry Potter*, J.K. Rowling wanted readers to dislike Snape to start with, so revealing his feelings toward the end played to her desired outcome.[2]

Whether structure is used to write an actual story, define a product experience, or plan out a presentation, it is part of the backbone of good storytelling.

Exercise: The Role of Dramaturgy in Storytelling

Think about a movie that has a slightly different, nonlinear structure; that is, it may start at the end or with a flashback:

- What effect does the chosen structure have on the experience of the story?
- How would the story and the viewer's experience change if the story was told linearly?

The Role of Dramaturgy in Product Design

All the products and services that we design—whether they are ecommerce sites, company websites, campaign sites, social sites, booking sites, B2Bs or systems, or anything else including apps—have certain product life-cycle stages. That life cycle may span from when the user first finds out about the offering to when they are a loyal or seasoned customer. Depending on the product and service, the life-cycle stages will be different (including their number). But what's common across all is that each stage in the product life cycle will have a different rhythm and character, just like the acts in Aristotle's three-act structure (Figure 5-1).

As we covered in Chapter 2, Aristotle's first act is the action act: the inciting incident happens and ensures that life will never be the same for the protagonist. The second act is the processing and reasoning act: the protagonist learns new skills, as well as a thing or two about himself while working toward a resolution to the dramatic question. The

---

2 *Khan Academy*, "Introduction to Structure."

third act is the finale: everything is concluded, and the protagonist and the other main characters look at the lessons learned and evaluate the whole experience.

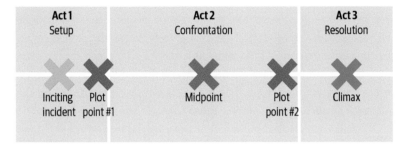

FIGURE 5-1
The three-act structure

APPLYING THE THREE-ACT STRUCTURE TO A PURCHASE LIFE CYCLE

Aristotle's three acts is similar to a traditional purchase life cycle, where you have your awareness, consideration, purchase, and post-purchase stages mapped across the three acts, as shown in Figure 5-2.

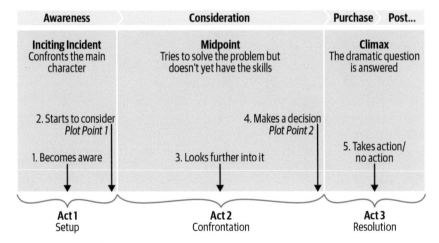

FIGURE 5-2
Three-act structure with a purchase life cycle mapped across it

Figure 5-3 ties a story into this model. In the first act, the user becomes aware of a need—let's say it's a desire to adopt a dog. The thought of how wonderful life would be with a small puppy and new best friend that would follow them everywhere is planted in their mind. In the second act, they start looking into adopting a dog. They research various breeds, look at costs and shelters with dogs close by, and maybe meet and play with a few. They learn a whole lot more about dogs and what it takes to be a dog owner, and perhaps start to doubt that having a dog will work with their lifestyle—the long work hours, the commute, and being out and about all the time. But then a friend comes along and says that perhaps a cat would be a better solution, as a cat wouldn't tie them down as much. After having learned more about dogs and cats, our user starts to make up their mind toward the end of the second act. In the third act, we find out whether the user did indeed adopt a dog or a cat, and what life is like with the new family member.

Although perhaps not the most captivating story, it is nonetheless a story. For the protagonist, it's a story about them and that time when they were going to adopt a dog. For us, the designers, it's a story about a potential user who might be visiting a cat and dog adoption website.

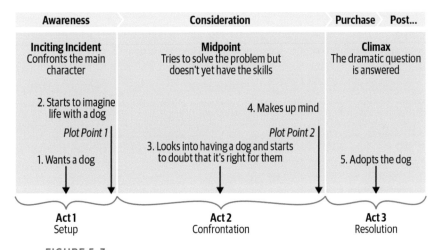

FIGURE 5-3

Three-act structure applied to the story about adopting a dog

Every single experience we design for is a story. The experience has a plot, characters, and a central idea that is brought to life. And just as Aristotle defined that a story should have three parts (a beginning, a middle, and an end), all of the experiences we design for also have three parts: a beginning (the user's need/goal is identified), a middle (the user goes on a quest to meet a need/goal), and an ending (a resolution occurs as the user's need/goal is either met or isn't met).

Using dramaturgy helps us identify a structure beyond this that, in turn, helps us shape the narrative of the experience in such a way that it's easier to define and design it. To fully understand how we can use dramaturgy in product design, there are a few more things to explore from traditional storytelling.

Exercise: The Role of Dramaturgy in Product Design

Taking the full end-to-end life cycle of your product or service, how would the life-cycle stages fall across the three acts?

Variations on the Three-Act Structure

As I mentioned in Chapter 2, there are many interpretations of Aristotle's three act structure. We'll take a look at three variations. Each can help us think about the acts within product and service experiences and how the more granular life-cycle stages fit into them.

YVES LAVANDIER'S MODIFIED THREE-ACT STRUCTURE

In the treatise *Writing Drama* (Le Clown & L'enfant), Yves Lavandier, a French writer and filmmaker, argues that every human action, whether real or fictional, has three logical parts: before the action, during the action, and after the action. Since the climax is part of the action, it must, according to him, take place in the second act. This makes the third act much shorter than what is traditionally found in screenwriting theories (Figure 5-4).

First Act	Second Act	Third Act
Inciting Incident		Climax

FIGURE 5-4
Lavandier's modified three-act structure

In a typical two-hour film, the first and third act usually last 30 minutes each, with the second act being around one hour. Today, however, many films start with the confrontation (the second act), or even the third act and then go back to the first act and the setup.

We can draw parallels to product design here. Every experience must also have acts a before, during, and after the action. However, though the after-the-action act is shorter, it still has critical things that are part of the continued experience; for example, in a post-purchase stage, if we use the purchase life cycle that we started working with earlier.

SYD FIELD'S PARADIGM STRUCTURE

Syd Field, an American screenwriter, posited a different theory around the three act structure in *Screenplay: The Foundations of Screenwriting*. He called this structure the *Paradigm*. Field noticed that in a 120-page screenplay, the second act was usually notoriously boring as well as about double the length of Act 1 and Act 3. He also noticed that an important dramatic event usually occurred about midway through the second act, which implied to him that the second act was, in fact, two acts in one. This divides Aristotle's three-act structure into four parts: 1, 2a, 2b, and 3 (Figure 5-5).

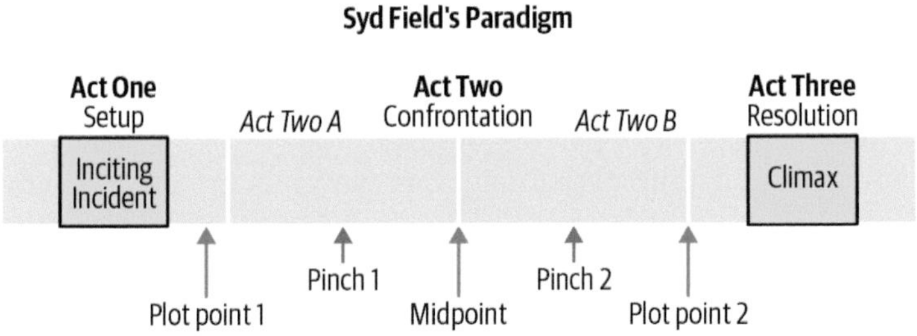

Syd Field's Paradigm

FIGURE 5-5
Field's Paradigm

FRANK DANIEL'S SEQUENCE PARADIGM

Another take on the three-act structure, and one of the most common ways of breaking down a film, is to divide it and its plot points into eight parts. This method, which is referred to as the *sequence paradigm*, was developed by Frank Daniels, a film director, producer, and scriptwriter, during his time as head of the graduate screenwriting program at the University of Southern California.

The eight parts stem from the early days of film, when a movie was divided into physical reels. Back then, films were shorter, and each reel held about 10 minutes of film. When each reel finished, the projectionist had to change the reel, as most theaters had only one projector. Early screenwriters incorporated this rhythm into their scriptwriting in such a way that individual sequences of a film lasted about the same length as that of a physical reel.

As films got longer, sequences got proportionately longer, too, but Daniel suggested that using eight sequences of 10–15 minutes was still a valuable way to structure a film. After he died in 1996, his disciple Paul Joseph Gulino described his approach in *Screenwriting: The Sequence Approach* (Continuum).

Definition of a sequence

Daniel referred to these sequences as *mini-stories* and encouraged his students to approach each sequence as a short movie, something we'll look at shortly that is also applicable to product design. Besides thinking of them as mini-stories, a sequence can be defined as "a series of related scenes that are tied together by location and/or time and/or action and/or the overall intent of the hero/ine."[3] Generally, the protagonist follows only one line of action during that sequence and, as such, each sequence has a beginning, a middle, and an end, with an inciting incident, a rising action, and a climax, respectively.[4]

The sequences usually follow a pattern with two in Act 1, four in Act 2, and two in Act 3, as shown in Figure 5-6. With the sequences providing the structure of the story, the five major plot points form the building blocks behind the sequence construction and propel the story forward.[5]

The Sequence Approach

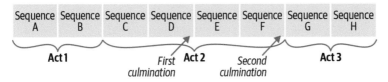

FIGURE 5-6
Daniel's sequence approach

3   Alexandra Sokoloff, "Story Structure 101," Screenwriting Tricks (blog), October 2, 2008, *https://oreil.ly/HT1B9*.

4   For more on this, see *Screenwriting: The Sequence Approach* by Paul Joseph Gulino (Continuum).

5   "Five Plot Point Breakdowns," *The Script Lab*, *https://oreil.ly/j4mxT*.

Star Wars Eight-Sequence Breakdown

This example is a simplified outline of the sequence structure of *Star Wars IV—A New Hope* (1977) developed by Neal Romanek, screenwriter and editor FEED magazine.[1] Each sequence begins with a problem and ends with a resolution that launches us into the next sequence:

Sequence 1

> Problem: The Empire is about to retrieve the Death Star plans, capture the Princess, and send R2-D2 and C-3PO to the spice mines of Kessel—in short, the movie is about to be over.
>
> Complicated by: The droids are captured by Jawas.
>
> Resolution: The droids find safety with Owen Lars and his nephew Luke.

Sequence 2

> Problem: Luke finds a mysterious message from an important person begging for help from someone he might know.
>
> Complicated by: R2-D2 runs away.
>
> Resolution: Luke decides to go with Ben Kenobi to Alderaan.

Sequence 3

> Problem: Luke and Ben have to find a way to get to Alderaan at Mos Eisley Spaceport.
>
> Complicated by: Imperial forces are searching the city for them.
>
> Resolution: The Millennium Falcon escapes Mos Eisley and heads for Alderaan.

Sequence 4

> Problem: Fly the droids and the plans safely to Alderaan.
>
> Complicated by: Alderaan is destroyed.
>
> Resolution: Our heroes are captured by the Death Star.

Sequence 5

> Problem: They discover the Princess is aboard the Death Star.
>
> Complicated by: The Princess is scheduled to be terminated.
>
> Resolution: The Princess is rescued.

---

1 Neal Romanek, "Introduction to Sequence Structure," Neal Romanek (blog), April 12, 2010, *https://oreil.ly/8j9Hn*.

Sequence 6

Problem: They must take the most important person in the galaxy to safety, starting from the bottom of a garbage masher.

Complicated by: Legions of single-minded fanatics are trying to kill them.

Resolution: They escape the Death Star and it's sentry ships.

Sequence 7

Problem: The Death Star is following the heroes to the Rebel Base.

Complicated by: Han is abandoning them.

Resolution: Luke and the rebels fly out to destroy the Death Star.

Sequence 8

Problem: The Death Star is going to destroy the Rebel Base and end the rebellion forever.

Complicated by: Darth Vader engages the rebel pilots in his own ship.

Resolution: Luke destroys the Death Star and becomes the hero of the galaxy.

Although not all movies will conform to a strict eight-sequence breakdown, adopting this structure can be a useful way of troubleshooting a script, as it makes you look at whether it has too few or too many sequences. Generally, the clearer the sequence structure, the better the movie and the story will be, and vice versa. As we'll cover shortly, these two insights also hold true for products and services, and it's one of the reasons that using dramaturgy in product design is so valuable.

Exercise: Variations on the Three-Act Structure

As Romanek allows, you may not agree with his breakdown. Do your own analysis of *Star Wars IV* or choose a completely different movie. Don't worry too much about forcing an eight-sequence structure on it. The key is to do the following:

- Identify where each new dramatic tension begins.
- Take note of how the character tries to solve that tension.
- Identify where that tension is replaced by a new one.

Applying Sequencing and Mini-Stories to Product Design

Sequences have many overlaps with UX and product design. Without necessarily thinking about it, when we work with user journeys and tasks, we're sequencing the user's experience into mini-stories. A typical purchase experience, for example, is often divided into the following:

- Research

- Registration/login

- Payment

- Support

Depending on whether we're working through these as user journeys (e.g., the payment user journey) or at a higher level as the product life-cycle stages a user goes through, we tend to name these slightly differently (e.g., awareness, consideration, purchase, and post-purchase, as the example earlier in this chapter showed). Sometimes, however, there's value in breaking down the life cycle even further.

USING DETAILED SEQUENCING IN UX DESIGN

When I was working with Sony Ericsson (now Sony Mobile) at Dare, the product life cycle was one of the key tools we used for getting an understanding of needs early on as well as of the different stages of the user's phone-buying experience. We defined each stage and mapped out both user and business needs against them. This process was simple but effective.

More important than that, we didn't stop at the purchase point, but broke down the post-purchase cycle into detailed stages that were typical for the experience of buying a new phone. The stages include the first hour, when you unbox and open your phone; the first day, when you start to set it up; the first week, when it starts to become yours; the first month, when it's pretty much embedded in your life; and so on until you consider upgrading or buying a new one.

This product life cycle provided us with a basic structure and story arc for the experience that helped ensure that we were all on the same page and both knew and considered what mattered to the users and the business at each point of the end-to-end product life cycle. For many experiences (e.g., a traditional purchase cycle of buying a sweater), you wouldn't necessarily need to include as many life-cycle stages; one post-purchase stage might suffice. Just as some argue that a play or film should have as many acts as the story requires, when it comes to using the product life cycle, there is no defined set of stages. As we'll explore later in this chapter, there are more common and typical product life cycles, but whatever benefits the project the most is what you should use.

DEFINING THE GRANULARITY OF SEQUENCES AND MINI-STORIES IN PRODUCT DESIGN

The previous example shows how we can break up the overall and full life-cycle experience of buying a new phone, from beginning to end, into detailed stages that help inform the UX design process. This breakdown is usually valuable as a high-level tool. But just as Daniel encouraged his students to think about sequences as mini-movies, we need to further break down each life-cycle stage into a mini-story in order to really work through the full experience. This process allows us to identify the narrative arc of each life-cycle stage and hence form a better understanding of what we need to consider at the each stage of the product experience.

As Daniel defined, each mini-movie or sequence, should have a beginning, a middle, and an end. If we take the first three life-cycle stages from the Sony Ericsson example, we can break these down as illustrated in Table 5-1.

As this breakdown shows, each stage can have a varying number of parts. Here, awareness and consideration have three, while purchase has four. The number of parts to include should be informed by what helps your project.

Each stage, or sequence in script-writing terms, has a conflict and a resolution that becomes the start of the next stage; for example, "Decides to look into it" in Act 3 of awareness leads to the user starting to research in the consideration stage.

TABLE 5-1. Breaking down the life-cycle stages into three acts

A	B	C	D
Stage/Act	Act 1: Beginning What's the conflict?	Act 2: Middle What happens then?	Act 3: End What's the resolution?
Awareness	First encounter	Starts to consider	Decides to look into it
Consideration	Research	Comparison	Decision
Purchase	Add to basket, checkout	Registration, login	Payment, confirmation

These breakdowns are getting into the high-level steps of each stage and they also start to sound like steps in a user journey. Depending on the complexity of each one, these mini-experiences might need to be broken down even further. The way to do that is to look at the mini-stories of each stage, with the left column now holding each step of the consideration stage (columns B, C, and D) instead of the life-cycle stage. For example, the consideration stage could be broken down in Table 5-2.

TABLE 5-2. Breaking down the stage into its own mini-story

A	B	C	D
Stage: Consideration step/part	Act 1: Beginning What's the conflict?	Act 2: Middle What happens then?	Act 3: End What's the resolution?
Research	Searches online	Reads reviews	Goes back to website
Comparison	Goes through products	Learns about differences, Selects products	Compares products
Decision	Makes a selection	Goes back over criteria	Decides "yes" or "no"

At times we'll also need to acknowledge that "how" the user chooses to interact with the product may impact the experience. For example, contacting support post- or prepurchase could take different forms that would result in different mini-stories, depending on the chosen medium:

- Via phone: Find contact details, inquire about order, get help

- Via form: Enter order details, submit help request, get help

- Via bot: Engage with bot, send query and order details, receive help

Just as conflicts and resolutions form the building blocks behind the sequence construction, for the preceding mini-experiences it's the main steps and goals of the experience that define the breakdown into stages and their related steps. How far we choose to break down the mini-experiences into further substories depends on the level of detail we require in order to add the most value to our project and product in question. Taking another look at traditional storytelling provides us with further useful references.

Exercise: Applying Sequencing and Mini-Stories to Product Design

Choose a project you're working on at the moment or a type of end-to-end experience that you're familiar with, such asswitching banks, grocery shopping online, or using an app, and work through the full high-level experience.

Step 1: Identify the main stages and their related mini-story.
Start with the stages and identify the beginning, middle, and end for each stage:

STAGE/ ACT	ACT 1: BEGINNING— WHAT'S THE CONFLICT?	ACT 2: MIDDLE— WHAT HAPPENS THEN?	ACT 3: END— WHAT'S THE RESOLUTION?
[Stage name]			
[Stage name]			

After you've had a go at this, identify which steps need to be broken down into their own mini-story and do the same exercise for these.

Step 2: Identify the main steps and their related mini-story.

Start with the step and identify the beginning, middle, and end for each step:

STEP/ ACT	ACT 1: BEGINNING— WHAT'S THE CONFLICT?	ACT 2: MIDDLE— WHAT HAPPENS THEN?	ACT 3: END— WHAT'S THE RESOLUTION?
[Step name]			
[Step name]			

The Difference Between Acts, Sequences, Scenes, and Shots

Alongside acts and sequences, we often talk about scenes and shots in screenwriting. *Shots* make up a scene. Scenes, in turn, are parts that contribute to a larger whole, namely the sequence.

A *scene* generally takes place in a single location over a continuous period of time and without a change of characters. A *sequence*, on the other hand, is made up of multiple scenes and has a coherent dramatic spine that begins when the character is faced with an uncertainty or imbalance. When that conflict is resolved or partly resolved, the resolution is what opens up a new conflict, and this becomes the subject of the subsequent sequence.[6]

Sequences are also what make up *acts*, and you generally have more sequences in the second act than in the first and the third. Acts, in turn, are what make up the film.

---

6 For more on this, see *Screenwriting: The Sequence Approach* by Paul Joseph Gulino (Continuum).

Translating Acts, Sequences, Scenes, and Shots to Product Design

Looking at the products and services we design in terms of acts, sequences, scenes, and shots is a good framework for thinking and working through the detail of the narrative structure of a product or service experience. If we translate acts, sequences, scenes, and shots to UX design, we get the following:

Acts

The beginning, middle, and end of an experience

Sequences

Life-cycle stages *or* key user journeys, depending on what you work with

Scenes

Steps *or* main steps in a journey *or* pages/views (as we'll look at in subsequent chapters)

Shots

Elements of a page/view *or* detailed steps of a journey

Exercise: The Difference Between Acts, Sequences, Scenes, and Shots

For your own product, come up with examples of sequences, scenes, and shots.

Understanding Plot Points

Identifying the events that take place in each life-cycle stage will help determine the number and type of life-cycle stages for the experience you're working on. Similarly, when it comes to storytelling, acts and plot points go hand in hand. Field developed the idea of plot points in *Screenplay: The Foundations of Screenwriting* (Delta, 1979) and defined plot points as "important structural functions that happen in approximately the same place in most successful movies."

FIELD'S MAJOR PLOT POINTS

In the books that followed *Screenplay*, and with the help of some of his students, the original list of plot points was further expanded and currently contains the following major plot points:

Opening image

Summarizes the entire film, at least in its tone. The writer usually goes back and rewrites the opening image as one of the last things in the screenwriting process.

Exposition

Provides the background of the story through information about the plot, the characters, and their history as well as the setting and the scene.

Inciting incident

The protagonist encounters the thing that will ultimately end up changing their life. For example, the boy meets the girl, or the comic hero gets fired from a job. The inciting incident is also referred to as the *catalyst*, and it's what opens the door and throws the character into the main action of the story.

Plot point 1

Usually the last scene in Act 1, this consists of a surprising development that radically changes the protagonist's life and forces them to face an opponent.

Pinch 1

A scene that usually takes place about three-eighths of the way into the script, which the central conflict of the story is brought up to remind us of the overall conflict.

Midpoint

This is an important part of the story that Field suggests will help ensure that the second act doesn't sag. Often a reversal of fortune takes place, or a revelation changes the direction of the story.

Pinch 2

This is another reminder scene that often takes place about five-eighths of the way through the script and that, similar to pinch 1, brings up the central conflict again.

Plot point 2

A dramatic reversal that signals the end of Act 2 and the beginning of Act 3 by focusing on confrontation and resolution. It's where the protagonist has finally had enough and is facing his or her opponent.

Showdown

The protagonist confronts the main problem and overcomes it, or a tragic ending occurs. The showdown usually takes place midway through Act 3.

Resolution

The issues of the stories are resolved.

Tag

Also known as the *denouement*, this is the epilogue; any loose ends are tied up and the audience is given closure.

Just as there are different interpretations of the three-act structure, various approaches exist when it comes to plot points.

Translating Field's Major Plot Points to Product Design

All experiences are different, and some will require more or fewer plot points than those that Field has defined. But determining the typical plot points can be a useful exercise for working through its basic structure.

Opening image

This is most typically the home page but can be any landing point or that first touch point that the user comes across.

Exposition

This is generally a module with a tag line that summarizes the offering, or brief About information for the product or service that might have a CTA to a page with more About information.

Inciting incident

This is the part of the experience/page/view where the user comes across the message associated with the main CTA that encapsulates the main proposition of the product and service and the value it offers the user; that is, how it could transform their lives.

Plot point 1

This is the main CTA and the point where the user is faced with making their first decision on whether to click/tap/select the main CTA.

Pinch 1

This is usually a contextual module or message that reminds the user of the main proposition and the value the product and main CTA offers them.

Midpoint

During the second act, the emotional aspect of the experience often dips, and the character learns a lot more about the subject and is slightly confused. The midpoint is usually a feature or content that helps get the user over any barrier they may be facing during the second act (such as choosing the right product). For example: a comparison tool that helps make a selection easier, a featured review, clearly listed product benefits.

Pinch 2

This is usually another contextual module or message that reminds the user of the main product benefit and CTA, as well as why they should take action.

Plot point 2

This is where the user starts to make up their mind in relation to the dramatic question and plot point 1 that was raised in Act 1. For example: an incentive to buy.

Showdown

The user wrestles with their main hesitation relating to their goal and has to complete a task in order to move forward or decide not to take action and abandon their quest. For example: the steps involved with completing a purchase, or abandoning it.

Resolution

The user gets an onscreen confirmation that they have indeed completed their task and that whatever benefit was promised is "on its way." For example: onscreen confirmation message.

Tag

The experience comes to a close, and any follow-up events in relation to the task or goal the user has just completed take place. For example: confirmation email with details about what happens next.

THE FIVE MAIN PLOT POINTS

Robert Towne, a screenwriter, producer, director, and actor who was part of the New Hollywood wave of filmmaking, has said:

> A movie is really only four or five moments between two people; the rest of it exists to give those moments their impact and resonance. The script exists for that. Everything does.

The Script Lab refers to these as the inciting incident, lock-in, midpoint, main culmination, and third-act twist, and maps them out over eight parts:[7]

Inciting incident

The first moment that shakes up the status quo and opens a new door for the protagonist. Even though the protagonist has not yet walked through it, we understand that they will have to do so in order to achieve their objective.

Lock-in

At this point in the story, the protagonist can no longer turn back and return to the status quo. The door that was previously opened slams closed, and the objective of the protagonist is established, which propels them into the second act.

Midpoint

The protagonist achieves their first major success or failure. If the midpoint is a success, it swings the story in favor of the protagonist. If it's a failure, it moves the protagonist even further away from the objective. The midpoint should generally mirror the outcome of the story and be a victory if the protagonist will win in the end, or a low point if the ending is a tragic one.

Main culmination

This is the highest or lowest point for the protagonist so far. This climax represents the pinnacle of the protagonist's journey and brings their second act objective to a close, as well as to a new goal in the third act.

---

7 The Script Lab, "Five Plot Point Breakdown."

Third-act twist

This changes the protagonist's trajectory in the final act. The third-act twist differs from other minor twists in that it actually changes the plot and it's often the ultimate "show down" scene.

No matter the approach, plot points in screenwriting teach us is that there are key points in all stories—including the product and service experiences that we design—that propel the person that the story is about forward. When looking at plot points for the experiences that we design, it's helpful to go back to Field's definition.

Plot Points in Product Design

Field defines plot points as "important structural functions that happen in approximately the same place in most successful movies." The key here is that plot points happen "in approximately the same place" in most "successful" movies. Just as patterns exist in successful movies, novels, and hit songs, patterns exist in successful product and services experiences. These patterns include the actions the user has to/tends to take, the steps involved, system responses, and the end outcomes that both the user and the business desire.

DEFINING PLOT POINTS IN PRODUCT DESIGN

Much of Field's plot point definition applies to product design with a slight modification: important structural functions that happen at a similar point in typical product and service experiences. While acts, sequences, scenes, and shots form the building blocks of the overall narrative structure of the products and services that we design, plot points are the events and triggers that propel the experience forward.

In the earlier example of the high-level purchase life cycle, the main plot points in that experience occur when the user becomes aware, starts to consider, looks further into it, makes a decision, and takes action/no action. These plot points are very high level, and when it comes to actually working through them for your product or service, you'll benefit from defining them in more detail.

Later in this chapter, we'll cover a few methods inspired by traditional storytelling that help to define the narrative structure of product experiences. However, in order to identify what plot points are in product design, it's useful to look further at what constitutes plot points in product experiences.

As we identified, plot points are the events and triggers that propel the experience and usually happen at a similar point in a typical product and service experience. Some examples of common plot point types are as follows:

Triggers
> Nudges that the user receives or encounters (e.g., a notification, a CTA, an email or a message)

Actions
> Measures that the user takes or things the user does (e.g., adds to basket, logs in, downloads app, pays, leaves website, closes app)

Barriers
> Potential road blocks that the user encounters along the way when using the product or service (e.g., asked to sign up, asked to enter payment details)

System events
> Events that happen in or by the system (e.g., confirmation messages, error messages)

Delights
> Unexpected moments of pleasure (e.g., emotional responses to what the user sees)

When defining the plot points in your product experience, it's useful to think about the user's emotional response at each part of the experience (Figure 5-7). There will be, for example, certain hygiene "steps" that have to be present but don't affect the user emotionally, and there might be conflict and resolution, or delights to have a greater impact on the user's emotional response. Thinking about it in this way can help you identify your plot points:

Major plot points in experiences
> These typically signal the end of one sequence—that is, stage in the life cycle, and the start of a new sequence, (e.g., "Starts to consider" during awareness, "Makes a decision" during consideration). You can often attribute "done," "completed," or "not done," "not completed" to major plot points. They have to occur before moving on to the next sequence. In other words, they need to be resolved before the experience continues.

Minor plot point in experiences

These typically occur during a sequence; for example, "becomes aware" (during awareness), "looks further into it" (during consideration). Minor plot points are more akin to intermediate events or steps that happen along the way rather than events that in a big way propel the user forward in the experience.

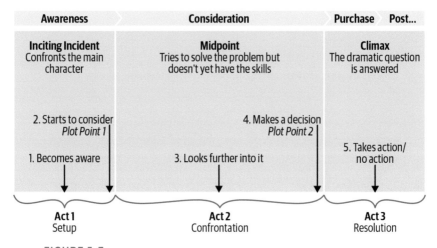

FIGURE 5-7

The three-act structure with a purchase life cycle mapped across it

---

Exercise: Plot Points in Product Design

With your own product in mind, think of examples of the following:

- A major plot point in the product experience
- A minor plot point in the product experience

Typical Experience Structures of Common Product Life Cycles

When it comes to presentations, Dan Roam, the author of five books on business visualizations, argues that which storyline you pick depends on what you're trying to do—change the audience's perception, abilities, actions, or beliefs. In the same way, which experience structure and life cycle we choose will depend on the type of products and experiences we work on.

While no project is the same, there are some typical narrative experience patterns that users will go through in their journey, based on the type of experience it is. Though the narrative pattern might differ slightly from project to project, just as with the structure of stories, these baseline product life cycles and their accompanying main and minor plot points can be mapped out and provide a foundation and reference point for similar experience structures.

The following are some typical product experience examples:

Ecommerce life cycle
> For example, buying from Amazon—from realizing a need to post-purchase

Video on demand (VOD) life cycle
> For example, Netflix—from signing up to using it regularly

Travel life cycle
> For example, Airbnb—from researching to returning home from a trip

Social-media life cycle
> For example, Instagram—from signing up to using it regularly

Software as a service (SaaS) life cycle
> For example, Slack—from trying it to integrating it into the company process

Help life cycle
> For example, contact support—from needing help to either getting or not getting it

Research life cycle
> For example, Google—from realizing the need to either finding or not finding the answer

Smart home device life cycle
> For example, Google Home—from first becoming aware to integrating it into everyday life

How to Use Dramaturgy and Plot Points to Define the Narrative Structure of Product Experiences

Screenwriters are generally encouraged to map out the plot points early on to help with the writing of their script, in the same way dramaturgy and plot points can help us map out the narrative of the experiences that we design for. The typical product life cycles covered earlier in this chapter provide us with possible foundational structures to start from. However, just as the story structures aren't meant to be followed down to every last detail, neither are the life cycles.

They provide insights into what tends to work well for that kind of experience, but should be adapted to the project in question. And as with everything, there are exceptions to every rule, so a typical ecommerce life cycle may not necessarily apply to all types of ecommerce experiences. So how do we go about defining and applying story structures and plot points to the product and services experiences we design?

First of all, we need to define the type of experience we're creating and break it down into its high-level stages; that is, sequences. Then we need to understand key moments—the plot points, be they pain points, opportunities, or actions that the user takes. Most often we'll perform these two steps in tandem, and each helps inform the other.

THE TWO-PAGE SYNOPSIS METHOD

Rumor has it that someone who studied with Daniel, who developed the sequence paradigm of screenwriting, said that one way to work with sequence breakdown is to start by giving each sequence a title that suggests the content; for example, "Meet Rocky," "Rocky and Adrienne," "A Chance of a Lifetime," "Rocky Trains," and "The Fight." These titles give you an idea about the content in the sequence. If you then write a short paragraph describing each sequence, you end up with a two-page synopsis.

We can apply the same principle to defining the narrative structure of our product life cycles. I tend to start by giving each phase a name and writing a descriptive line for each. This helps ensure that the purpose of each stage is clear to me and everyone else. This doesn't have to be in a fancy-looking document. A sketch or list of bullet points in an email or similar will do just fine. The key is to give each sequence or stage of the product life cycle a title that gives an idea of what will happen in it.

Once that is done, list the main moments, or plot points, that will happen in each stage. A simple way of going about this, just as in the two-page synopsis method, is to write out what happens at each stage as a short narrative. By focusing on and highlighting the user's actions (e.g., "signs up," "searches for," "looks through," "enters," etc.), you can start to visualize the main points in the user's experience. As a general rule, only one or two plot points should occur in each sequence. If you have more, you can likely break the sequence into two sequences.

THE INDEX CARD METHOD

The *index card method* is used by many screenwriters. You can use either a pack of index cards or a stack of sticky notes. If you want to go one step further, use multicolored sticky notes. You also need a big table, an empty floor, or a wall that you can use to put your index cards or sticky notes on. We'll first explore how this method works for screenwriting and then how you can adapt it to product design.

In traditional screenwriting, you would lay out your story in four acts or in eight sequences. If the former, you'd create four vertical columns with 10–15 cards in each. If the latter, you'd use eight vertical columns of 5–8 cards. To structure it, make a grid by drawing lines between the columns, or use a few marker cards at the top of each column.

If you work with four acts

Write "Act 1" at the top of the first column, "Act 2: Part 1" at the top of the second, "Act 2: Part 2" at the top of the third, and "Act 3" at the top of the fourth.

After that, take another card and write "Act 1 Climax" and place it at the bottom of column 1. Use another card for "Midpoint Climax" and pin it at the bottom of column 2, "Act 2 Climax" at the bottom of column 3, and "Climax" at the very end. In traditional screenwriting, these are the scenes you know that your movie must have and where. If you already know what they are, you should write a short description of them.

If you work with eight sequences

Write "Sequence 1" at the top of the first column, "Sequence 2" at the top of the second, "Sequence 3" at the top of the third, and so forth until you have your eight columns.

After that, take another card and write "Act 1 Climax" and place it at the bottom of column 1. Use another one for "Midpoint Climax" and pin it at the bottom of column 2, "Act 2 Climax" at the bottom of column 3, and "Climax" at the very end.

Common for both approaches

After this point, you would start to brainstorm scenes and write each scene on a sticky note. You don't have to worry too much about putting them in order just yet. But if you know roughly where they go, it can be helpful to place them in approximately the right spot from the beginning. This exercise help you get a full picture of the sequences and your story as a whole. It also provides a way to review and play around with the structure and narrative in a way that's very easy and cost-effective.[8]

For product design, this method helps designers get a full picture and overview of the experience we're working on and allows us to review it before we go into the level of detail that eats up more time and budget. We can adapt this method for product design by using it to define the main life-cycle stages of the experience we're working on. If you have different colored sticky notes, use a specific color for these stages and write the name of each stage (sequence) on separate sticky notes. Just as in the index card method, lay them out horizontally across the table, or across the wall as the top row (Figure 5-8).

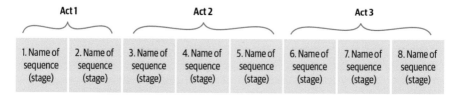

FIGURE 5-8

Step 1: Define the main sequences of the experience

Next, take another stack of sticky notes in a different color and write down the main plot point (action, event, or outcome) of each stage and place them at the bottom. Leave a fairly big gap (at least four sticky notes high) in the middle, between the name of the stage and the plot points. Do this for each stage and leave them blank if you're not yet

---

8 Sokoloff, "Story Structure 101."

sure what some of them are. This bottom row contains the plot points of your experience and signals the end of one stage and the start of the next one (Figure 5-9).

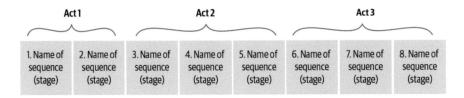

1. Name of sequence (stage)	2. Name of sequence (stage)	3. Name of sequence (stage)	4. Name of sequence (stage)	5. Name of sequence (stage)	6. Name of sequence (stage)	7. Name of sequence (stage)	8. Name of sequence (stage)

Plot point 1 Name of plot point	Plot point 2 Name of plot point	Plot point 3 Name of plot point	Plot point 4 Name of plot point	Plot point 5 Name of plot point	Plot point 6 Name of plot point	Plot point 7 Name of plot point	Plot point 8 Name of plot point

FIGURE 5-9
Step 2: Define the main plot points

Once that is complete, just as in the index card method, brainstorm what the different steps (scenes) will be for each column. Write each one on a separate sticky note, preferably using a different color. At the end, you'll have something that looks a little like Figure 5-10.

Act 1			Act 2			Act 3	
1. Name of sequence (stage)	2. Name of sequence (stage)	3. Name of sequence (stage)	4. Name of sequence (stage)	5. Name of sequence (stage)	6. Name of sequence (stage)	7. Name of sequence (stage)	8. Name of sequence (stage)
Name of scene (step)	Name of scene (step)	Name of scene (step)	Name of scene (step)	Name of scene (step)	Name of scene (step)	Name of scene (step)	Name of scene (step)
Name of scene (step)	Name of scene (step)	Name of scene (step)	Name of scene (step)	Name of scene (step)	Name of scene (step)	Name of scene (step)	Name of scene (step)
Name of scene (step)	Name of scene (step)	Name of scene (step)	Name of scene (step)	Name of scene (step)	Name of scene (step)	Name of scene (step)	Name of scene (step)
Plot point 1 Name of plot point	Plot point 2 Name of plot point	Plot point 3 Name of plot point	Plot point 4 Name of plot point	Plot point 5 Name of plot point	Plot point 6 Name of plot point	Plot point 7 Name of plot point	Plot point 8 Name of plot point

FIGURE 5-10

Step 3: Identify the scenes

Summary

By combining the practice of dramaturgy and sequencing with product life-cycle stages, you can create a framework for thinking through the high-level, end-to-end stages and mini-stories of the product and service experience you're working on. This, in turn, forms a thorough foundation for defining it further.

As you will learn when you start working through this type of breakdown for varying types of products and services, sticking to a strict three-act structure or number of stages in the life cycle won't always work or make sense. Just as it's argued that a play or film should have as many acts as the story requires, your product experience should also have as many acts as benefits the product design process.

Which method you choose is up to you. Just as with most things when it comes to product and UX design, some methods are more suitable than others. How you get there doesn't really matter as long as you get there. If you're not working with a predefined typical product life-cycle structure as the basis, you might find that it's easier to start by listing the key moments before you identify the stages they will fall in. However you go about it, by defining your product life cycle structure early on, you help ensure that your product narrative is thought through. Just as this upfront work helps define the plot in screen- and playwriting, in product design it helps ensure you have a deeper understanding of the problem area and the way your product can and should help the user.

But, as *The Guardian* has written, "A plot is only one aspect of its screenplay. Plenty of other elements can claim to change, and even determine, overall meaning."[9] As we'll explore in more detail in Chapter 7, when it comes to designing experiences, we need to take multiple elements into consideration in addition to the structure and main points of the experience we're creating. As we know from Aristotle, the characters are on par with the plot, in terms of importance for a good story, and that's what we'll look at next.

---

9 Adam Mars-Jones, "Terminator 2 Good, The Odyssey Bad," *The Guardian*, November 20, 2004, *https://oreil.ly/z8QH9*.

Using Character Development in Product Design

Reluctance to Use Personas

Over my years working as a UX designer, I've seen a reluctance to create user personas, and more specifically, detailed personas. I've met this reluctance in the teams and companies where I've worked, with people that I've mentored and coached, and have come across it in articles and in social media posts. Many of you who read this book will probably be skeptical of personas, too. Part of this skepticism comes down to how they're used, or rather not used, on projects, but part of it is also due to a common belief that the team knows who their audience is, so there is no need to articulate it. There are better and more important things to get on with, like an actual solution or creative idea.

I write this with no judgment because I get it. Sometimes the audience feels so obvious that the need to spend time on personas is lower, all things considered, than "doing the actual work." However, doing the actual work is dependent on knowing who that work is for and why. Freelance UX researcher Meg Dickey-Kurdziolek writes, "Being a user-centered designer means that you deliberately seek out the stories, data, and rationale behind your users' motivations."[1] Many organizations believe that they have a good understanding of their users and customers, there are some big surprises usually arise when you do more detailed research into who they actually are and go beyond the stereotypes. Assumptions often lead us in the wrong direction, or if we don't look into the data, we might miss a key part of the audience. One

---

1 Meg Dickey-Kurdziolek, "Resurrecting Dead Personas," *A List Apart,* July 26, 2016, *https:// oreil.ly/kQRq2.*

big department store, for example, realized only after looking into its data that although women represented the largest volume of sales, it was actually men who drove the most value.[2]

Now, breaking down our audience into larger segments like "men" and "women" doesn't do us enough good when it comes to shedding light on the needs of both current and potential users and customers. In marketing, we're increasingly moving away from demographic-based segmentation and turning traditional classification on its head. Instead, we're starting to turn to data and the networks of consumers who are similar to each other, not forming stereotypes like we're used to, but archetypes that are based on data and insight. This type of segmentation provides far more value and a more accurate picture of the people our products and services are intended for than any broad classification like "millennials," "mums," or "entrepreneurs."

As the story about the user who was going to buy a dog in the preceding chapter started to tell us, no user's story is the same. The use case, or Jobs To Be Done (JTBD), might be the same—research and buy a dog—but everything else that goes into making that story come to life will, with 100% certainty, be different for every single user. No matter how simple and generalized we want to keep things, people aren't simple or general.

The things we need to do and the reasons we use websites, apps, and other products and services aren't simple either. We're increasingly talking about end-to-end experiences and about CX. To ensure that we can provide value and help users throughout their "end-to-end" experience, we need to understand all the moments that go into it—all the different touch points and what will influence each moment and determine the outcome of the next.

Users bring not only varying existing knowledge into an experience, but also different past experiences. With two first-time visitors, one might have no previous knowledge or experience, and one might have a wealth of previous knowledge and experience from, for example, other similar sites. The former will need more hand-holding and background information, whereas the latter might prefer a

---

2 Kevin O'Sullivan, "The Netflix Approach to Retail Marketing," *FutureScot*, April 29, 2016, *https://oreil.ly/fuhy3*.

"straight-to-what-I'm-looking-for" kind of experience. The opposite, with regard to background knowledge, can also apply to your returning users, with the gist of it all being that every user goes on their journey. Rather than making broad statements and decisions about what users as a group want, we should acknowledge that factors like prior knowledge, backstory, and mindset also play a role in a user's experience and expectation alongside the other factors that we hopefully define.

Chuck Sambuchino, a freelance editor and former editor with Writer's Digest Books, offers a really nice metaphor for developing characters. He remembers when cameras had something inside of them called *film*, and that in order to get the pictures off the film, a technician had to treat it with some chemicals inside a "mysterious darkened room," and as if by magic, the image would appear on the special paper. But, if the process didn't go as planned, you could end up with fuzzy or dark or overexposed images. The key to getting a clear photograph depended largely on how the technician developed the film. "If we want readers to have a vibrant mental image of our characters, we have to spend some time in the dark room," Sambuchino explains.[3] The same goes for doing research into our users and what matters to them in the multidevice experiences that we design: "If you don't understand your users, you will never build great products."[4]

The Role of Characters and Character Development in Storytelling

In Aristotle's seven golden rules of storytelling, the plot and the characters are on par with each other in terms of their importance to the story. Without compelling characters, there won't be any story to speak of. It's the characters that we follow throughout the story, the ups and downs that they go through. We follow their personal development, the people they meet and fight along the way, and the lessons they learn. We cheer for them from the moment the dramatic question is asked to

---

3 Chuck Sambuchino, "The 9 Ingredients of Character Development," *Writer's Digest*, March 30, 2013, https://oreil.ly/N2Qsi.

4 Brandon Chu, "MVPM: Minimum Viable Product Manager," *Medium*, April 3, 2016, https://oreil.ly/y7ma4.

the moment it's answered. It's them we invest in emotionally, and why we care so much that we keep watching or turning the page until we find out how the story will end.

It's not a given, however, that we will care about the characters in the stories that we watch or read. Some characters we don't like because of the actors who play them, and other times we simply don't connect with them.

For the writer or creator, this is, of course, not ideal. Even if we don't think about it, a relationship is created with the audience in every story we're telling, or at least that's what we're hoping to do.[5] The surest way to do that is through the emotions of the characters that the story is about. Martha Alderson of The Writer Store, an online resource for writing and filmmaking tools, tells us, "Thoughts can lie. Dialogue can lie, too. However, emotions are universal, relatable and humanizing. Emotions always tell the truth."[6]

While it's the character's motivations that fuel the story and propel it forward, John Truby, a screenwriter, director, and screenwriting teacher, argues that in some instances, particularly for superhero stories, what makes us care about the character is their weakness. According to Truby, what we as an audience want to find out most is not whether the character accomplishes their goal, but whether they overcome their weakness.[7] This weakness can be closely linked to the protagonist's goal and motivations, but also to their emotions and the challenges they faced in overcoming that weakness.

This journey to accomplish their goals must affect the character emotionally. Only then do we connect. This goes for all the characters in the story, not just our main protagonist. The change that the character goes through is often referred to as the *character arc*, which Wikipedia describes as "the transformation or inner journey of a character over the course of a story." Further on in this chapter, we'll look closer at character arcs and character development.

5 Diego Crespo, "Spoilers, Schmoilers: The Narrative Design of Plot Twists," *Audiences Everywhere*, October 1, 2014, *https://oreil.ly/9f4-G*.

6 Martha Alderson, "Connecting with Audiences Through Character Emotions," The Writers Store, *https://oreil.ly/ynM1f*.

7 Film Courage, "The #1 Most Important Element in Developing Character," YouTube Video, September 24, 2012, *https://oreil.ly/cgevp*.

One of the reasons why it's so important to pay close attention to your characters is summarized quite well by director and cinematographer Samo Zakkir:

> If you've done your homework, really enveloped yourself within the character iceberg, and you know your characters intimately, the rest is easy. The character tells you. All you have to do is listen.[8]

This is something we can learn from when it comes to product design.

The Role of Characters and Character Development in Product Design

When we talk about characters in relation to product design, we often think of personas, whether they are *user personas* used to represent key user types, or *marketing personas* (also referred to as *buyer personas*) used to represent ideal customers. Today, however, there are a growing number of types of actors and characters to consider. For example, new input methods are present in the form of voice UIs and conversational UIs, with the "system" increasingly taking on human traits through the form of AI and machine learning.

Many roles that were previously filled by people, such as the support team over the phone, are now handled via chats and bots through AI and machine learning. Though we may not automatically think about it, whether we like it or not, and whether we define those personalities it explicitly or implicitly, users will infer some personality on each point of interaction. The way the bot writes and the way a VUI sounds impacts a user's perception of the same, and that perception matters because it impacts a user's emotional response. We should define intentionally rather than leave up to the users to interpret on their own, because it impacts the success of the experience as well as the brand. As brand strategist Jess Thoms writes, "If you don't spend the time crafting that character and motivation carefully, you run the risk of people projecting motivations, personality traits, and other qualities onto your App and brand that you may not want associated with them."[9]

---

8 Samo Zakkir, "Screenwriting 102 (Character)," *313 Film School*, February 25, 2014, *https://oreil.ly/KW6rH*.

9 Jess Thoms, "A Guide to Developing Bot Personalities," *Medium*, May 29, 2017, *https://oreil.ly/JQtdS*.

Regardless of whether our products and services involve a conversational interface, the case for defining the characters and actors is less about avoiding users projecting unwanted characteristics onto our products and services and more about acknowledging that personality, and a growing number of actors, increasingly play a role in the product experience. Additionally, it's also about really understanding the people who we're designing for.

Just as Walt Disney paid attention to the smallest of details as well as the whole, we need to do the same. To truly cater to user and business needs, and to address the challenges we covered in Chapter 3, we need to take ownership of the bigger picture as well as the small details in the products and services that we design. That has a lot to do with understanding what plays a role for whom, when, and where, and that "what" is increasingly related to a particular "who."

In this chapter, we'll look at the importance of characters and character development in relation to product design.

THE ROLE OF CHARACTERS IN CREATING A SHARED UNDERSTANDING

One of the main reasons to pay attention to characters is to ensure that everyone is on the same page when it comes to who we're designing for. As an extension of that, we want everyone involved to know personas we're working with. Making sure that the team and the client, if applicable, share a deep understanding of who you're designing the product for, and what matters to those people, is critical. This knowledge ensures not only that you're developing and designing the right thing, but also that you get buy-in for the solutions that the team is proposing and that they indeed get implemented.

A famous picture by Luke Barrett is used in numerous articles about personas and *proto-personas* (or *ad-hoc* or *improvised personas* as they are also called), and the importance of having them articulated (Figure 6-1).

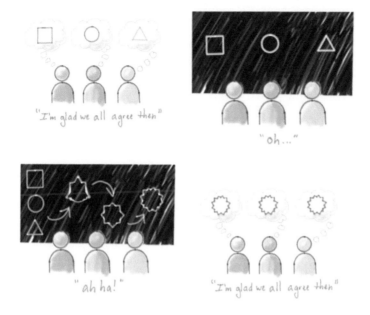

FIGURE 6-1
Cartoon by Barrett illustrating the importance of shared understanding

Having well-defined personas ensures that the internal team and that of the client have a shared understanding of who you're designing for and what they need, rather than each person walking around with their own understanding in their heads.

THE ROLE OF CHARACTERS IN CREATING EMPATHY

One of the reasons character development in product design is so important is that it includes the characters' emotions. Bringing these emotions to life through the character is one of the most powerful ways of reaching an audience.

In product design, we often talk about the importance of empathy. *Empathy* is about being able to see the world through the eyes of others, and as best as possible to imagine what they see, think, and feel. Empathy maps, shown in Figure 6-2, are one type of tool used to help create this understanding. IDEO's *Human-Centred Design Toolkit* defines empathy as a "deep understanding of the problems and realities of the people you are designing for," and the importance of it lies in being able to set aside our own preconceived ideas.

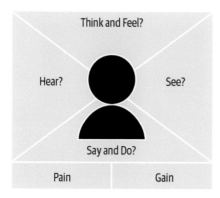

FIGURE 6-2

An empathy map, which is used as a low-fidelity tool to help create empathy and understanding for the users of our product and service

As mentioned earlier, personas have been getting a bad reputation as of late for being superfluous and not adding anything to the design process, but instead simply being a deliverable that gets shoved away in a drawer after they're done. Part of that is related to the process in which personas are created. In my view, a lack of true empathy for the people we design for, and their personification through personas, also plays a role. We tend to focus on the functional bit in terms of features, and even though we work with user stories or JTBD that include a qualification of the requirement, without linking these to a personification of a user, they tend to be too generalized.

Just as we need to connect emotionally to the characters in a story for it to have an effect on us, in product design we need to connect emotionally with the people we're designing for. Beyond making sure that we see the needs of the people we design for through their eyes rather than our own, empathy is also critical for getting other people vested in the process and vested in the people we're designing for. Without empathy, we don't care, and if we don't care, then we won't bother paying attention to the personas, or use them in the product design process. And without that, the end result is very likely to fail to meet the needs, motivations, worries, barriers, and more of the people we're designing for.

THE ROLE OF CHARACTERS IN UNDERSTANDING NEEDS AND MORE

The more we define experiences that need to work for specific users, their devices, and scenarios, ensuring that it fits into the users' own personal stories, the more we need to understand the specifics of the users. Our aim should not be to define a user group as a whole, or to define a one-size-fits-all solution, but to really understand who our customers are and what they need at specific points in their journey. Only then can we make them the true heros of the experience.

As we've talked about throughout this book, users now expect experiences that work for them, and them specifically. As advances in technology progress, with devices and experiences on these devices that increasingly feel like they know us, the more this expectation of "just for me" is going to increase.

As Alan Cooper, founder of Cooper Professional Education, "Father of Visual Basic," and inventor of design personas, says: we need to look at personas as individual users and dig in deep to identify what matters to them, how the experience should feel when and where, and the overarching principles that should guide the story that we're telling that specific user.

THE ROLE OF CHARACTERS IN HELPING DEFINE THE PRODUCT EXPERIENCE NARRATIVE

For script writing, it's often said that your story will come to life only when you know your characters inside out and can imagine them in every possible situation, from the mundane to the extraordinary. That same principle applies to creating product and service experiences that truly meet user needs. When you get to the point where you can imagine the relationships your users have with others (including the product), how they'd behave and react, and what they'd need in certain situations, you start to really explore the world of your product's story. Then just like that, scenes start to emerge that will help inform the experience narrative, what it needs to include, when, and how.[10]

THE IMPORTANCE OF IDENTIFYING ALL THE CHARACTERS AND ACTORS IN THE PRODUCT EXPERIENCE

Think back to the sequences, scenes, and shots we covered in Chapter 5. For every scene in a play, movie, or TV series, certain members of the cast have to be present. They have a particular part to play, lines to deliver, actions to perform, and often a specific place (or *mark* as they are called) to be at a specific time for everything to come together and

---

10 Michael Schilf, "Reveal the Tip, Know the Iceberg," *The Script Lab*, April 6, 2010, https:// oreil.ly/etLJm.

for the hero's journey to progress. It's choreographed and designed, and everyone is, clear on who the cast is and when the different actors are supposed to be on set/stage, and what roles they have.

That same kind of choreography and cast approach is immensely beneficial to product design as well. For every scene of a product experience, certain "cast members" need to be present. It may just be the user, but more often than not, more characters and actors play a part than we immediately think about, as we'll be looking at next.

The Different Actors and Characters to Consider in Product Design

Usually, more actors are at play than you would immediately think when it comes to product design. We see this in traditional storytelling as well. The majority of stories have more than one character, even if some of these other characters aren't actual people.

In *Cast Away*, Wilson the volleyball serves as Chuck Nolan's (played by Tom Hanks) sole companion during his time on the desert island. The character of Wilson the volleyball was created by screenwriter William Broyles Jr., and from a screenwriting point of view, Wilson helps ensure realistic one-on-one dialogue in the otherwise one-person situation presented in the majority of the film. Similarly, a character that isn't a person plays a big part in the movie *Her*. "Her" refers to the operating system that the main character, Theodore (played by Joaquin Phoenix), develops an unusual relationship with. Though Samantha, as the operating system is called, has dialogue and is played by Scarlett Johansson, you never see her.

Just as the hero will meet people on their quest, the users of our products and services will always come across different "characters" and actors on their journey. The users will see the characters that play a part in the products and services we define—from first hearing about our product or service, to whatever and wherever the end of that experience story will be. These characters will vary based on the type of product or service. The following is a good starting point to help you see the "who" and "what" that may need to be considered as part of your product's cast of characters and actors:

The user

The user is the protagonist and the hero of our product or service.

Other users

The actions of other users (e.g., commenting, liking, posting, etc.) have an effect on the user's experience.

Friends, family, partners, colleagues

Friends, family, partners, and colleagues are the allies that the user turns to for advice, or to share joys and frustrations with.

The system

The software systems, or external software system, with which the user or other systems interact.

The brand

The brand can be personified through TOV, look and feel, a VUI, animations, messaging.

Bots and VUIs

Bots and VUIs are part of both the system and the brand, but they are treated separately because of their prominence and distinct personality-based characteristics.

AI

Also part of the system and the brand, but treated separately because AI needs to be taught, initially, by people.

Touch points and drivers

Touch points and drivers include the people, platforms, interactive installations, points of sale, physical stores, etc., that users will interact or engage with on their journey with our products and services.

Devices

Devices are all things smart that are more than a mere "prop" and whose "when," "where," and "how" play an actual role in an experience; for example, smart phones, smart watches, smart home devices, and IoT.

The antagonist

The antagonist isn't always visible, physical, or digital, but present by putting obstacles in the way of what the user is trying to accomplish. Can be internal (e.g., doubt) or external.

Next we'll take a look at each type of character in a little more detail, in terms of what to consider and why they play a part. Before we do that, however, we need to define what a character is when it comes to product design and distinguish between characters and props.

A DEFINITION OF CHARACTERS AND ACTORS IN PRODUCT DESIGN

In traditional storytelling, the distinction between characters and props isn't so much of a problem. A *prop* is "an object used on stage or on screen by actors during a performance or screen production. In practical terms, a prop is considered to be anything movable or portable on a stage or a set, distinct from the actors, scenery, costumes, and electrical equipment."[11] However, as the following examples demonstrate, some props in traditional storytelling will at times be treated as characters in product design.

A *character*, or *actor*, in product design can be defined as someone who plays a direct part in one or many of your product's storylines and scenes. They should also be present for the scene to work as intended.

[NOTE]

I say "should be present" and not a "must be present" because the particulars of any given project always depend on the needs and specifics of that project.

Throughout the rest of this book, we'll work with the following definitions when it comes to characters and actors in product design:

Characters
Personified players in the product experience that interact with or influence other characters, one of which may be our protagonist, the user

Actors
Nonpersonified systems that the product we're working on interacts with or depends on

---

11 "Theatrical Property," *Wikipedia*, *https://oreil.ly/wXch2*.

Props

Elements—stationary or movable—that are used by characters or just in the product and that help further the action of the product experience

---

Exercise: A Definition of Characters and Actors in Product Design

- Using the preceding overview, take 10 minutes and write down a list of the characters and actors that come to mind for your product.
- Refer to the index card method in Chapter 5, where you defined the main scenes for your product, and define who the characters and actors are in those main scenes.

THE USERS

Just as there has to be a protagonist present in a story (or there wouldn't be a story), when it comes to product experiences, there wouldn't be any experience or product to speak of if it weren't for the users (Figure 6-3). You'll have primary, secondary, and, at times, tertiary users for any product. Whether we place a primary focus on them and their needs, or cater to them as a secondary audience, they are the ones the product and service is really about.

There's an ongoing debate in the UX field of what to call, or not call, users. Throughout this book the term "user" is used in a broad and general sense, complemented with the following distinctions:

Users

People who—in the past, present, or future—will use our product or service, but might not necessarily complete a monetary transaction in doing so.

Customers

People who either paid, are currently paying, or will pay for our product or service. Customers, however, will not necessarily have used the product.

Audience

Passive "onlookers" who are either indirectly or directly subject to our product or service; for example, through marketing.

FIGURE 6-3
The users

Exercise: The Users

Think about your product or service:

- Do you have both customers and users?
- What makes them customers or users?
- Who is your product's or service's audience?

THE OTHER USERS

The majority of stories have supporting characters that help either the protagonist or the plot of the story. In product design, and experiences in general, there are always other users who form part of the main user's team, company, or network—either on a first-, second-, or third-degree level. The main user may have no connection to them other than a shared interest, topic, or location that connects them indirectly. For example, the other users might have left a review or comment, or all be part of the same Slack group or local Facebook group (Figure 6-4).

The other users are generally important when products have a social aspect (e.g., LinkedIn and Slack). They also play a significant role when trust in the product and its offering is influenced by other users' reviews or comments (e.g., about a positive or negative experience on an ecommerce or restaurant site).

Here are some examples of other users to consider:

Peers

Users who are similar to the main users. They can be active or passive; for example, first-, second-, or third-degree contacts on LinkedIn or members of a Slack channel.

Contributor

Users who have an official role that involves creating content or in other ways adding to the product; for example, a contributing writer for your product's blog.

Passive users

Users who don't create or add to the product or service offering but engage through simply using the system in its intended way; for example, liking things on Facebook but not posting updates or content on their own.

Influencers

Power users and/or early adopters with a large audience who actively share or contribute by creating content, sometimes in a formal capacity as someone hired by a brand or as their main job; for example, a YouTube or Instagram creator who is considered to be one to follow related to a topic.

Promoters

Users or customers who are advocates of your product or service and who can influence others; for example, sharing a positive message related to your product or service on their social accounts.

Detractors

Users or customers who are critical of your product or service and who can influence others; for example, sharing a negative message related to your product or service on their social media accounts.

Though other users will almost always play a role—at least as promoters or detractors—there are a number of types of products where they don't have any impact on the user's experience or use of that product besides influencing a decision to go with the product and company in question. Accounting software for freelancers and banking are two such examples where the other users might recommend a specific software but aren't part of the product experience beyond that.

FIGURE 6-4
The other users

Exercise: The Other Users

With your own product or service in mind, answer the following:

- Who are the other users for your product or service?

- Are there any groups not mentioned in the preceding list that apply?

- Are they active or passive? For example, do they contribute directly to the growth/value of the product or service by creating content, actively sharing, or commenting? Or are they passive users who use it for their own interest but rarely engage beyond, for example, liking someone else's post?

- What can you provide to help them play their part? For example, consider how to make it easy for the active sharers and engagers to contribute or take part. Is there something that you could do to help the passive users feel comfortable and become more active in their use?

FRIENDS, FAMILY, PARTNERS, COLLEAGUES

In traditional storytelling, friends, family, partners, and colleagues are often some of the other main characters (Figure 6-5). Because they are the people closest to the protagonist, they usually play a big part in the protagonist's life.

In product design, friends, family, partners, and colleagues tend to be the main user's most trusted allies. They are the ones whom the user turns to for advice and recommendations, and whose opinions the user seeks out (or in some instances doesn't seek out but still gets). Though they play a big role in the protagonist's life, in product design these characters tend to take on more of a one-string character form, appearing in only one part of the product experience; for example, research.

FIGURE 6-5
Friends, family,
partners, colleagues

However, friends, family, partners, and colleagues can become more like subplot characters when a certain part of the product experience story involves both them and our protagonist, the main user. The main user might consult with others when making a decision on whether to buy one product over another, or seek help with setting it up. In many cases, the role they play doesn't involve any direct engagement with the product itself. Instead their part usually concerns an offline experience, such as offering advice on whether to buy the product or not.

Considering friends, family, partners, and colleagues in the product design experience is important mainly because of the role they play in influencing the user's key decisions by providing subjective opinions (or objective ones, for that matter).

Exercise: Friends, Family, Partners, Colleagues

Think about the full experience of your product, including where things may go wrong, and identify, where applicable, the following:

- At which parts of the experience do friends, family, partners, and/or colleagues become subplot characters?

- At which parts of the product experience are they more like minor, or one-string, characters?

THE SYSTEM

As we covered earlier in this chapter, the system, or more precisely the operating system called Samantha, was one of the main characters in the movie *Her*. Back when I studied computer science and business administration at Copenhagen Business School, one of the subjects we studied was systems analysis and design. We created Unified Modeling Language (UML) diagrams and use case diagrams, and the system and its components (including the database system, client application, application server, etc.) were defined as actors and represented as little stick men.

The purpose of use case diagrams is to identify the ways a user might interact with a system (Figure 6-6). It's not a detailed step-by-step representation, but a high-level overview of the relationships between use cases (e.g., make a purchase or log in), actors, and systems.

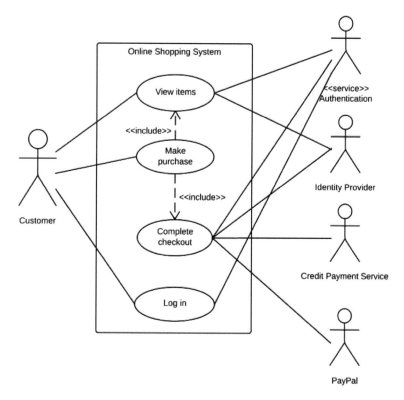

FIGURE 6-6

Example of UML use case diagram

When we talk of actors in relation to the system, there are both primary and secondary actors (Figure 6-7):

Primary actors

Actors who use the system to achieve a goal; for example, the user, or customer referred to in Figure 6-6.

Secondary actors

Actors who the system needs assistance from in order for the primary actor to achieve their goals; for example, PayPal, or the Credit Payment Service shown in Figure 6-6.

FIGURE 6-7
The system

Because we are referring to the main user as either the "user" or the "protagonist" throughout this book, instead of as "primary actors" as per the preceding definition, we'll use the following definitions of "system" and "actors" in product design:

System

The product or service that we're working on as a whole and when this acts intelligently and communicates with the user; for example, Gmail and its "Received 5 days ago. Reply?" nudges.

Actors

Other systems or technical actors that the system needs assistance from in order for it to enable users to achieve their goals; that is, the same as "secondary actors" in the preceding definition; for example, payment gateways, using existing login systems like Facebook and Gmail.

THE BRAND

As we discussed in Chapter 1, storytelling was one of the earliest forms of branding. Anyone who's worked with branding is used to defining and giving the brand a personality through the TOV and the look and feel. We define what the brand should and shouldn't say in terms of the language that is being used and what it should look like in terms of colors and the imagery style.

With the rise of bots and VUIs, the personality of the brand (Figure 6-8) is increasingly more important. Though we're far from the world that we saw in the movie *Her*, we're not that far from it. As technology takes on more human traits and becomes more intelligent, defining the personality of the brand—the dos and don'ts in terms of its behavior—is becoming more important for ensuring that we deliver the right experience to our users and customers at the right time.

FIGURE 6-8
The brand

Who and what the brand stands for should be communicated and felt by the people using the product in ways beyond the TOV and look and feel. Both should be apparent in micro interactions, in error messages, and micro copy. It should also be part of how the brand behaves across different input methods and touch points.

In some cases, including with VUIs and products that have chatbots as part of the experience, the brand will increasingly be one of the main characters, or at least a key supporting character. However, even when the brand takes on a more prominent role with its presence, it should never be the hero. The hero is always the user. The user is who the story is about, and that's why the product exists.

When we're talking about "brand" in relation to character, we're talking about the brand's overall personality, which in particular can be seen and felt in the following ways:

The brand's TOV
From micro to long-form copy

The brand's look and feel
From color palette to animations

The brand's conversational UIs
From text and avatar-based to voice-based personifications

Any other personification of the brand
Customer service representatives, sales reps, etc.

Exercise: The Brand

Think about your product and the experience the users will have with it:

- In which parts of the product experience does the brand particularly matter?
- How does the brand manifest itself?

BOTS AND VUIS

In the movie *2001: A Space Odyssey*, the computer HAL 9000 speaks in a soft, calm, and very conversational manner. Yet, when combined with its face plate and actions, it becomes quite clear that HAL 9000 is an antagonist. As soon as something is given a voice, whether an actual voice or in written format, it needs a personality. Whether we like it or not, people will project human traits onto anything that has a voice or human characteristics, such as a bot interface.

As Oren Jacob, founder and CEO of PullString, says, "We cannot separate having a conversation from thinking about whom we are having that conversation with."[12] Everyone we've talked to, or as Jacob points out, everyone who has talked to us—has had a personality, a tone, a mood, and a style that's influenced the way they talked. When we communicate, he says, we communicate both above and below the surface. What's said below the surface, in the subtext, often makes up the majority of our long-term perception of the experience. We're accustomed to using subtext to read the people we talk to, and we can't help but use the same strategy to understand bots and VUIs, too (Figure 6-9).

FIGURE 6-9

Bots and VUIs

When we talk about the personification of bots and VUIs, we consider both the nonseeing aspect and the seeing aspect. Some bots have an avatar, whereas some conversational interfaces consist of just a voice or text from which we infer the personality. Whether we see or hear something talk back to us, it's only natural for us to project human traits onto it. This personification triggers us to start building our relationship with the thing in question.

As mentioned earlier, this personification will happen regardless of whether we like it or not. Therefore, it's to the product's and the users' advantage if we put some actual work into it. We have the opportunity to make chatbots and VUIs particularly effective by creating them to match the situations, contexts, and outcomes that we need them for—and increasingly, we have to define their personality.

Some of the aspects that we create personalities for bots and VUIs through are:

---

12 Google Developers, "PullString: Storytelling in the Age of Conversational Interfaces," YouTube Video, May 19, 2017, *https://oreil.ly/bEy9x*.

The bot or VUI's TOV
> How it talks or writes in general

The actual voice of the VUI
> Making sure it matches the defined TOV and the product

Situational responses
> What and how it responds in various situations, both happy and unhappy ones

Behavior
> If and how it should behave differently under certain circumstances; for example, when specific subjects are asked about

Appearance
> What the personification should be, considering the type of product

---

Exercise: Bots and VUIs

Think about the various contexts in which your bot or VUI will be used and how, if it were human, it would behave and respond. Think particularly about these situations:

- The intent wasn't fully understood; for example, how and what should the bot or VUI respond to, and how will the way it responds influence the user's perception?

- The intent was understood, but the ask is out of scope; for example, how do you best deliver that response in light of the desired action you want the user to take next?

AI

When it comes to making a distinction between bots/VUIs and AI in traditional storytelling, the waters get a bit muddied. Without an actual voice to the AI, there wouldn't really be an AI to personify (Figure 6-10). Ava, the robot HAL 9000, and Samantha in the movie *Her* are two other examples. However, I'm treating the AI separately because AI needs to be taught and we have a responsibility in teaching it well.

What AI is really good at is dynamic personalization: it can tailor specific recommendations based on a user's actions, or lack thereof. What AI is really bad at is understanding nuances and filtering them out, as well as responding in a humane way, which requires empathy.

Increasingly, designers will be less of the creators but more of the curators of the AI. It's our job to ensure we bring an empathetic context to the AI as well as establish what relationship the AI should have to the product and the user.[13]

FIGURE 6-10
A representation of AI inspired by *2001: A Space Odyssey*

When designing AIs, we need to be particularly aware of the following:

What AI learns from

AI learns from what is fed into the system. If it's told only about apples, it will deal only with apples. As designers, we need to be on the lookout for bias in the data we feed into the AI.

Understanding user states

Currently, AIs aren't great at identifying, understanding, or responding accordingly to different user states such as sad, happy, angry. Until we reach a point where they are and can adjust and respond in empathetic ways, some scenarios will be better handed off to humans.

---

13 Miklos Philips, "The Present and Future of AI in Design," Toptal, *https://oreil.ly/s9wds*.

Exercise: AI

For your product, think about the following:

- What particular bias should you avoid transferring into the AI?
- What scenarios would be better handled by a human than by an AI-powered system?

DEVICES

Devices and technology have so far played a primary role in sci-fi literature and in movies like *Her* and *Iron Man*. In these stories, devices often play the role of assisting in the main protagonist's endeavor. They are more than mere technology that the protagonist uses, and the words *assistant, companion,* or *extension of [the user]* describe them better.

The more advanced that AI and machine learning get, and the more integrated they become in driving real value in product design, the more devices move from being a prop to being an actor or character in the product experiences that we design (Figure 6-11). We covered bots and VUIs earlier, and smart speakers are an obvious example of a device as a character. There are, however, many more. What makes a device a character rather than a prop is its role as a personified players in the product experience that interacts with or influences the main user, or other users.

FIGURE 6-11

Devices

Here are some examples of devices as characters:

Smartphones

What makes the smartphone a character rather than a prop is the enabler aspect of the device and that its role can change with the context of use. The more intelligently the operating system acts, the more helpful the device becomes and the greater its role (e.g., the Pixel and Android 10).

Smart watches

These devices often play a very similar role to smartphones, though generally more akin to an assistant that notifies you of key things because of the limitations in the tasks you can carry out on the device. Just like smartphones these devices are highly personal (e.g., Apple Watch).

Smart speakers

These often get referred to by name. Though very closely linked to the AI that powers them, they become a character in themselves that lives in a specific place in the home (e.g., Amazon's Alexa and Google Home).

Robots

Though very few of us so far have robots in our home, these devices, similar to smart speakers, will often perform a specific role or task (e.g., the Roomba vacuum cleaner, and mobile webcams that let you speak to your pet).

IoT

A good way of thinking about IoT as characters is to think of IoT as objects that talk to each other and hat we can interact with by using voice, an app or other means (e.g., Nest and Hive).

As these examples show, a very close connection exists between the device and the product that the user is using on the device, as well as a connection with the AI that powers it. However, maintaining a separation between them during design is still important, as the specifics of the device itself will have an impact on the "how" and "where" of the user's experience. For example, the use of Google's voice assistant on a smartphone has a different context than the use of Google's voice assistant on a smart speaker (Figure 6-12). With this in mind, devices should be thought of as the enabler to the product or service.

Google Assistant is
now available on
Android and iPhone

To get started, touch and hold the home button on
eligible Android phones* or download the Google
Assistant app on the App Store

FIGURE 6-12
The Where to Find It section on the Google Assistant website showing all the
types of devices that have Google Assistant available

Exercise: Devices

With your product or service in mind, define the following:

- Are there any devices that can be considered a character?
- If not, can you think about another product that you've come across
  where devices are more like characters than props?
- Does your product interact with the digital assistant of any device?

TOUCH POINTS AND DRIVERS

In all stories, the protagonist comes across other people in the journey.
These people have a role to play, however minor: in one way or another,
they assist (or try to sabotage) the protagonist's quest. Similarly, all
experiences include multiple "meet-along-the-way" touch points and
drivers that the user will come across (Figure 6-13).

Some touch points are involved in creating awareness and in driving
action (or no action), around the product in question, while others are
best thought of as props that are present but don't really play an active
part in the scene other than to further the action. An example is an ad

that you see in a magazine or online that may remind you or nudge you into doing a Google search. Though these touch points are important, the touch points and drivers that are of interest when it comes to characters and actors are those that play a more active role. These touch points are more akin to minor characters in traditional storytelling.

FIGURE 6-13
Touch points and drivers

We defined touch points and drivers as the people, platforms, interactive installations, points of sale, physical stores, etc., that users will interact or engage with on their journey to and with our products and services. What these touch points and drivers have in common is that, in one way or another, they have a message or opinion directly or indirectly associated with the product or service that may influence other people's opinions and actions. That opinion may be good or bad.

Here are some examples of touch points and drivers:

Direct touch points and drivers
> Any touch point that has a voice, albeit not necessarily a physical one, and that the user interacts with through a more active choice and as such helps drive their journey (e.g., blogs, news sites, magazines, ads that the user clicks).

Indirect touch points and drivers
> Any touch points that the user comes across and that they don't actively interact with, but that still may influence the user through their messaging (e.g., billboards, ads that the user doesn't click).

Exercise: Touch Points and Drivers

With your product experience in mind, think about the stages that the user will go through and identify the following:

- What direct touch points and drivers are there?
- What indirect touch points and drivers are there?

THE ANTAGONIST

In traditional storytelling, the *antagonist* is the person who wants things to go badly for the protagonist. They might take direct action to sabotage the protagonist (Figure 6-14).

In product design, we often don't think about antagonists, and we often design for the best-case scenarios. However, there are multiple antagonists to consider:

Internal antagonists

The "devil-on-the-shoulder" thoughts and feelings that influence users in a negative way in relation to taking action or achieving their goal (e.g., the user's doubt or lack of confidence in their ability to succeed).

External direct antagonists

Those that actively attempt to sabotage the main user (e.g., trolls and haters on social media that post negative comments in reply to the main user, or about the product with the aim of causing pain).

External indirect antagonists

Those that are indirect in that they don't assist the user in achieving their goals (e.g., badly written error messages or instructions that confuse users rather than guide them).

FIGURE 6-14
The antagonist

Exercise: The Antagonist

Think about your product and the experience the user has with it and identify the following:

- The internal antagonists for your main users
- The external direct antagonists
- Any external indirect antagonists

This overview is a helpful reference for identifying the characters and actors in a product experience. The next step is to define and develop these characters and actors further.

The Importance of Character Development

One of the main goals in traditional storytelling is to create characters that the audience or the reader will care about. Without such characters, there usually isn't a good story, and if there is no emotional connection, then the story will fall flat. Screenwrite and director John Truby says that one of the biggest mistakes writers make when developing their characters is to make them as detailed as possible by giving them too many traits. According to Truby, these are just superficial elements of a person. Though they help us see who the character is, they're not what makes us care about a character.

What makes us care are two things: the character's weakness (i.e., the need of the character and that deep personal problem inside), and the character's goal in the story (which will eventually also deal with their weakness and problem).[14]

The goal, or objective, of the character is an important aspect of who the character is and how they will develop. Each character will have one, just as each user will have an objective when it comes to product design. This objective is also related to the big "why." We're always advised to dig into the "why" in product design. In traditional storytelling, the why is an important part of establishing why the character is in the story and, in turn, who they are.

By trying to answer the questions that we have around the characters, or users, we start to do our research into their context, culture, and occupation. We start to add in details around their values, attitudes, and emotions, and we develop the characters' backstories covering physiology, sociology, and psychology. With these details (partly) defined, their personality and behavior become defined, and you can imagine them in a range of situations, from the extraordinary to the mundane. And then all you have to do is listen, as I said at the beginning of this chapter. The characters will help tell you their story.[15]

Next let's look at a few terms that often appear in discussions about character development in traditional storytelling.

DYNAMIC VERSUS STATIC CHARACTERS

In traditional storytelling, a distinction is made between dynamic and flat characters. *Dynamic characters* go through some form of change that can be seen. Most protagonists are usually dynamic characters.

Static characters, in contrast, don't change throughout the course of the story. Instead, they remain the same and serve to ensure contrast to the dynamic characters. Antagonists are often static characters.

14 Film Courage, "How To Make The Audience Care About Your Characters," YouTube Video, September 5, 2012, https://oreil.ly/csDLE.

15 Samo Zaakir, "Screenwriting 102 (Character)," *313 Film School*, February 25, 2014, https://oreil.ly/Uy2cl.

ROUND VERSUS FLAT CHARACTERS

Related to dynamic and static characters are round versus flat characters. *Round characters* are fully developed and show a true depth in personality. They are often complex and more realistic and undergo changes that at times may surprise the audience or reader.

Flat characters have less depth to them. They are two-dimensional and relatively uncomplicated. They don't usually undergo any changes but remain the same throughout the work.

CHARACTER ARC

The changes in a character are often referred to as the *character arc*, which Wikipedia defines as "the transformation or inner journey of a character over the course of a story." Essentially, if a character starts as one person and changes, that's a character arc. Though less important characters can have a character arc too, the character arc is most common for the protagonist and the lead characters.

There are also different types of character arcs:[16]

A change arc

> The classic "hero's journey," where the character changes from more of a nobody into a hero. The change that is happening here is transformative and most aspects of the character change throughout the story.

A growth arc

> The character overcomes an inner battle (e.g., a weakness or fear) while facing external opposition. At the end of this "change," the character is a fuller person but otherwise the same.

With a better understanding of these terms, we'll take a look at what traditional storytelling teaches us about making the characters come to life.

---

16 Veronica Sicoe, "The 3 Types of Character Arc—Change, Growth and Fall," Veronica Sicoe (blog), April 29, 2013, *https://oreil.ly/gPqNE*.

What Traditional Storytelling Teaches Us About Characters and Character Development

Some stories will begin with the plot and narrative evolving around the characters, their needs, motivations, weaknesses, and secrets. In these types of stories, the trick is to make sure that the story that unfolds doesn't result in "a beginning, a muddle and an end," as the author and poet Philip Larkin says. More often than not, however, novels will begin with an idea for a story. Some writers, or pantsers as they are also called, prefer to just sit down and write the story as it comes to them. To them, the characters will develop as the story unfolds. Others, the outliners who prefer to outline their novel or book first, will know a lot more about the characters before they start writing. We've previously referred to this as *character-driven* versus *plot-driven* stories. Regardless of the approach you take, characters need to be defined and developed.

Whether you're working on a film, TV show, book, or animated movie, the advice is often to draw from your own personal experience when you build out your characters. It's quite the opposite when we talk about product design. For product design, we're often told that we are not our users. While drawing from own experience is a great starting point, both product design and, traditional storytelling emphasize the importance of research. To develop well-rounded and believable characters, you need to not only be able to describe them, but also know the motivations and reasons for their actions, thoughts, and feelings, and how these, in turn, affect the protagonist's friends and family. You're not as likely to get these details just by doing online research, but may need to have face-to-face conversations.

As for how to develop and introduce characters, you can take insight and inspiration from the way characters are developed in books, animations, games, TV, and film scripts, and in how actors make them come to life.

BUILDING AND INTRODUCING CHARACTERS IN BOOKS AND NOVELS

In novels, the advice is to introduce your characters slowly. The main character is the one you should meet first, and many writers make the mistake of introducing them too late. Not everything about the character should be described with words, however.

Novelist Jerry Jenkins says that imagination is part of the joy of reading and that you should trust your readers to deduce the qualities of the character through what they see in your scenes and hear in your dialogue. The old saying "Show, don't tell," Jenkins explains, applies here too. "Show who your character is through what he says, his body language, his thoughts, and what he does."[17] Furthermore, don't force your readers to see the character exactly the same way you do. It doesn't matter if your audience imagines your main character with dark or blonde hair, Jenkins says:

> Thousands of readers might have thousands of slightly varied images of the character, which is all right, provided you've given him enough information to know whether your hero is big or small, attractive or not, and athletic or not.

What will help your readers, however, is to give your character a *tag*, a repetitive verbal device, as many readers will struggle to differentiate one character from another.

Applying it to product design

We recognize the use of tags from the personas we work with in design. We often give them a name that helps us put them in perspective in terms of the product or service we're working on, as well as in relation to the other personas. For example, we may have "Sarah, the social shopper" who's different from "Karen, the carefully considered shopper." Giving our key users these tag lines helps us remember who they are and what distinguishes them from other users.

As for how to introduce your character, the advice for novels doesn't apply to product design. In product design, it is important that the core team, clients, and key stakeholders share a common understanding of who the users of the product are from the start of a project, as the image by Luke Barrett earlier in this chapter illustrated. Everyone, and the core team in particular, should be able to reference who the main users are without looking at the deliverable that specifies this. Some seeing the user with brown hair and others seeing the user with blonde

---

17 Jerry Jenkins, "The Ultimate Guide to Character Development," Jerry Jenkins (blog), *https://oreil.ly/8ZEbJ.*

hair is less of an issue, but sharing the same deep understanding of who you're designing for is crucial. We can take this lesson from traditional storytelling:

> The goal is to make your readers feel something for your character. The more they care about them, the more emotion they'll invest in your story. And maybe that's the secret.[18]

WELL-DEVELOPED CHARACTERS FOR TV AND FILM

Many of us have read a book that was later made into a movie. Sometimes it's a disappointing experience. What was magical when we read it does nothing for us when we see it up on the big screen. This difference might come down to the way the film is directed. Other times the problem lies with the cast and the characters. Maybe they're too different from what we imagined in our heads when we first read the book. Or maybe they simply don't connect with us.

In storytelling, it doesn't matter how good the plot is in principle, if it's not brought to life through the characters of that same story. This is of particular importance when it comes to film, TV, and theater, where the images created in our heads by the words we have read in a book are replaced with what we see on screen or on stage. If the characterization falls flat, or is badly acted, then the storyline will become unbelievable and we won't connect emotionally.

In contrast, if the characterization is really well done and acted, it can make the whole film or TV episode/series. The movie *Gone Girl*, based on the best-selling book of the same name, is a great example. The character of Amy Dunne, as written in the novel and as portrayed onscreen by Rosamund Pike, is one of the most frightening and hated villains.[19] Another example of well-developed characters is the American drama series *True Detective*. Here every character has intentions and obstacles that help make them feel like living and breathing people.

---

18 Sambuchino, "The 9 Ingredients of Character Development."

19 David Shreve, "B2BO: Gone Girl," *Audiences Everywhere*, September 17, 2014, *https://oreil. ly/FtIE7*.

True Detective creator Nic Pizzolato says that bad writing looks like characters running around delivering and trading information with no life in the plot. Daniel Netzel, who makes videos about movies and publishes them on Film Radar on YouTube says *Rogue One* is an example of this. One of the reasons for its flat characters stems from the way director Gareth Edwards, approached making the movie, Netzel says: "Most of the sequences felt like they were there to serve the purposes of the writer, and not the characters."[20] This assessment fits rather well with the way Edwards describes his approach himself:

> The way I like to work is, you try and come up with visual milestones of like...Well I'd love to see this, and I'd love to see this, and I'd love to see this. I'm not sure how they'll connect. And then what you do is, you create visuals of the things that would be great. And then you try and find a way of linking them all in.

According to Netzel, this is a mistake: although this process can certainly produce something that's visually stunning, like *Rogue One*, a plot that is driven by the aesthetic needs of the writer or the director rather than the characters' motivations will inevitably leave us feeling that something is missing.

Director and producer Ridley Scott, who has a background in directing commercials, is another example of a director who is famous for being more interested in the shot and how it looks than how the characters develop. That's not to say you can't produce a box office hit this way. Both *Rogue One* and the *Alien* movies show that you obviously can, but focusing on the shot is not what's going to create the strongest emotional connection, and that, as we've covered, is where the power of stories lie.

Applying it to product design

Moviemakers and writers can forget about the power of a character's emotional development and instead get swept up in specific scenes, or in including high-tech special effects.[21] Likewise, in product design we can get too excited about the latest animations or design trends and for-

---

20 Film Radar, "True Detective: How to Develop Character," YouTube Video, June 12, 2017, *https://oreil.ly/g0VS*.

21 Alderson, "Connecting with Audiences Through Character Emotions."

get to question whether they are right for our users. Or we let features, "the big idea," or business requirements drive our work instead of anchoring it in the users' needs and goals and the bigger "why."

To deliver product experiences that really engage the user, and to get the product design process to be really user-centered, it has to be a character-driven (i.e., user-driven) experience instead of a plot-driven (i.e., idea-driven) product.

As for working with character-driven plots and developing characters, novelist Stephen King advises to "put interesting characters in difficult situations and see what happens."[22] This is along the same lines as the general advice for script writing that we referenced earlier: your story will come to life only when you know your character inside out and can imagine them in every possible situation.

ACTORS AND BUILDING A CHARACTER

Drama schools teach a number of techniques to help actors empathize with the character; this empathy helps create believable emotions and actions in the characters that they portray. One of the methods is the *Stanislavski method*, which is used to build believable characters in seven steps by asking these questions:

- Who am I?
- Where am I?
- When is it?
- What do I want?
- Why do I want it?
- How will I get it?
- What do I need to overcome?

The method is based on first reading the script carefully to get a good understanding of the character's motivations, needs, and desires, and this in turn helps the actor identify the role that they're playing. After that, the actor starts working out how the character would behave in situations and how they'd react. The actor must keep in mind the character's objective, and the obstacles that stand in the way of achieving

---

22 Jenkins, "The Ultimate Guide to Character Development."

their objective. These also determine just how far they are willing to go to get what they want. The actor is advised to break down the script into *beats*, which are individual objectives of the character. These could be as simple as getting on a train. The next step is to determine the character's motivation for this action, as this in turn helps portray the emotion that the character is experiencing while completing the objective.

In addition to this, Konstantin Stanislavski created the *Magic If*, which asks, "What would I do if I found myself in this (the character's) situation?" The actor steps into the character's shoes in a given situation and asks this simple question; the answer will help the actor understand the thoughts and feelings that they need to portray for each scene. Stanislavski came up with this method because one of the jobs of an actor is to be believable in unbelievable circumstances.[23]

Applying it to product design

Being able to imagine ourselves as one of our users is incredibly valuable for creating empathy and a deep understanding of what matters to the user or user group in question. Stanislavski's Magic If in particular is a useful question for product teams to ask themselves throughout the design process in order to better understand where a user may be coming from and what they may or may not want.

One piece of advice when working with personas throughout the product life cycle is to allocate one persona to one member of the team. It then becomes that person's role to play that persona and to ensure that the persona's needs, concerns, motivations, and goals are being considered in what's being designed and developed. Though this doesn't replace the need for testing the product or service with real users, it can be an effective way to ensure that the users you're designing for are considered throughout.

---

23 "The Stanislavski System, Stanislavski Method Acting and Exercises," Drama Classes, *https://oreil.ly/YV4cT*.

Exercise: Actors and Building a Character

For your next project/design review, assign each persona to a member of the team. At discussions and meetings, it's their role to look at what's being discussed through the lens of that persona (as well as through the lens of their role in the project, of course). Ask each team member to answer the Magic If—"What would I do if I found myself in this (the user's) situation?"—to ensure that the needs, concerns, motivations, and goals of each persona are considered and met.

CHARACTERS IN ANIMATIONS

Animated movies are a great example of the personification of nonhuman "things," whether animals, toys, or other objects. Many of us have magical, or at least fond, memories of particular animated films, that have brought these nonhuman "things" to life.

Khan Academy's Pixar in a Box feature provides a behind-the-scenes look into how Pixar develops its animations into fully developed characters; that is, those that you can imagine in almost any situation.

The lessons cover the following topics:

External versus internal features

External features are the character "design" (their clothes, what they look like), whereas inner features are their beliefs and preferences.

Wants versus needs

Wants and needs can be in conflict with each other. The wants are often what we say that we want, whereas the needs are sometimes the things we don't realize or don't like to admit we need. For example, in *Toy Story*, Woody wants to be Andy's favorite toy, but what he needs is to learn how to share and not always be the best. In terms of their role in the story, wants often provide the entertainment, whereas the story's emotional heart lies in the need.

Obstacles

These stand in the way of wants and needs and can be anything, including something internal like fear.

Character arc

This is how the character changes as a result of the choices they make, based on the obstacles they come across, in their quest for what they need.

Stakes

These are the things that add drama and that, together with obstacles, can often spark subplots. However, stakes can be divided into three categories:

- *Internal stakes*—What's going on emotionally or mentally

- *External stakes*—What's going on in the world

- *Philosophical stakes*—What is impacting the world, what is making the values and the belief system of this world change (or not change), and what happens then[24]

Applying it to product design

Wants and needs hold a lot of relevance in design. Often users think that they want something in particular when, in fact, what they need is slightly different. By making the distinction between wants and needs, we're able to go one level deeper and separate out what users often say they want from their underlying need, and hence, identify the real value that our product and services (can) offer.

External features are usually not something we need to consider in persona development, as it doesn't matter if we have an exact shared mental picture in our head of what our target audience actually looks like. But when we do need to consider external features when designing other characters and actors that have a role in the experience. One such example is in developing avatars for bots. What might appeal to some users will feel alienating to others, and getting the balance right, as well as allowing the user to potentially choose from a range of avatars, can help ensure that the product or service resonates with specific users. Just think of the growing number of emojis that we now have.

---

24 "Introduction to Character," *Khan Academy, https://oreil.ly/5ezW6*.

Just as in games, which we'll touch on shortly, users want to be able to identify with the personification of the bot avatar. This want to identify has to do with trust and overall perception of what they're experiencing, and as an extension of that, the brand.

Exercise: Characters in Animations

For a current or recent product or service that you've worked on, start to identify the main user, the protagonist:

- What is their backstory? This helps explain the user's goals, barriers and motivations.
- What are their external features? This is what they look like.
- What are their inner features? This is their beliefs, what they enjoy.
- What are their wants? These are the things that drives a character to act.
- What are their needs? These are the things they need to do or learn to succeed.
- What are their obstacles? These are the things that stand in the way of their wants and needs.
- What are their stakes? These are the consequences of any choice they make (e.g., risks, impacts and rewards).

CHARACTERS IN GAMES

In some games, the avatars of the characters are predefined. In others, choosing or designing your own avatar based on predefined elements is part of the game. Gabriel Valdivia, a designer at Canopy, writes that one of the best avatar-creating flows puts the process of actually creating your avatar into the storyline. Creating the character this way is an opportunity to showcase the tone of the game and help inform the decisions the players make as they create their avatar. In Grand Theft Auto Online, for example, avatars are posing to get their mugshots taken which, as Valdivia writes, is "a cheeky way of introducing players to the sensibilities of the game."[25]

---

25 Gabriel Valdivia, "The UX of Virtual Identity Systems," *Medium*, July 1, 2017, *https://oreil.ly/hylrR*.

Applying it to product design

A key difference between "normal" product design and game design is that for games, the player has almost always chosen to play the game. This is unlike the users of the products and services that we work on. This active choice means that the game designer needs to truly understand the player and what will get them engaged. We'll talk more about what we can learn from player personas in the last part of this book.

Building out a detailed picture of who our personas are is not far from how the characters in adventure games are shown. We know exactly what tools or weapons they have at their disposal, and what their energy levels are at any point. Throughout their quest, our game personas will engage in fights and activities that deplete their energy levels. If they get hurt, their energy decreases even more, but when they come across the good stuff, their energy levels get recharged.

This similar to what our users are experiencing in their adventures of the products and services we design. As we talked about in Chapter 5, throughout the life cycle and the stages of the experiences we're creating, there are bound to be barriers, whether they're mental ones related to what the user doesn't like doing or physical ones like forms that have to be filled in, or a choice that needs to be made. To help us narrate and plan out an experience and a storyline that resonates with our specific users, we need to know their likes and dislikes, and the kinds of encounters that will give or take energy from them.

Much more can be said about what traditional storytelling can teach us about characters than the material covered here, but that is beyond the scope of this book. Next we'll take a look at methods and tools used in traditional storytelling in relation to characters that can benefit the product design process. Before doing so, however, we'll explain the difference between character definition, character development, and character growth.

Exercise: Characters in Games

For your product or service, either use an existing persona, or if it hasn't been defined, start by identifying who they are. Once done, do the following:

- Grab a pen and paper and draw a very simple picture of your persona that includes their name, a picture of them, and a quote that summarizes who they are.

- Identify the different factors that either motivate them or pose barriers for them by drawing them out as bars that indicate their starting level.

- With the overall experience in mind, or a specific sequence of it (e.g., a defined user journey), either add or subtract to their bars at key points in the experience.

Character Definition Versus Character Development Versus Character Growth

There is a bit of ambiguity in each of these terms. Both "definition" and "development" possibly evolved around defining and working on who the character really is, whereas both "development" and "growth" possibly refer to how the character actually develops and grows throughout the story. For the purpose of clarity, in this book we're using the following definitions:

Character definition
> The process of identifying, and at a high level defining, the characters and actors

Character development
> The process of creating believable characters by giving them depth and personality

Character growth
> The process of defining how the character develops and grows throughout the story

Tools for Character Definition and Development in Product Design

Most of us are fairly comfortable with the process of identifying and, at a high level, defining who all the main users of our product or service actually are, but we rarely look beyond these users to the other characters and actors that play a smaller part. Similarly, we're used to developing personas or proto personas for our users, but with the rise of conversational UIs, we need to start developing personas for bots and voice assistants, too. What we do less often is to look wider and define and develop more than the main user personas to include other characters and actors. And we very rarely look at how our personas, and other characters and actors, develop and grow throughout the product experience story, or what their relationships are and how these affect the product experience.

The grouping that we covered earlier in this chapter of the various characters and actors in product design is a good starting point when it comes to thinking through who plays a role and the kind of role they may play. In many instances, there is no need to define these characters and actors further than simply being aware of them, or by mapping them to when they play a part in the experience; for example, as part of a customer experience map that looks at the whole end to end experience across touch points and channels. That's often the case with "other users," "friends, family, partners, colleagues," and "touch points and drivers." The system, the brand, bots and VUIs, AI, and the antagonist may need more defining, depending on the type of product or service. The key here is that it should help define the product experience and what's needed when and where.

Next we'll take a look at three methods and tools from traditional storytelling and how they can help us with character definition, character development, and character growth.

CHARACTER HIERARCHY FOR CLARIFYING ROLE AND IMPORTANCE

In screenwriting, a *character hierarchy* indicates how characters rank in relation to other characters in terms of their importance for the screenplay (Figure 6-15). The most important one is your protagonist, as it's their story, and without that character, there really is no story. But then you have the villains, friends, rivals, and mentors, all of which can be divided as follows:

- Main characters
- Supporting characters
- Subplot characters
- One-string characters

Who follows whom in the hierarchy will depend on the variables of the specific story. However, just as certain types of stories tend to have a certain shape (as author Kurt Vonnegut and others have defined), there are typical patterns of character hierarchy based on the type of story it is. In disaster movies, for example, friends, mentors, and rivals rank closely behind the protagonist; and in slasher movies, the rule tends to be that the longer a character survives, the more important they are. The Script Lab references that in some movies, the villain ranks nearly as high as the protagonist; Hannibal Lecter in *The Silence of the Lambs* is one example of a clear supporting character. Other times, the villain is actually the protagonist and becomes an anti-hero. A prime example of this is Alex in *A Clockwork Orange*. In buddy pictures like *Lethal Weapon*, Riggs and Murtaugh are partners, both with clear character arcs, but Rigg's story is the obvious one that we follow through the film.[26]

Working through a character hierarchy is a useful high-level exercise to go through in conjunction with the defined plot of the product experience. It helps you think of who really matters when and why, and often results in realizations that a certain part of the experiment needs more focus to match with its importance, from, for example, the role of other users early on in the product life cycle to help drive awareness and build trust, to how the antagonist shouldn't be forgotten. By using a simple character map sheet like the one in Figure 6-15, you get an overview of just how many characters and actors are part of the product experience and, as with many things, going through the experience will help you think of more characters.

---

26 "Character," *The Script Lab*; Schilf, "Reveal the Tip, Know the Iceberg."

The Protagonist: our target persona
Alex, the Tech CEO and Father of One

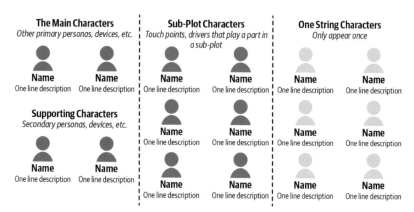

FIGURE 6-15

Sample character hierarchy map

Exercise: Character Hierarchy for Clarifying Role and Importance

Define the character hierarchy for the product and service you work on.

CHARACTER QUESTIONNAIRES FOR CHARACTER DEVELOPMENT

One of the best ways to get to know your characters is to ask a lot of questions about them. One of the tools that writers use to develop their characters is a *character questionnaire,* or character development questions (Figure 6-16). This list of questions is designed to make sure the characters in the story don't become flat, but are memorable, as well as making sure the changes they go through are linked to the broader story arc. Many writers complete these questionnaires before they start to write the story, as the more you know about your characters, the richer they'll be and, at times, the more the story will come to you.[27]

---

27 "Character Development Questions," Now Novel, *https://oreil.ly/18t8K.*

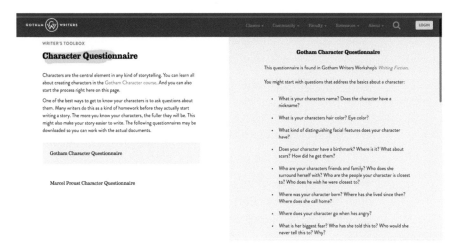

FIGURE 6-16

Sample character questionnaire from Gotham Writers (*https://oreil.ly/uC7_U*)

Several character questionnaires are available for download online. Some are more in depth, and others are more abstract. Many also break up the questions into sections such as:

- Basics about the character (name, hair color, their friends, and family)

- Personality (good and bad habits, strongest and weakest character trait, catchphrases)

- Past and future (ambitions, greatest achievements, strongest childhood memory)

- Daily life (eating habits, what their home is like, what they do first thing on a weekday morning respectively weekend morning, drink of choice etc.)

Editor Chuck Sambuchino writes of nine ingredients for character development for novels:[28]

Communication style
    How does your character talk?

---

28 Sambuchino, "The 9 Ingredients of Character Development."

History

Where does your character come from?

Appearance

What do they look like?

Relationships

What kind of friends and family do they have?

Ambition

What is their passion in life? What goal are they trying to accomplish through your story? What is their unrecognized, internal need and how will they meet it?

Character defect

What's their personality trait that irritates their friends or family?

Thoughts

What kind of internal dialogue does your character have? How do theye think through their problems and dilemmas? Is their internal voice the same as their external?

Everyman-ness

How relatable is your character?

Restrictions

More than a personality flaw, what physical or mental weakness must your character overcome through their arc?

Quite a few overlaps exist between these steps and the way we define personas. However, Sambuchino's ingredients can add a few nuances to the character development of personas for multidevice projects. *History* is a good one that we often don't do enough with in our personas—describing their backstory, their prior key experiences, and what got them here today.

Restrictions are also relevant for helping us think through how to make the individual users of the experiences we design into the hero of the story. As the "hero's journey" outlines, the protagonist will come across help along the way in the form of a mentor or a co-hero. While we shouldn't aim to make ourselves the co-hero in the experiences we design, or an actual mentor, we can offer help through the content and features of what we design, as well as how we design them. But in order to do that, we need to know what kind of help the users need.

How to go about it

For product design, just as for character development in storytelling, it's about identifying what questions that will help develop the persona. We're used to working with persona groups, demographics, tasks and goals, barriers, and more, but beyond that, using character questionnaires in product design is about what will help bring light to a persona in relation to the full end-to-end experience.

Just as traditional storytelling tends to group different questions, a good starting point is to do the same in product design.

Exercise: Character Questionnaires for Character Development

For the personas for your product and service, identify the following:

- What are five basic questions to ask about them?
- What are five questions to help clarify their backstory?
- What are five questions to learn more about the different scenarios related to use of the product or service?
- What are five questions to learn more about their use of the product or service?

QUESTIONS TO HELP DEVELOP THE CHARACTER ARC

As we've talked about earlier in this chapter, a character arc maps the evolution of the character's personality over the course of the story. Depending on the type of story, the character arc can either be positive or negative.

In a positive character arc, such as that of the hero's journey, the protagonist overcomes external obstacles and internal flaws and ends up a better person for it. At its core, this arc is made up of three points:[29]

---

29 "How to Write a Compelling Character Arc," Reedsy (blog), September 21, 2018, *https://oreil.ly/m3TAg*.

The main goal that the character has in the story; it may be to fall in love or to become rich. No matter what the goal is, their journey will be hindered by it. Using Bilbo Baggins in *The Hobbit* for reference, his goal is to help the dwarves retrieve the treasure that was stolen and guarded by Smaug.

The lie

The lie is a deeply rooted misconception that the character has about themselves or about their world, and this misconception keeps them from reaching their true potential. To reach their goal, they need to overcome or acknowledge this lie and face the truth. Bilbo's lie is a belief that hobbits belong in the Shire, where they are surrounded by their comforts, and that the outside world is dangerous and for braver men who can fight with a sword and take on goblins.

The truth

The truth is related to the positive change arc's goal itself, which is self-improvement. This self-improvement is achieved when the character learns to reject the lie and embrace the truth. Bilbo's truth is the heroic qualities that he possessed heroic qualities all along and that heroism is as much about the inner strength to follow your own moral compass when faced with adversity as it is about facing dangers.

This has some resemblance to Pixar's wants versus needs, although in product design, an antagonist usually isn't deliberately designed into the product experience narrative to focused on ruining things for the protagonist. However, as we've covered, the antagonist can be internal too, and just as Pixar explains, what users think they want is often slightly different from what they actually need.

How to go about it

Working through the goal, the lie, and the truth for each of your main personas is a quick and easy exercise to help identify what it is that they are overcoming, be that external obstacles or barriers, or internal ones.

You may do this by just sitting down and discussing or thinking through what each of these may be. Another way to approach this is to do it in relation to your product experience narrative.

Exercise: Questions to Help Develop the Character Arc

For the main persona for your product and service, identify the following:

- What is your character's goal?
- What is your character's lie?
- What is your character's truth?

Summary

Though there are different ways to come up with a story, all stories are better with a focus on characters. Similarly, all products are better when we focus on the users that we're building them for, and when we are clear on all the other actors that play a part in that product experience. Starting to define the personas of your characters and actors is the first step in understanding what will matter in the experience. To get a more complete picture that helps identify the bigger picture as well as the details throughout the different points in their journey, we need to go one step deeper, and that is really where the fun begins.

What's common in both the design and the storytelling world is that we have to do research into the characters of the stories we're telling, and into the users of the products and services that we're designing for. We must know our characters/users inside out not just to be able to tell a good story, but to ensure we know all the whys. Why does the character want to be in the story? Why does the user want to use your product and service?

As this chapter has covered, there's more than what immediately meets the eye when it comes to characters and actors in the products and services that we define. The more complex these become, the more important it is that we've defined who plays a role, when, and where, so that we can ensure that the experience flows. By considering and accounting for all aspects that should be defined, we can ensure the most optimal outcome for users and the business.

Character development is something that we very rarely get involved with in product design. However, significant benefits could be reaped if we continuously spend time throughout the product design process on character development of our personas.

It's the characters of a story that we invest in emotionally. We want to know what happens to them. Whether we root for the good or the bad guy, we develop empathy for them through the challenges they face, the weaknesses they overcome, and, of course, through their quest to reach or achieve their goal. We want to know what happens and how the story is going to end, and in most cases, we want things to go well for them.

[7]

Defining the Setting and Context of Your Product

Once Doesn't Mean Always

IN 2014 I WENT to the Swedish Embassy in London to vote in the election back home. It was one of those moments where I wanted to share my check-in with the world—or in this case, the Twittersphere. I opened up Foursquare, as it was still called back then, added a comment, and tapped the Twitter icon on the check-in screen and checked in.

A few days later, I was on my way to Berlin to speak at a conference and, as usual, I checked in to Heathrow T5 on Foursquare. We boarded the plane, and as I scrolled through my Twitter feed, I saw that Foursquare had shared my check-in on Twitter. I quickly deleted the tweet and opened up Foursquare to see what had happened. It turned out that since that time at the Swedish Embassy, where I'd chosen to share my check-in, sharing check-ins was now turned on by default.

It may seem like a small and silly thing, but these little things really make a difference. As the world we live in, and design for, becomes ever more filled with noise, it's our responsibility as designers to make sure that we don't add to it unnecessarily but instead help users do what they want and not make assumptions or decide for them. The right and nice way for the Foursquare app to have behaved in this instance would have been to look at my past behavior in the app and use a simple algorithm to decide how to handle the check-in scenario. As a rule of thumb, apps should not change the default behavior and setting unless the user has specifically asked for it—and definitely not without telling them.

If Foursquare had analyzed my behavior in its app, it would have noticed that I very seldom share my check-ins. As a result, the default assumption of the app should have been that if I share a check-in, it's probably a one-off or a special occasion. However, if I'd also chosen to share my next check-in, and the check-in after that, the start of a pattern would have been established, which Foursquare could have confirmed by asking if I'd like to change the default setting to share all check-ins on Twitter.

Because technology increasingly takes the form of useful assistants, this is a simple example of an opportunity to nudge users with a friendly "Hey, we noticed that... Would you like to...?" style of communication. These simple if-then scenarios, otherwise known as *conditional statements*, can be quickly mapped through a decision tree or user flow, and it's both in the user's and Foursquare's interest to do so. When we design experiences, we should always strive to do that which will provide the user with a positive one.

Accidentally sharing every single Foursquare check-in can make you feel like a fool, and it also creates spam. Unintentional shares provide very little value, and it's likely that sharing every single check-in on Twitter isn't actually in Foursquare's interest. A check-in without an accompanying comment is pretty much just useless noise, and the small value it can provide in brand awareness is far outweighed by the negative response many users have to this kind of spam broadcast. Not all check-ins are created equal.

To understand what creates and drives value and what doesn't for both users and the business, we need to look into context and the reason(s) behind the action(s), or lack thereof. In the case of Foursquare, it's important to understand why people check in and why people share check-ins so it can try to leverage those aspects that drive value for the user, other users, not yet users, and for Foursquare. Foursquare could make and quickly validate a range of hypotheses, from how to identify social moments to how to measure how active a sharer a user is in general.

Personally, I used to use Foursquare as a way to remember certain places I've gone to, or times I've been there, as well as to log what I've done. While writing this, it was helpful to be able to look at when I checked in at the embassy and just how many days later I flew to Berlin. However, I generally don't want to share those updates, even inside Foursquare. With a simple decision tree, Foursquare should be able to identify, and make sure, that I don't accidentally share something I don't want to share. Figure 7-1 shows another example of a check-in

I accidentally shared on Twitter after deliberately having shared, and added a comment, to my check-in prior to that about landing at Copenhagen Airport and being home.

FIGURE 7-1
Another example of a check-in I accidentally shared on Twitter

Understanding all of these parameters comes down to context, which is one of the most powerful and important aspects we have at our disposal as UX designers and product owners. Through context, we have the ability to ensure that we deliver value at the right time, in the right way, and on the right device. This also applies to trying to anticipate users' needs before they themselves have realized they have them. Context can be used to create products that seem to know you, not in a creepy way, but in a helpful and friendly way of being one step ahead and there when the need arises.

For a long time, I've advocated that we should design with the individual in mind. Most of the time, this suggestion is met with some skepticism, just as when you talk through something that's fairly complex: "It's too complex. Keep it simple. Don't design for everyone. Focus on our key audience groups." But my passion lies in the complete opposite direction. It lies in digging into the complexities to find the simple little things, and the big ones, that will really make a difference and to truly understand how a specific individual might want to use a product or service, and what will really make a difference to them, specifically, not to everyone as a whole. This is where context plays a crucial role and where you need to go into detail and look at the complexities of it all to really find the thing that will make a difference.

The Role of Setting and Context in Storytelling

In traditional storytelling, the setting, or place, is one of the main elements, together with plot and characters,[1] whereas context is often talked about in the interpretation of literary works or films. However, that is not the type of context we're talking about here. We're talking about context in relation to how to create and tell a story to an audience.

Merriam-Webster defines *context* as "the parts of a discourse that surround a word or passage and can throw light on its meaning" or "the interrelated conditions in which something exists or occurs [namely] environment, setting." Julien Samson explains for *The Writing Cooperative* that context is a tool that helps authors build trust and interest with their readers. Context, as Merriam-Webster defines it, can be anything that helps give a story meaning, or that is related to the environment or setting in which the story takes place. Here are some examples of context in traditional storytelling:[2]

- The backstory

- Details about your character

- An event or situation

- A memory

- An anecdote

- An environment or setting

Context, in other words, serves to ensure that the story works, that the reader or audience understands the "why" of characters' actions or events that take place, and that a relationship is formed with the reader

---

1 Courtney Carpenter, "Discover the Basic Elements of Setting in a Story," *Writer's Digest*, May 2, 2012, *https://oreil.ly/QGxrg*.

2 Julien Samson, "Why Context Matters In Writing," *Medium*, June 28, 2017, *https://oreil.ly/8Ekoi*.

or audience by creating meaning and empathy for the characters and the plot. Context also helps push the story forward and is an integral part of the story itself, and the telling of that story.

The Role of Setting and Context in Product Design

Before social media, we didn't have to worry or think as much about the environment in which our website would be used. We knew that users would be sitting in front of a computer, most likely a stationary one, and that they'd use a mouse to interact with what they saw on the screen. Fast-forward to today, and we can't be sure of anything except that how, where, and when our users will use our product or service will vary. There is no one size fits all, and no two journeys are the same.

With this in mind, coupled with often tight schedules and budgets, it's easy to think that the need to really work through the bigger picture and the detail is less important. The journey will vary so much from user to user, so what's the point? However, it's more important than ever to make sure that we have an understanding of the full end-to-end experience as well as the small contextual details that make a difference along the way. Here the setting and context of the experience play a big part.

In Chapter 5, we talked about acts, sequences, scenes, and shots as a metaphor for thinking through the bigger picture and the smaller details in product design and defined them as follows:

Acts
> The beginning, middle, and end of an experience

Sequences
> Life-cycle stages *or* key user journeys, depending on what you work with

Scenes
> Steps *or* main steps in a journey *or* pages/views

Shots
> Elements of a page/view *or* detailed steps of a journey

When we talk of *setting* we'll be using the preceding list as a reference and defining setting as the environment and context in which the product experience takes place.

This is slightly broader than the definition of *setting* in traditional storytelling, as that's primarily focused on time and geographic location. What makes for a nice parallel, however, is that setting is at times referred to as *story world*, and that is very much one of the aspects we increasingly need to include as part of the product experiences that we design.

A Look at Context in Product Design

As Samson so eloquently put it, context is about the relationship between the reader and the writer. In Chapter 1, we talked about purposeful stories; that is, stories created with a specific purpose in mind. In product design, all parts of the experience should be purposeful, from the overarching aim of the experience to the smaller aspects related to individual user journeys.

Between September 2017 and February 2018, Google looked at the clickstream data from thousands of users as part of an opt-in panel related to the marketing funnel. What Google found was that no two user journeys were the same. In fact, even when the user journeys took place within the same category, they took different shapes. Traditionally, we've been thinking that a user's search starts wide and then narrows down, and in some instances it does. But in other instances, it widens and narrows, widens and narrows, as shown in Figure 7-2. It all depends.

These types of patterns aren't just typical for purchase-related journeys. They illustrate how users in general behave both online and offline. Entry and exit points vary, as do the touch points, including how many, that the user comes in contact with along the way.

What we've experienced with the rise of mobile technologies, and still are experiencing, is similar to what happened after the introduction of the printing press in 1440. Before the rise of print, a storyteller had a fair bit of control over how their story was told, as the storyteller was typically the one who told the story. Since the invention of writing, but with the rise of print in particular, stories have been able to travel, not just through the storyteller, but through the medium in which they were experienced. Mass communication and the printing press meant that stories could be enjoyed and experienced by many more people, in a various places and contexts—not just the specific ones that the story-teller was in for that storytelling performance.

FIGURE 7-2
Think with Google user search journeys for a candy bar, where even the smaller details related to the search are verified (top), and a makeup journey, where the user is searching for the best brand (bottom) (*https://oreil. ly/G5OoO*)

Today social media plays a primary role in ensuring that stories, in whatever format, travel. But we also see people consuming more tra-ditional stories in what would previously be considered new environ-ments. It's not uncommon in many cities to see fellow commuters binging on the latest Netflix series on their way to and from work.

And just as we can jump straight into a later episode on Netflix and skip the beginning, the users of our products and services can land right smack in the middle of a user experience, rather than at page 1, otherwise known as the home page. Additionally, the way users end up on our product or service in the first place is often through search or social media. Rather than being taken to the home page, where the carefully crafted background for the user is presented, they'll click a link, and whatever accompanies that link is often what provides the contextual backstory for them.

It's been a good few years since users needed to be at home, at work, or in school to experience the web. At the time of writing, we're seeing an increasing shift in the way people search. As covered in Chapter 3, users are increasingly expecting results that work for them, at that location and point in time. They're expecting contextual search results and contextual products and services. To meet their needs in the best possible way, designing for context is crucial.

Exercise: A Look at Context in Product Design

With the Think With Google examples in mind and by referring to either data that you have or by making an assumption, identify two different journeys that the users of your product take when approaching a similar task (e.g., finding a product).

A Definition of Contextual Products and Context-Aware Computing

Ami Ben David, co-founder and CEO of Owner, defines context for product design as "A contextual product understands the full story around a human experience, in order to bring users exactly what they want, with minimal interaction."[3]

In *The Grand Budapest Hotel*, the new lobby boy is asked to "anticipate the client's needs before the needs are needed"—and Ben David says that this is exactly what we mean when we talk about context with

---

3 Ami Ben David, "Context Design: How to Anticipate Users' Needs Before They're Needed," *The Next Web*, April 28, 2014, *https://oreil.ly/_jZOi*.

regard to our users. There is no need to wait for them to ask a question. Instead, we should just deliver what they want, before they know they want it. Ben David goes on to suggest that when we typically think about user interface design, we think about user-initiated interactions: a user makes a request, and the system or service responds. With contextual products, he argues, the user never has to tell the system. The system just knows. That's the kind of experiences we have the ability to create when we focus on context in multidevice design.

THE HISTORY OF CONTEXT-AWARE COMPUTING

In the early days of mobile computing, back in the '80s and '90s, the focus was on making mobility transparent for the user and automatically making the same service available everywhere. In this case, *transparent* meant that users wouldn't need to worry or care about the changes in their environment, but could rely on accessing the same functionality, regardless of their location.

Research into ubiquitous computing that took place at Xerox PARC in the early '90s caused a shift in thinking, and researchers started to discover the potential of exploiting the context of use for how systems could be adapted. In 1994 Bill Schilit, who introduced context-aware computing, described it as follows:

> The basic idea is that mobile devices can provide different services in different contexts – where context is strongly related to the location of a device.[4]

CONTEXT-AWARE COMPUTING TODAY

To this day, we still often think of location when we think about context, but it's increasingly about much more as well. The more technology is embedded into our surroundings and everyday lives, moving beyond the screen and into objects in our home as well as encompassing more and more services talking to each other, the more complex context becomes. The things we interact with and the ways we do so expand into new areas. In addition, the products and services as well

---

4 Albrecht Schmidt, "Context-Aware Computing," The Encyclopedia of Human-Computer Interaction, 2nd Edition, *https://oreil.ly/Y2raZ*.

as devices that we use will increasingly have access to rich contextual information about us—from where we are, and indeed, our physical location, to social, health, and other data via sensors.

There's a tremendous opportunity, not the least to do good, that can come from incorporating this kind of data into the products and services we design. Through the intelligent and ethical use of data, we'll be able to offer personalization at scale in the form of one-to-one experiences that are tailored to the individual. No more unnecessary noise, or stating the obvious. Just the right content at the right time, for specific users.

In many of the films we see that take place in the future, the protagonist lives in a world full of data. In *Minority Report,* the machines know everything about Tom Cruise, and as he walks down the streets, he is surrounded by billboards that target him with ads. Digital designer and leaderhsip coach Tutti Taygerly argues that in many movies, such as *Minority Report*, the interfaces that we see leave much to be desired as the burden of attention and the effort involved with controlling these interfaces is on the user. Taygerly compares *Minority Report* to the movie *Her,* where the interface between the protagonist and the operating system is so seamless and so natural that he in fact falls in love with it. Rather than overwhelm, the machine complements the human by being aware of everything, and based on this contextual awareness, it provides relevant suggestions.[5]

Larry Page of Google shows a video of a man in Kenya, Zack Matere, who says "information is powerful, but it's how we use it that will define us."[6] Besides making sure that we use the data responsibly and ethically, the power in using data and what we know about users doesn't just lie in showing them tailored recommendations of content, including products we know they're more inclined to like and buy. It also lies in how we can tailor interfaces over time through progressive content and progressive reduction. Through clever use of technology, we're able to deliver a bit of everyday magic. But for that to happen, the system behind the experience needs to know what matters, and

---

5 Tutti Taygerly, "Designing Big Data for Humans," *UX Magazine,* June 24, 2014, *https:// oreil.ly/m2MtW.*

6 Larry Page, "Where's Google Going Next?" TED2014 Video, March 2014, *https://oreil.ly/ aRfqG.*

when. Only then can we deliver the kind of experiences that anticipate users' needs before they are there, just like the lobby boy in *The Grand Budapest Hotel*.

Working Through the Context

Context impacts everything across every stage of the product or service life cycle, and its effect is not limited to digital products. In "Emotion and Design: Attractive Things Work Better," Don Norman talks about his three teapots and when he tends to use which one. First thing in the morning, efficiency trumps everything else, which results in him using his Japanese hot pot and a little metal brewing ball. At other more leisurely times, or when with guests or family, he uses one of the other ones and says, "Design matters, but which design is preferable depends upon the occasion, the context, and above all, upon my mood."[7]

Context is essentially about considering the humans that are about to use or already are using our product or service and taking into account what matters to them, how we can remove obstacles, barriers, and worries so that we help them best meet their needs and goals. Just as humans are complex, so too is understanding context, but that is good. As Page Laubheimer, a UX specialist with Nielsen Norman Group, writes:

> When we're doing our day-to-day design work, we rarely consider our users' real context. We often assume that people who use our product will be focused on it, with no distractions. But that's simply not how people interact with digital products.[8]

Context often plays a critical role in delivering value, but also in helping users avoid situations or alert them to something that seems out of the ordinary. No matter what the scenario, as the Foursquare example in the beginning of this chapter illustrated, we have multiple considerations to make when we anticipate a user's needs and deliver or carry out what we believe the user wants. A good use case for thinking

---

7 From: Norman, D. A. (2002). Emotion and design: Attractive things work better. *Interactions Magazine, ix* (4), 36-42.

8 Page Laubheimer, "Distracted Driving: UX's Responsibility to Do No Harm," *Nielsen Norman Group*, June 24, 2018, *https://oreil.ly/rJ_TW*.

through contextual experiences and products is that of designing a TV-viewing experience across devices. With Netflix being a household name, most of us can relate to some of the considerations we have to make in terms of content recommendations. For instance, there's often a big difference in what we watch if we watch alone, with a special someone, or with kids.

A few years ago during one of my freelance contracts, I was fortunate enough to work on such a project. One of our tasks was to look at how to best personalize the viewing experience across both live and on-demand content for different viewers. As part of this work, we looked into several aspects that might influence what we showed them. The most obvious ones were as follows:

- Who's watching?
- What are their viewing preferences?

But in order for us to provide suitable recommendations, we needed to know a bit more:

- Are they watching alone or with someone?
- If they are watching with someone, who are they watching with (e.g., partner, friends, the kids)?

As you start to ask these questions, other questions pop to the surface:

- What day of the week is it (e.g., weekday versus weekend)?
- What time of the day is it (e.g., morning versus evening)?
- Where are they watching?
- What are they watching on?

All of these factors influence what a user might want to watch. But the process doesn't end there. To truly deliver great recommendations and consider the full context, we need to know even more:

- What did they watch before (e.g., episode in a series or a film)?
- What do we know about their behavior (e.g., what did they start but didn't finish watching, and why)?

All of this impacts the continuous experience and how to make it easy for the user to pick up from where they left off. However, it doesn't tell us everything. We also need to know the following:

- What did they think about what they watched before?

- What might they want to watch next?

- How is this influenced by day of the week and time of day and who they are watching with?

- What was the reason for their action, or lack thereof (e.g., why did they stop watching a show or film)?

These were just some of the things that came up during the discovery phase of that project. The list of questions could go on, and rightfully so. Getting these types of experiences right requires digging into the details and embracing the contextual complexity of the products and services that we design.

Exercise: Working Through the Context

With your own product or service in mind identify 10 questions that help define the aspects that influence the context of use for your product or service.

Embracing the Complexity of Context

As the preceding sections illustrate, there are so many different combinations. To design an experience that is simple, intuitive, and feels as if it knows what the user wants—which is just the kind of experience a user wants when watching video and on-demand content—you need to embrace the complexity and dive straight in. You need to work through what matters step-by-step, what doesn't, and how it's all interlinked. The process is complex, but after you've worked on figuring out all the different pieces of the product experience, connecting all those detailed parts can be simple. But understanding the context and what will constitute a great experience in different scenarios requires work, including research and talking to people.

An example that I would not have considered until I myself had a child is that what to recommend next for kids versus for adults is very different. Our daughter, who at the time of this writing is under two years old, wants to watch two shows on Netflix—*Peppa Pig* and *Little Baby Bum*. However, even on Netflix's Children profile, the system works in the same way, meaning that if you finishing watching a show like *Peppa Pig*, it will disappear from your "Continuously watched" row (Figure 7-3).

For an adult, this is right. You seldom want to watch the same show or film straight after you've just finished watching it. For a soon-to-be two-year-old, it's the exact opposite. The implications of the show automatically disappearing is that when we're with an impatient toddler who says "Piggu," as she calls Peppa Pig, on repeat, rather than Piggu being one or a few clicks away, we have to go into search and find it, which takes substantially longer. Netflix will, without a doubt, have multiple reasons for working this way (metrics, ease of build, etc.), but it's not ideal from our, the users', point of view.

FIGURE 7-3
The desktop UI of our Netflix's Children profile showing the Continue Watching for Children row as the second row

Be it VOD, recommendations through bots, or just general content recommendations, making the right recommendations requires much more than just data. We need to truly understand the context, the relationship, and any value or nonvalue that an interaction has. It's far too easy to generalize and make assumption-based decisions about what a user does or doesn't do, but actions don't necessarily say anything about what users actually value.

In 2016, for example, Facebook changed its newsfeed to show more articles that users actually want to spend time viewing. But getting an understanding of what people want to see wasn't as easy as it first appeared. Facebook noted:

The actions people take on Facebook—liking, clicking, commenting or sharing a post—don't always tell us the whole story of what is most meaningful to them. For example, we've found that there are stories people don't like or comment on that they still want to see, such as articles about a serious current event, or sad news from a friend.[9]

When it comes to analyzing user behavior and providing personalized and tailored experiences, we need to get under the hood in order to understand what drives the user's action and put it into context.

The Factors and Elements That Make Up Context in Product Design

In traditional storytelling, the context of the story has to do with what story is being told, by whom or what, and how. For product design, context runs along the same lines. It's about who you're telling what part of the product story, in what way, when, and where. Depending on the type of product or service, what matters in terms of context will vary.

If you search online, at least at the time of this writing, there is no universal definition of *context* in design. Ben David defined the building blocks of context as follows:

User context
    How people are different

Environmental context
    Any physical aspect that influences the application

World context
    What is happening elsewhere that may be related to the user

A whole book can (and has been) written on the subject of context—see *Understanding Context* by Andrew Hinton (O'Reilly, 2014)—so for the purpose of this book, the preceding categorization and a reference to the *Understanding Context* book will suffice. The key takeaway is that when it comes to product design, context is all about relevance, timing, appropriateness, and value to the person on the receiving end. It

---

9 Moshe Blank and Jie Xu, "More Articles You Want to Spend Time Viewing," Facebook, April 21, 2016, *https://oreil.ly/mDwSW*.

requires a deep understanding of who they are and where they are in their journey and own personal story, and how best our product or service can help them.

What Storytelling Teaches Us About Setting and Context

Aristotle, as mentioned in Chapter 2, was the first to point out that the way we tell stories has a profound influence on the human experience of the same. Restrictions of a medium can force a one-size-fits-all approach to the way the story is told. For example, in a book, every word, picture, and paragraph is the same, regardless of who the reader is. Similarly, in film and on TV, the viewer is presented with the same images, sounds, etc., on the screen as all the other viewers. How the readers of the book or the people watching the film or TV program experience it, though, differs.

From what we pay attention to and remember, to what resonates with us, no two people will experience a story in the same way. This all comes down to context—context of who the person is, their likes and dislikes, their backstory, where they're experiencing it and with whom, etc. The power of a great storyteller lies in the ability to identify and bring these factors to light so that they can be considered in the way that the story is told. This is what the great storytellers back in the Middle Ages were masters at and why being a professional storyteller was so well regarded.

Context in relation to how we tell stories, however, has to do with both the medium and the techniques we use to tell that story, what we include in the actual story (e.g., in terms of backstories, details, etc.) and how we actually tell it, and, of course, the practicalities related to budget, team, equipment, and so on.

When we look at how we tell stories in our day-to-day life—how our day was, what we dreamt about at night, or what we're thinking about—the approach always differs based on who the story is told to. If we're talking to close friends, we may share some additional details that we'd leave out if we told the same story to our parents. We often assume a warmer, softer voice when we tell or read a story to a child. And, we'll jump over or speed up certain bits if part of the group we're telling a story to has heard it before. Without thinking about it, we're assessing the situation and the context in which our story is about to be told, and based on our often subconscious assessment, we adapt how we're telling it so that it's appropriate for the audience and the situation.

How we tell a story is closely related to what we're trying to get across with the story and, as Samson suggests, the relationship we want to create with our audience. As we covered in the previous chapter, sometimes a story will be plot driven, and the desire to include particular special effects helps shape it and starts to build up the environment or setting in which the story takes place, as was the case with *Rogue One*. Other times a particular character drives the plot, and in those instances the context around the character helps inform the story itself and how it's told, as was the case with *Finding Nemo* that we referenced in Chapter 5.

Next we'll look at three areas where product design can draw from traditional storytelling.

DEFINING YOUR SETTING AND CONTEXT

Just as it's crucial to be able to create a shared mental image in everyone's head of the people we design for, making sure that everyone is on the same page about the setting and context of the product experience is imperative. Often silos between teams and different parts of the organization are due to the individuals not having a shared understanding, or a common language that bridges the gaps and makes the respective parties see the value or importance of what the other party is talking about. Here, using some of the tools from traditional storytelling such as questions to ask, and developing a setting and context chart can be extremely useful, particularly if visualized in the form of a customer experience map.

CREATING A WORLD

The power of the word and our imagination lies in the images and the worlds that these create in our heads. My dad often talks about how the books he read to us when we were kids didn't have that many pictures and, as a result, they sparked our imagination and made us create our own images in our heads of the worlds and characters that he was reading about.

In Chapter 2, I said one of the really distinctive aspects of video games is that the user is immediately immersed into the world of the game. When Pixar story artists talk of a world, what they really mean is the environment or the set of rules in which the story takes place.[10]

How to go about it

When we talk about product design, worlds can be viewed in different lights. There is the broader world, as in context and setting, in which the product experience resides, but there's also the world that has to do with branding and other guidelines, such as platform guidelines. These are more in line with the way both game designers and Pixar designers talk of "the set of rules" that govern the world in which the story takes place.

One of the story artists in the Pixar in a Box series says the character should always come first. if you have a blind person forgetting their pants and going to work, she says, that person will have a completely different story than a seeing person forgetting their pants and going to work. The objects and the setting will be the same, but the two characters will have completely different stories. Her colleague, who's a director, prefers to come at it from the world first and then find the character to go into that world. This is similar to what we experience in product design. We all have different preferences of how to work and the key isn't so much in which order it happens, but that it does happen. There should always be a bit of back and forth, as one will inform the other. In the Pixar in a Box series references, the story is born when the world and the character meet.

DESIGNING THE SET

Though *set* and *setting* are different, there is a close connection between them, particularly when we look at them in relation to product design. The *setting*, as we've covered, is all about the time and the place in which a story takes place. *Set*, on the other hand, is the scenery that is created to help support and tell the story. In some films, like *Star Wars* and the original *Blade Runner*, the set itself has become iconic.

For theater as well as film and television, the creation of the set is referred to as *scenic design, scenography, stage design, set design,* or *production design.*

---

10 "Your Unique Perspective," *Khan Academy, https://oreil.ly/gimne.*

How to go about it

The importance of thinking of the setting for product design, and taking it one step further to think of the actual set that has to be designed for each part of the product experience story, has to do with identifying, based on the plot, characters, and the context, what should be present at different parts of the product experience to make sure it all comes together to meet both user and business needs. It's about identifying both what should be there (and not there) and how to design it, even if it's something offline and nondigital. And it applies to both the bigger picture as well as the small details. As *Evening Standard* reported, "A set is more than a backdrop. It can become a storyteller itself, with plot-twisting reveals or intricate attention to detail."[11] With this in mind, it's important to start planning out the set early on in the product experience discovery and definition phase as, just as in a good story, everything is connected.

Summary

In all good stories, there are key moments when everything just comes together. One of the best things we can do for the people we're designing for is to fully understand the context. It touches on and influences everything we've covered so far. To some extent, combining two words from film, TV, and theater—*set* and *stage*—provides a more active and accurate description of the JTBD and the role it plays for planning out and defining the types of product experiences we're working with.

To fully understand the bigger picture as well as the small details of the experiences we work with, we need to identify all the elements of the set that influence the product or service experience. Then we need to stage that experience in light of what we know about the users, other characters, and actors, and the different contexts in which the experience takes place, so that it all comes together and we deliver against it.

No matter how simple the experience might be (and even if we're just designing a landing page), being more explicit and including set design and staging as part of our work helps ensure that we have a good foundation when we start defining our content strategy and information architecture and the steps that come after that.

---

11 Zoe Paskett, "London Theater," *Evening Standard*, February 15, 2019, *https://oreil.ly/ho5U-*.

Increasingly, as offline and online blend and influence each other, we need to ensure that we understand the world in which the people live who will come across and use our products or services.

Setting and context form a big part of the experience narrative. They influence not only how our users will experience our product or service, but also what and how we should tell our story to make sure it comes together. It's by thinking through the context in which people will use our product and services that scenarios are born. Then we're able to really start visualizing and adding detail to the narrative that surrounds the use of our product and service; our imagination is sparked. And, if we really listen, the story will start to tell itself. Next, we'll look at how to use storyboarding to help visualize and aid this process.

[8]

Storyboarding for Product Design

One Document to Capture It All

OVER THE LAST FEW years as I've been coaching and mentoring teams on UX-related matters, one of the UX tools that I've been the strongest advocate of is experience maps. *Experience maps,* also called *customer experience maps,* visualize and capture the full end-to-end experience that a user goes through in order to complete a goal.

The benefit of an experience map is that the process of working through one, and the finished result, help you understand the full end-to-end experience and force you to think beyond the page or view that you're working on. Experience maps are also about more than what happens on the screen. They cover the offline aspects and, if done well, show how everything is intricately linked and how a change on one end will impact something somewhere else. The more the products are services we design need to work on any device used anywhere and at any time, the more we need to be able to dip into a specific point in a user's journey and understand what matters then and there. This is another thing that experience maps are really great for.

One of the most, if not *the* most, famous experience map is the Rail Europe Experience Map, which was developed as one part of an overall diagnostic evaluation for Rail Europe, Inc (Figure 8-1). The company wanted to get a better understanding of its customer's journeys across all touch points in order to define where to focus design and development resources, as well as its budget. What the Rail Europe Experience Map helped to do was, in the words of author and designer Chris Risdon, "create a shared empathic understanding of the customers' interactions with the Rail Europe touch points over time and space."

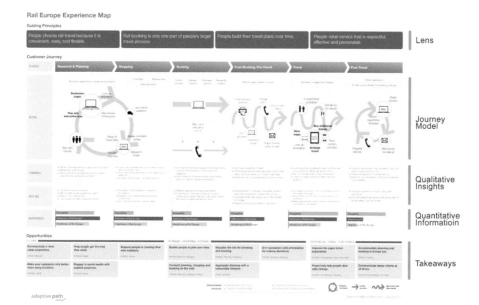

FIGURE 8-1

The Rail Europe Experience Map, courtesy of Chris Risdon and Adaptive Path

The Rail Europe Experience Map holds a great level of detail for that project. To the unfamiliar eye, it's the kind of document that some would consider complex. They are right. Experience maps *are* complex, but that's because we as human beings are complex. There is no one journey or one experience of the products and services we define that will be the same as that of someone else. There will be the ideal path, and more common and likely journeys, but the story of how our products and services are used, how they come into people's lives, and the role they play will change with every single user.

The initial reaction of many of the people I've introduced experience maps to is that it's too complex and that the level of detail they hold isn't needed for the project in question. There is no denying that experience maps, at times, can look quite complex and scare people, but the complexity that goes into creating an experience map is its beauty. When you work and talk through them, most people and teams find them incredibly valuable. They can often be one of the first steps in breaking down organizational silos.

Additionally, just as the product experiences we design are never really finished, experience maps are never really done. Rather than an end point and a conclusion, experience maps should be seen as a catalyst, says Risdon, something that is actionable and will get people talking.

One of the great benefits, and opportunities if used correctly, is that experience maps are brilliant as a *do-once-and-keep-on-using* kind of document. They are living and breathing documents that the team and project can derive great value from by constantly evaluating and improving, not to mention use as a reference point throughout the project as various aspects are being worked through. To make this process easier, print out the map in large format and put it up on a wall if you have access to one, where it's easy for the team to see and get to it.

Done right, experience maps provide a snapshot of what you're dealing with. Name one person who wouldn't rather have one thing to look at and go "Ah!" than 10+ pages requiring them to mentally put everything together at the end. And as for how to make them look less complex, this is a matter of visual presentation and how you talk through it. Most experience maps have a visual element that captures either touch points, as shown in Figure 8-1, or the emotional flow that the user will go through. Another opportunity is to include a storyboard as the visual element.

The Role of Storyboarding for Film and TV

Storyboards are linear sequences of illustrations used to visualize a story. They were made popular in the form they are known today by Walt Disney Studios in the 1930s. Since the 1920s, Disney Studios used sketches of frames to help create the world of the films before they actually began building it. Disney was also the first to have a specialist story department that was separate from the animators. This department was introduced as Disney had realized that audiences wouldn't care about the film unless the story itself gave them reason to care about the characters.

Storyboards are commonly used in films, theater, and animatics. In theater, storyboards are used as a tool to help understand the layout of the scene. In films, they are also known as *shooting boards* and often include arrows to indicate movement as well as instructions. Storyboards play an important part in helping the director, cinematographer, and advertising clients visualize the scenes. For the live-action filmmaker, they also help in identifying which parts of the set needs to be created versus which parts will never come into the shot. Using storyboards for films also helps identify any potential problems before shooting begins, as well as estimate costs. In this sense, storyboards can be seen as the low-fidelity prototype of a film.

In animations and special effects, storyboards are often followed by animatics (Figure 8-2). *Animatics* are simplified mock-ups that are created to develop a better idea of how a scene will look and feel when motion and timing have been added. In its simplest form, an animatic is made up of a series of stills, usually taken from the storyboard, and new animatics may be added until the storyboard is complete. Just as in films, the storyboards and animatics help ensure that time and resources are used well instead of being spent on scenes that may end up being cut from the film later. In computer animations, the storyboards also help identify which parts of the scene components and models need to be created.

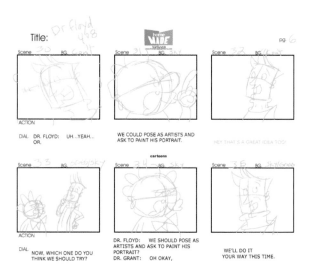

FIGURE 8-2

Storyboard for *The Radio Adventures of Dr. Floyd* (*https://oreil.ly/HrYMH*)

To what level of detail the storyboards are followed during production varies. Some directors use a storyboard as a reference point together with the script, from which a detailed shot list is created. A *shot list* is a document similar to the one in Figure 8-3 that maps out all the shots, together with who and what will be included.[1] Such a document is particularly useful when a film is shot in multiple locations, as it helps directors to organize their thought before filming begins. For this reason, creating the shot list usually done in conjunction with the script and other activities in the preproduction process.

Script /SB Ref.	Shot #	Interior Exterior	Shot	Camera Angle	Camera Move	Audio	Subject	Description of Shot
1	1	Exterior	WS	Eye Level	Static	VO	Paul and son	Paul and his young son are at the la fishing
6	2	Exterior	WS	Eye Level	Static	VO	Paul	Paul at the lake, fishing alone. He pl out a photo of him and his son; he smiles.
9	3	Exterior	WS	Eye Level	Static	VO	Paul, son, grandson	Paul, his son, and grandson at the la fishing
2	4	Exterior	VWS	High Angle	Static	VO	Paul and son	Paul and son playing baseball in a backyard
3	5	Interior	MCU	Eye Level	Static	VO	Paul and son	Paul teaching his son how to drive
4	6	Interior	WS	Eye Level	Pan	VO	Paul, wife, and son	Paul and his wife at their son's high school graduation
5	7	Exterior	WS	Eye Level, Birds-Eye view	Static	VO	Paul, his wife, and son	Paul's son packs up a car, clearly leaving for college. He hugs Paul an his wife, and they both watch him a he drives away.
7	8	Interior	MS	Eye Level	Pan	VO	Paul at his son's wedding	Paul hugs his son before he walks o to the alter; they smile
8	9	Interior	MS	OTS	Static	VO	Paul's son and his	Paul's son is at the hospital with his

FIGURE 8-3
Screenshot of a shot list template from the TechSmith Blog

Exactly how storyboards are used in preproduction and production varies. Pixar, for example, doesn't begin a new movie with a script but instead starts with a storyboard.[2] Others follow a script–storyboard–shot list path, and what's in the storyboards may change after they are done. On the other end of the spectrum, productions treat the storyboards as a bible. The film *The Matrix* is an example of this. To convince the suits at Warner Bros Entertainment to buy the script, the Wachowski sisters hired two underground comic book artists named Geof Darrow and Steve Skroce to draw up a shot-by-shot storyboard of the script, something that ended up being six hundred pages. During the filming they didn't allow the director to deviate from the storyboards, except during the editing process.[3]

---

1 Justin Simon, "How to Write a Shot List," *TechSmith*. https://oreil.ly/Y44kH.

2 Ben Crothers, "Storyboarding & UX: Part I," Johnny Holland (blog), October 14, 2011, https://oreil.ly/UvmuA.

3 Mark Miller, "Matrix Revelation," *Wired*, November 1, 2003, https://oreil.ly/7If-y.

Whether the storyboards are used as a way to help define the narrative, or are seen as an end product, there are a lot of overlaps and benefits of storyboarding for product design.

The Role of Storyboarding in Product Design

During my career as a UX designer, I've worked with a lot of digital and full-services marketing agencies. In those companies, storyboarding has often been carried out by the creatives in concepting as part of the process of coming up with and selling ideas to the rest of the team and the client. Very seldom have I seen it being used by any UX or product team. However, I've come across many other companies that use storyboards as part of the UX and product design process, including Airbnb and *The Atlantic*. This is great as the benefits of using storyboards for product design is very similar to the benefit of using storyboards in theater, film, and animatics.

Just as in theater, film, and animatics, through storyboarding you start to explore the world in which the experience will take place, and you start to explore the structure. By storyboarding parts or the whole experience narrative, you both explore and define the experience the user has with the product, and the aspects that matter around it. By adding emotions and making it come to life through the drawings, you both visualize and help create empathy, understanding, and buy-in within the team as well as stakeholders and clients. And just as with film and animatics, storyboards as part of the product design process are a great tool for spotting gaps or new opportunities, as well as to help determine costs and identify what you'll need.

Here are some of the other reasons that make storyboards so great:[4]

- Help you understand the problem space you're working with

- Bring a solution to life

- Are an effective communication tool that almost anyone understands and can engage with

- Combine multiple elements, such as personas, behaviors, requirements, and solutions

---

4 Crothers, "Storyboarding & UX."

- Make conceptual ideas tangible, which helps us, clients, and stakeholders to connect the dots

Just as storyboards are used in various ways in theater, film, and animatics, they can be used in various ways in product design as well. We'll cover some of those ways a bit further ahead in this chapter. No matter how they are used, however, just as experience maps are great as a team activity, or for involving different parts of the business and/or the client, storyboards are equally great as something that not just one or two people work on but that instead include various people. By collaborating on storyboards, you help create buy-in, understanding, and empathy. Because each storyboard can be related to a specific persona, it helps to continuously ensure that the people the product is for are actually considered.

Exercise: The Role of Storyboarding in Product Design

With your own product or service in mind, think about the following:

- What role could storyboards play for your product or service, or what role have they played?

- What would be some initial skepticism by others on the project, if you suggested it?

Using Storyboards to Help Identify the Invisible Problem and/or Solution

When you start to storyboard an experience related to a product, the simple act of having to draw it requires you to include a lot of things in order to make the narrative come to life. Having to think about the experience in this narrative way is what led Airbnb to its big insight: that its service isn't a website, as most of the Airbnb experience in fact happens offline.[5]

Far too often we jump straight in, thinking that we have a solid understanding of the people we design for and the content, features, and overall solution that will best meet their needs. And hopefully we

---

[5] Sarah Kessler, "How Snow White Helped Airbnb's Mobile Mission," *Fast Company*, November 8, 2012, *https://oreil.ly/DmuSp*.

do. However, as offline and the *dance*, as the Airbnb team refers to it, between offline and online experiences increases for a large number of products and services, there is also an increased need to take a step back and create an actual picture of the overall experience that different parts of the team, the business, and the client can engage with. It's no longer enough to just have the UX or product team working on experience maps or storyboards. To create really great products that best incorporate both user and customer insight, as well as business requirements, we need the different parts of the business to come together and for everyone to share their knowledge and expertise.

Tony Fadell, one of the originators of the iPod, says that "as human beings we get used to things really fast" and that as a product designer it's his job to see those everyday things and improve on them.[6] The reason we have to get used to everyday things is that, as human beings, we have limited brain power. To deal with this, our brains encode things we do on an everyday basis into habits, using a process called *habituation*. This process allows us to free up space to learn new things, and what's originally hard becomes easier and easier until it's eventually second nature and we're able to relax more by thinking less about what we're doing.

Fadell says driving a car provides a good example of habituation. When you first start driving a car, you pay close attention to the ten-to-two position of your hands, turn off music or the radio, and limit talking and anything else that might distract you from what you're doing. Over time we become more used to driving. Our ten-to-two grip loosens up, we start to listen to music or the radio at the same time, and even talk to the passengers in the car. In these instances, habituation is good. Without it, we'd notice every single little detail, all the time.

Habituation is not a good thing when we stop noticing the problems that are around us. Our job, Fadell says, is to go one step further and not just *notice* the problems, but *fix* them. To do that, Fadell tries to see the world the way it really is rather than the way we think it is. Solving problems that almost everyone sees is easy, but "it's hard to solve a problem that almost no one sees."

---

6 Tony Fadell, "The First Secret of Design Is…Noticing," TED2015 Video, March 2015, *https://oreil.ly/CK4eg*.

An example of solving a problem that almost no one sees is the "charge before use" label that used to come with the electrical products we bought. Apple and Steve Jobs noticed it and said that they weren't going to do that. Instead, the battery of Apple's products came partially charged. Today, that's the norm for most products. The importance in this story, Fadell says, is that it sees not only the obvious problem but the invisible one.

Fadell's advice for noticing all the invisible problems is to first look broader and examine the steps that lead up to the problem and all the steps that come after. Second, look closer at the tiny details and ask whether they are important, or are simply there because that's the way we've always done it. Last, think younger—be more like kids and ask the optimistic, problem-solving questions like the one Fadell's daughter asked: why doesn't the mailbox just tell us when there's mail rather than us having to walk out each day to check it?

Storyboarding is a great tool for helping spot these invisible problems, or solutions. Through the act of creating and bringing the narrative of specific personas to life, we start to see the experience through the user's eyes. The act of drawing itself is also usually a fun activity that lowers people's guards and allows you to have a bit of "what if..." with it. In the world of stories, anything is possible, and adding that dimension to the product design process helps us see things in a different light from what we're used to.

Exercise: Using Storyboards to Help Identify the Invisible Problem and/or Solution

With your own product or service in mind, think about the following:

- What are some details in your product's experience that are simply there because that's how it's always been done?

After reading the next section, return to this exercise and do a storyboard for part of your product's experience:

- What, if any, invisible problem or opportunity did the storyboard you created make you identify?
- What solution, if any, did you include to help solve it?
- Could this solution be relevant as a future iteration of your product?

Creating Storyboards

Some people will be put off by the idea of storyboarding simply because they don't think that they can draw. However, there are a number of ways to draw, and if you don't feel comfortable drawing, perhaps someone else who'll be part of the storyboarding process does. There are other ways to contribute to the storyboarding process besides drawing, from helping define the purpose of the storyboard (e.g., whether it's carried out to help think through an experience or a communication tool), to identifying all the elements and details that should go into it.

In 2011, UX writer Ben Crothers did a three-part series around storyboarding and UX for the Johnny Holland blog. The second part, which focused on how to create your own storyboard, shared some useful advice: while storyboarding can be used for ideation, just as it is in concepting and at times for Pixar, you'll get the most out of your storyboards and storyboarding process if you first have a clear point of view. If you're going to use storyboards for ideation or as a thinking exercise, you will get the most out of the exercise if you're clear on who the storyboard is about and what goal that character, or user, has.

Crothers continues to advise that if you're going to use storyboards as a communication tool, it helps to be clear on what you're communicating. More precisely, if you're using your storyboard, do the following:[7]

- Solve an existing user experience problem

- Identify the impact of an existing situation or issue on the user experience

- Define a desired user experience for a particular solution

These three scenarios apply, in my opinion, if you're using your storyboards as an ideation or thinking tool too.

Once you have a clear point of view, the next step is to identify the story structure. You may choose to do a high-level end-to-end storyboard for the full experience, similar to the shopping experience we covered in Chapter 5, or you may choose to do it for a specific journey, or sequence, as we referred to it earlier. If you've carried out some of the exercises in

---

7 Ben Crothers, "Storyboarding & UX: Part II," Johnny Holland (blog), October 17, 2011, https://oreil.ly/oqF4G.

Chapters 5 or 6 related to narrative structure and character, you'll have plenty of your narrative already defined and it's just a matter of bringing it to life.

In terms of what to include, Crothers recommends that you include the following, which is inspired by Aristotle's seven golden rules of storytelling:

Character

> The user or customer personas that the plot is about

Script

> Aristotle refers to this as *diction*, is the inner dialogue that the character is having, what they say, and what others around them say

Scene

> The scenario that the character finds themselves in

Plot

> The narrative that unfolds in relation to your character's goal

In addition, you can add the environment or setting of the scenario and the solution.

Exercise: Creating Storyboards

With your own product or service in mind, think about what role your storyboards would play:

- Would storyboards be most beneficial as a thinking or communication tool, or both, for your product?

- Why one over the other, or both?

- What would you use the storyboards for? For example, to solve an existing user experience problem, identify the impact of an existing situation or issue on the user experience, or define a desired user experience for a particular solution.

Ways to Incorporate Storyboards into the Product Design Process

As we covered earlier, the role of storyboards and to what level of detail they are followed varies in traditional storytelling, all depending on what is being created and who is working on it. As with all deliverables and tools, when it comes to the UX and the product design process, it's about choosing the one that is best for the job, including the team, and about using it for what the deliverable and tool itself is great for. While storyboarding can be a great activity to include, for example, developers in, that doesn't mean that storyboards should substitute other deliverables like flow charts that developers are used to working with.

Every deliverable and tool has its own part to play, at a specific time, during the product design process. Next we'll look at three ways that storyboards can be included in the product design process.

STORYBOARDS AS THEIR OWN DELIVERABLE

For comics, storyboards are seen as the end product rather than the means to an end. But even if storyboards will never be the end product in product design, they can be the end product in the sense of them being their own deliverable (Figure 8-4). It all depends on what you include and why.

As we covered earlier in this chapter, you'll get the most out of the storyboarding process if you're clear on the purpose of the storyboard and its point of view. Using storyboards as their own deliverable works well both when they are used as a thinking tool and a communication tool. The key is to identify what the storyboard should capture, with regard to the overall narrative and any additional details and notes that you may want to add in order for the storyboard to be as valuable as possible to the project, and the people who will refer to it.

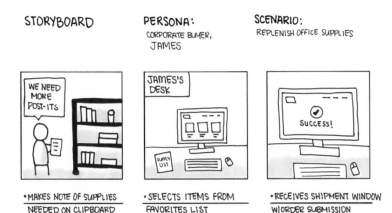

STORYBOARD

PERSONA:
CORPORATE BUYER,
JAMES

SCENARIO:
REPLENISH OFFICE SUPPLIES

WE NEED MORE POST-ITS

JAMES'S DESK

SUCCESS!

- MAKES NOTE OF SUPPLIES NEEDED ON CLIPBOARD
- PHYSICAL INVENTORY

- SELECTS ITEMS FROM FAVORITES LIST
- USES DESKTOP & SUPPLY LIST AS TOOL

- RECEIVES SHIPMENT WINDOW W/ORDER SUBMISSION
- SETS PLAN FOR RESTOCK

FIGURE 8-4

A low-fidelity storyboard created as its own deliverable by Rachel Krause, "Storyboards Help Visualize UX Ideas" NN/g, *https://oreil.ly/7ttZg*

STORYBOARDS AS PART OF CUSTOMER JOURNEY MAPS

Earlier in this book, we covered customer journey maps as a common tool for capturing the user's emotional response to part of an experience. As with most (UX) deliverables, you get the best outcome and value when you customize and adapt that deliverable to your need. The internet is filled with various takes of what they can include and how they can be visualized. One take on a customer journey map is to further add to it by including a storyboard that helps bring the narrative of the experience to life (Figure 8-5).

This can be done in numerous ways, depending on what information you need to add to best further the project. As the example in Figure 8-5 shows, you can use just a few visual elements if that is all you need to get the key point across.

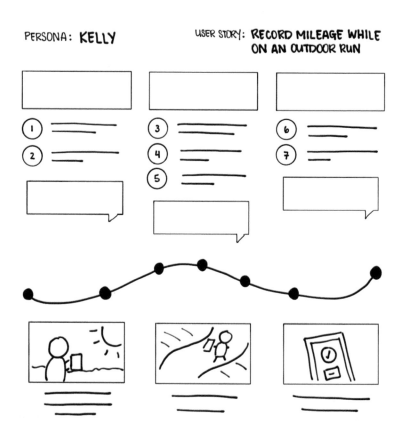

FIGURE 8-5

A storyboard (bottom) is included as an additional visual element in the customer journey map (top) by Rachel Krause, "Storyboards Help Visualize UX Ideas" NN/g, *https://oreil.ly/7ttZg*

STORYBOARDS AS PART OF EXPERIENCE MAPS

Just as storyboards can be included as an additional element to customer journey maps, storyboards can also be added to experience maps. The storyboard could be the main visual element (i.e., the user journey representation) or an additional one.

According to Adaptive Path, there are four overarching steps for mapping experiences:[8]

Uncover the truth
   Study customer behavior and interactions across channels and touch points.

Chart the course
   Collaboratively synthesize key insights into a customer journey model.

Tell the story
   Visualize a compelling story that creates understanding and empathy.

Use the map
   Follow the map to new ideas and better customer experiences.

With regard to the fourth point—use the map—one of the strengths of customer journey maps is that they can be adapted to best fit the needs your specific project. In *Mapping Experiences* (O'Reilly), James Kalbach provides an extensive account of the process involved with mapping experiences as well as examples of what they can include and look like. A simple search online will show many takes on what detail and what type of visual to include. The more captivating the visual, and the experience map as a whole, the more favorable other people tend to be toward getting involved.

Summary

In the words of Fadell, our challenge is to "wake up every day and experience the world better." By taking a step back, thinking and working through experiences end to end, we help create the best possible conditions for noticing and capturing the kinds of problems and opportunities that no one else sees and turning them into something great. This is about making sure that we don't stop at a certain point (e.g.,

---

8 Patrick Quattlebaum, "Download Our Guide to Experience Mapping," *Medium*, February 7, 2012, *https://oreil.ly/FLjPm*.

purchase), but consider the needs of the user as well as the business throughout the full product life cycle, and even before it officially begins by looking at the user's backstory.

What we might even set a new standard, just like Apple's charged products did. While leaving a lasting legacy that influences how other companies do things would be nice, it shouldn't be our goal. Often it's the little things that make a big difference. Just as Walt Disney acknowledged that small details are what make a story come together, paying attention to minor elements of product experiences is how we're able to define problems and opportunities, and deliver value and products that really work for our users, and as a result, positively impacts our bottom lines.

Doing this requires that we bring the experience to life for everyone that is involved with working on the product—using a storyboard as its own deliverable, or as part of a customer journey map or experience map, or just through the use of an experience map. Whatever format it takes, these types of tools and outputs help ensure that we're being more explicit and take that holistic end-to-end approach that brings different aspects of the product experience to life, creating more empathy and understanding for the end users' situation in the process.

[9]

Visualizing the Shape of Your Product Experience

"The Website Knows Me and What I Want"

I FIRST CAME ACROSS *experience goals* in 2009 while working on the Sonyericsson.com redesign. The internal UX team at Sony Ericsson used them as a way to work through their vision for the user experience and its division across the life cycle stages of the product.

By defining goals for what we wanted the experience to feel like, we had a different starting point for approaching requirements. Rather than jumping straight in and defining what a need would correspond to in terms of content or features, we defined three overarching experience goals that should apply to the website and a user's experience; one of them was "The website knows me and what I want." Next we broke down each overarching experience goal into more specific experience statements for certain points across the product life cycle. For example, the experience goal "It knows me and what I want" was broken into "It gives me recommendations" at the consideration stage in the product life cycle.

Many organizations and projects are driven by the business's needs and a list of requirements or user stories. The latter is not to be confused with user needs; just because it has the word *user* in the title doesn't mean they are grounded in actual user needs. Writing user stories, in whichever format they take, is easy in the sense that we can all write "As *a* <type of user> I want to <goal/ desire/capability> so that <benefit/why>." User stories can, however, become something that we almost churn out, and because we're constantly writing, and therefore also thinking *"As a user...,"* we can fool ourselves into thinking that we're automatically considering user needs. What users need, however, often starts at a deeper level.

To fully understand what users need, we first need to understand the humans behind the users. We need to know their backstories and be able to identify their desired outcomes at each point, as well as what it is they are trying to avoid. Insights about these backstories and pleasure and pain points for specific users provide us with more valuable information than a simple statement around what a user should be able to do.

That's not to say that user stories aren't valuable. The part of user stories that includes the "...so that <benefit/why>" helps ensure that a reason for the requirement is included, of course. But starting one level above that—by defining an overall vision for the experience through the use of something like experience goals—enables the product team to add a more nuanced perspective to the requirements. It also helps ensure that a through line runs through the experience, that red thread. Experience goals are also a great tool for mapping out what the experience across your website and app should feel like: they can help you visualize the desired emotional shape of the experience for the user, something that helps make it more tangible for the whole product team.

The Shape of Stories

In all types of narratives, there's an ebb and flow. At times, things are tough, and we're not exactly sure how the story is going to turn out. Then something happens that lifts the mood, and it seems more likely that the protagonist will achieve their objective. As Nancy Duarte suggests, all great talks have a certain shape to them. The same applies to stories.

Going all the way back to the time of Aristotle, people have tried to define the optimal structure of films, plays, and stories in general. Some stories start with the status quo, others in a more dire situation, and still others in times of good fortune or happiness. When it comes to product design and the problems and opportunities we help our users with, the experiences we design also tend to have a shape to them, even if we don't think about them that way.

By looking at typical structures from traditional storytelling, we can draw inspiration and learn a lot about how to define and visualize the experiences we're designing. As the saying goes, "A picture is worth a thousand words." When it comes to aligning teams, clients, and internal stakeholders, having something visualized can help ensure that everyone is on the same page. As we'll cover, visualizing the experience also helps us think it through from the start, identify typical patterns compared to other similar experiences, and determine where we want or need to place an emphasis. In the same way, typical structures in traditional storytelling help storytellers and scriptwriters in their work. What follows are some of the most well-regarded story structures.

CAMPBELL'S THE HERO'S JOURNEY

One of the most famous story structures is Joseph Campbell's *The Hero's Journey* (Figure 9-1). In his 1949 book *The Hero With a Thousand Faces,* Campbell describes the basic narrative pattern as follows:

> A hero ventures forth from the world of common day into a region of supernatural wonder: fabulous forces are there encountered and a decisive victory is won: the hero comes back from this mysterious adventure with the power to bestow boons on his fellow man.[1]

The Hero's Journey is typically illustrated as a circle with a dividing line, symbolizing the divide between the known and the unknown world, also referred to as the *ordinary world* and the *special world*. The hero's journey begins in the known world, where he gets a call to adventure that leads him over the first threshold and into the unknown world. In total, the hero goes through 17 stages and returns back to the known world with his reward after having undergone *the ordeal*, where he overcomes his main obstacle or enemy. In addition to the outer journey, there is also an inner journey for the hero that starts with a limited awareness of the problem and ends in mastery (Figure 9-2).

---

1 "Hero's Journey," *Wikipedia, https://oreil.ly/gN2d1.*

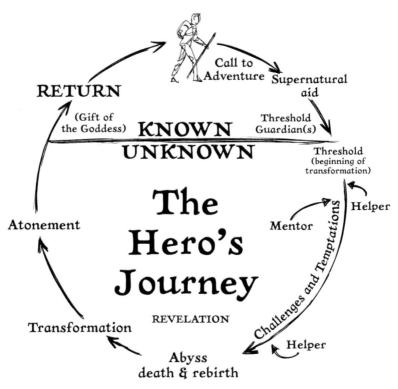

FIGURE 9-1

The Hero's Journey

The inner and outer journey is similar to what our users may experience while using the products and services that we design. The *outer journey* includes the steps and actions that a user takes in completing a task or achieving a goal. The *inner journey*, on the other hand, consists of the user's thoughts and emotions while moving through each step. It's the inner journey that, in the end, governs what the outer journey —determining, for example, whether the user decides to takes action or not, or leave your website in favor of a competitor's.

The unique combination of the inner and the outer journey is what results in no two journeys being the same. Outer journeys tend to bear more similarities among users than inner journeys, which is why we tend to focus on them more. However, with a growing number of touch points, even outer journeys don't always follow one clear path, and this also places increasing emphasis on the inner journey and understanding each user's scenarios.

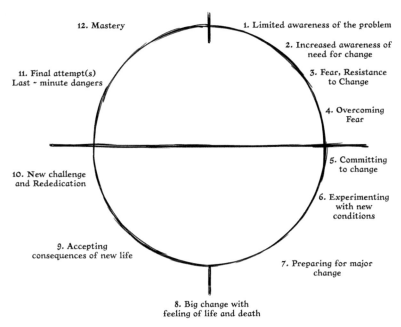

FIGURE 9-2

An interpretation by screenwriter Chris Vogler of the Hero's Inner Journey, in which he argues that the protagonist changes right from the beginning[2]

Exercise: The Shape of Stories

For your product or service, or one you use on a regular basis, define the high-level outer and inner journeys for one of your main types of users.

KURT VONNEGUT'S SHAPES OF STORIES

American novelist Kurt Vonnegut went one step further and looked at types of scenarios in traditional storytelling. During his time at the University of Chicago, he pitched a master's thesis on the shapes of stories. Although it got rejected, reportedly because it looked like too much fun, what Vonnegut aimed to do was to plot all the stories of

---

2 Allen Palmer, "A New Character-Driven Hero's Journey," Cracking Yarns (blog), April 4, 2011, *https://oreil.ly/Ldk-_*.

mankind onto a simple graph. The vertical axis represented ill to good fortune, and the horizontal axis moves from the beginning to the end of the story.

While nothing came of the thesis, Vonnegut spent the rest of his life championing the theory and describing it in his lectures and writing.[3]

Man in Hole

In *Man in Hole* (Figure 9-3), the main character gets into trouble and has to get out of it, ending up better for the experience. *Harold & Kumar Go To White Castle* and *Arsenic and Old Lace* are examples of this type of story.

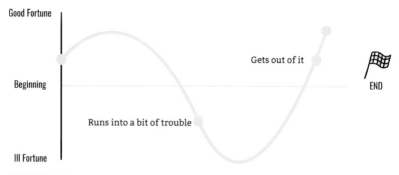

FIGURE 9-3
Man in Hole (Illustration by Eugene Yoon courtesy of fassforward)[4]

Boy Meets Girl

In *Boy Meets Girl* (Figure 9-4), the main character comes across something wonderful, gets it, loses it, and then gets it back forever. Examples are *Jane Eyre* and *Eternal Sunshine of the Spotless Mind*.

3 Kurt Vonnegut, "At the Blackboard," *Lapham's Quarterly*, 2005, *https://oreil.ly/FFHZ2*; Robbie Gonzalez, "The Universal Shapes of Stories, According to Kurt Vonnegut," *Gizmodo*, February 20, 2014, *https://oreil.ly/Q5DEz*.

4 Originally published in "Use these story structures to make messages people talk about," *https://oreil.ly/xiHml*. Illustrations by Eugene Yoon.

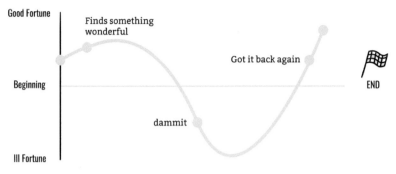

FIGURE 9-4

Boy Meets Girl (Illustration by Eugene Yoon courtesy of fassforward)

From Bad to Worse

In *From Bad to Worse* (Figure 9-5), things start out poorly for the main character and get continuously worse, with no hope for improvement. *The Twilight Zone* and *The Metamorphosis* are examples of this type of story.

FIGURE 9-5

From Bad to Worse (Illustration by Eugene Yoon courtesy of fassforward)

Which Way Is Up?

Which Way Is Up? (Figure 9-6) stories have an ambiguity that keeps us wondering about, and from knowing whether, any new developments are good or bad. Examples of this type of story are *Hamlet* and *The Sopranos*.

FIGURE 9-6
Which Way Is Up?

Creation Story

In *Creation Story* (Figure 9-7), humankind receives incremental gifts from a deity. First major ones, like the earth and the sky, and then smaller things. This is not a common structure in Western stories, but it appears in the creation story of many cultures.

FIGURE 9-7
Creation Story (Illustration by Eugene Yoon courtesy of fassforward)

Old Testament

In *Old Testament* (Figure 9-8), which is similar to the Creation Story, humankind receives incremental gifts from a deity, but is suddenly ousted from good standing in a fall of enormous proportions. *Great Expectations* is an example of this type of story.

FIGURE 9-8
Old Testament (Illustration by Eugene Yoon courtesy of fassforward)

New Testament

In *New Testament* (Figure 9-9), humankind also receives incremental gifts from a deity and is suddenly ousted from good standing, but receives off-the-chart bliss following it. *Great Expectations* with Dickens' alternative ending is an example of this kind of story.

FIGURE 9-9
New Testament

Cinderella

Cinderella (Figure 9-10) is similar to New Testament and is also what thrilled Vonnegut for the first time in 1947 and continued to do so over his years.

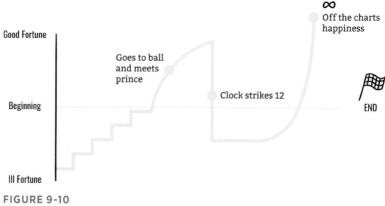

FIGURE 9-10
Cinderella (Illustration by Eugene Yoon courtesy of fassforward)

Exercise: Kurt Vonnegut's Shapes of Stories

For each of Vonnegut's story shapes, think of one product experience example that follows a similar storyline.

BOOKER'S SEVEN BASIC PLOTS

Someone else who dedicated a large part of his life to the shape of stories is the British journalist and author Christopher Booker. In 2004, he published *The Seven Basic Plots*, in which he argues that every myth, every film, every novel, and every TV show follows one of seven story structures. It took Booker 34 years to complete the book, which is an analysis of stories, their psychological meanings, and why we tell them.

Overcoming the Monster

In *Overcoming the Monster* (Figure 9-11), the protagonist sets out to defeat an often evil monster that is threatening the protagonist and/or the

protagonist's homeland. Examples of this type of story are the *James Bond* series, *Harry Potter* series, *Star Wars: Episode IV—A New Hope*, *Jaws*, and *The Magnificent Seven*.

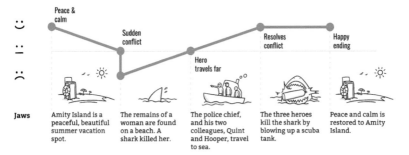

Jaws

| | Amity Island is a peaceful, beautiful summer vacation spot. | The remains of a woman are found on a beach. A shark killed her. | The police chief, and his two colleagues, Quint and Hooper, travel to sea. | The three heroes kill the shark by blowing up a scuba tank. | Peace and calm is restored to Amity Island. |

FIGURE 9-11

Overcoming the Monster (Illustration by Eugene Yoon courtesy of fassforward)

Voyage and Return

In *Voyage and Return* (Figure 9-12), the protagonist travels to a strange land. On that journey, the protagonist overcomes the threats that the strange land poses before returning with nothing more than the experience, but is better off for it. Typical examples of this type of story structure are *The Odyssey, The Wizard of Oz, Alice in Wonderland, The Hobbit, Gone with the Wind, The Chronicles of Narnia, Apollo 13,* and *Gulliver's Travels.*

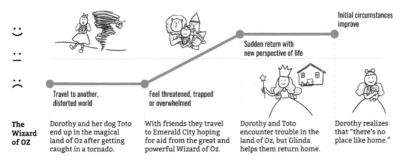

The Wizard of OZ

| Dorothy and her dog Toto end up in the magical land of Oz after getting caught in a tornado. | With friends they travel to Emerald City hoping for aid from the great and powerful Wizard of Oz. | Dorothy and Toto encounter trouble in the land of Oz, but Glinda helps them return home. | Dorothy realizes that "there's no place like home." |

FIGURE 9-12

Voyage and Return (Illustration by Eugene Yoon courtesy of fassforward)

Rags to Riches

In *Rags to Riches* (Figure 9-13), the poor protagonist acquires the likes of wealth, power, or a friend, loses it all, and then gains it back, growing as a person in the experience. *Cinderella, Aladdin, Brewster's Millions, David Copperfield*, and *Great Expectations* are all examples of the Rags to Riches story structure.

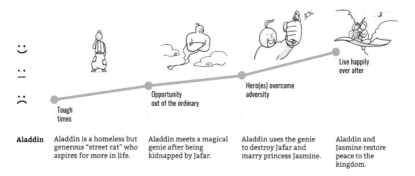

	Tough times	Opportunity out of the ordinary	Hero(es) overcome adversity
Aladdin	Aladdin is a homeless but generous "street rat" who aspires for more in life.	Aladdin meets a magical genie after being kidnapped by Jafar.	Aladdin uses the genie to destroy Jafar and marry princess Jasmine.	Aladdin and Jasmine restore peace to the kingdom.

FIGURE 9-13

Rags to Riches (Illustration by Eugene Yoon courtesy of fassforward)

The Quest

In *The Quest* (Figure 9-14), the protagonist sets out with companions to acquire an important object or to get to a specific location, facing many obstacles, dangers, and temptations along the way. Examples of this type of story are *The Lord of the Rings, Indiana Jones, The Illiad,* and *The Land Before Time.*

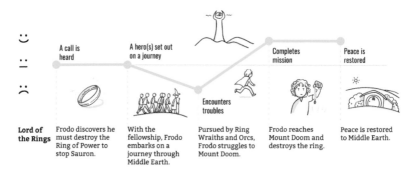

	A call is heard	A hero(s) set out on a journey	Encounters troubles	Completes mission	Peace is restored
Lord of the Rings	Frodo discovers he must destroy the Ring of Power to stop Sauron.	With the fellowship, Frodo embarks on a journey through Middle Earth.	Pursued by Ring Wraiths and Orcs, Frodo struggles to Mount Doom.	Frodo reaches Mount Doom and destroys the ring.	Peace is restored to Middle Earth.

FIGURE 9-14

The Quest (Illustration by Eugene Yoon courtesy of fassforward)

Tragedy

In Tragedy (Figure 9-15) the protagonist is a hero with one major flaw, or great mistake, that ultimately is their undoing and leads them on a downward spiral, evoking pity along the way. *Macbeth, Anna Karenina, Romeo and Juliet, Hamlet*, and *Breaking Bad* are all examples of tragedies.

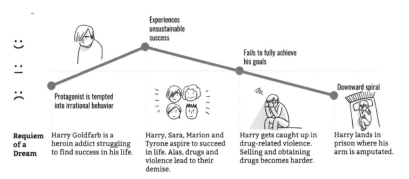

Requiem of a Dream: Harry Goldfarb is a heroin addict struggling to find success in his life. | Harry, Sara, Marion and Tyrone aspire to succeed in life. Alas, drugs and violence lead to their demise. | Harry gets caught up in drug-related violence. Selling and obtaining drugs becomes harder. | Harry lands in prison where his arm is amputated.

FIGURE 9-15

Tragedy (Illustration by Eugene Yoon courtesy of fassforward)

Comedy

In *Comedy* (Figure 9-16), which has a light and humorous nature, the protagonist triumphs over adverse circumstances that often get more and more confusing but always lead to a happy ending. Most romances

fall into this category. Some examples of the Comedy story structure are *Four Weddings and a Funeral, Bridget Jones's Diary, Mr. Bean, A Midsummer Night's Dream*, and *Much Ado About Nothing*.

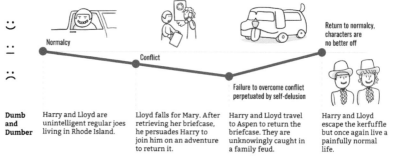

| Dumb and Dumber | Harry and Lloyd are unintelligent regular joes living in Rhode Island. | Lloyd falls for Mary. After retrieving her briefcase, he persuades Harry to join him on an adventure to return it. | Harry and Lloyd travel to Aspen to return the briefcase. They are unknowingly caught in a family feud. | Harry and Lloyd escape the kerfuffle but once again live a painfully normal life. |

FIGURE 9-16

Comedy (Illustration by Eugene Yoon courtesy of fassforward)

Rebirth

In *Rebirth* (Figure 9-17), an important event forces the main character to change their ways, often leading them to becoming a better person. Typical examples are *Beauty and the Beast, The Snow Queen, A Christmas Carol, Peer Gynt, The Secret Garden, Despicable Me,* and *How the Grinch Stole Christmas.*

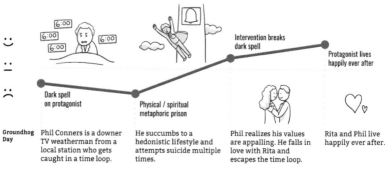

| Groundhog Day | Phil Conners is a downer TV weatherman from a local station who gets caught in a time loop. | He succumbs to a hedonistic lifestyle and attempts suicide multiple times. | Phil realizes his values are appalling. He falls in love with Rita and escapes the time loop. | Rita and Phil live happily ever after. |

FIGURE 9-17

Rebirth (Illustration by Eugene Yoon courtesy of fassforward)

Exercise: Booker's Seven Basic Plots

- Think about one of your favorite books or movies. Which of the preceding story shapes best fits its storyline?

- Think about your product or service. Which story shape best describes the overall experience with it?

The Shapes of Experiences

In 2016, a group of students at the Computational Story Lab at the University of Vermont set out to test whether Vonnegut's thesis held true. Vonnegut hypothesized that the emotional arcs invoked by the story structures he defined could be fed into a computer. However, the group of students used computers to find the shapes. Rather than look at the story structure, they analyzed the emotional arc that is invoked by the words that are used, using a filtered subset of 1,327 stories from Project Gutenberg's fiction collection. Their test concluded that there is strong support for six core emotional arcs. One of their conclusions was that understanding emotional arcs can be beneficial when constructing arguments, but also when teaching artificial intelligence.[5]

Although some of the story structures may be less relevant for the types of product or service experiences we work on (hopefully, there isn't too much tragedy by deliberate design), we can take a great deal of inspiration from some of them, even if we don't work with artificial intelligence. The Quest, for example, applies well to a situation where the user needs to find information, book something, or buy something, like the bath my partner and I had to first research and then buy.

Two Ways to Define the Shape of an Experience

Visualizing and knowing the shape of the story and experience that you're designing helps make it more tangible. These types of visualizations can help us define, and identify with, the user's emotional journey when using our product or service. They are also great for thinking through when the user is in a mindset where our product or service can be of relevance and help to them. Additionally, visualizations can help us make sure we consider and define the state of mind/need the user was in before coming to us—an aspect we often don't include, but one that can have a profound impact on the user's overall experience and expectations.

Mapping part of an experience is something we know from customer journey maps and, to some extent, customer experience maps, depending on what they include in the visualized part of the map.

---

5 Andrew Reagan et al., "The emotional arcs of stories are dominated by six basic shapes," EPJ Data Science 5, no. 31 (2016), *https://doi.org/10.1140/epjds/s13688-016-0093-1.*

In the former, you evaluate an experience, most often a specific user journey, and map it across an emotional spectrum, usually spanning from happy to unhappy. In the latter, you look at the whole end-to-end experience.

Both are great tools for mapping out the current experience and the future desired one. As both are covered elsewhere in detail (see, for example, *Mapping Experiences* by Jim Kalbach and Chapter 8), we won't go into detail here but instead look at two other ways related to storytelling that can help you map, plan, and visualize what the experience should feel like:

Using experience goals to map the emotional journey
By using experience goals and mapping these across emotional spectrums for each stage of the product life cycle, we create a shared view of what the experience of the product we're working on should feel like. It's a great tool for helping prioritize requirements as well as for aligning teams, stakeholders, and clients on a shared and clearly articulated product vision.

Mapping the happy and unhappy journey
We tend to focus on and design for the ideal scenario, in which things go smoothly. The reality often looks somewhat different. Mapping the happy and unhappy paths helps us think through what an experience would be like if everything really went the ideal way, as well as what it would be like if everything went wrong. The most realistic scenario is that we'll end up somewhere between the two. Going through this exercise is great, not just for multidevice projects, but also for campaigns and product launches. This process also forms a solid basis for thinking through and creating a customer service action plan and for communications in general.

USING EXPERIENCE GOALS TO MAP THE EMOTIONAL JOURNEY

Just as films, books, or TV series often have a number of storylines that run through them, you can define multiple experience goals for your website or app experience. On the Sony Ericsson project, we had four overarching experience goals, one of them being ".com knows me and what I want." By subsequently breaking these down into experience statements for each product life cycle stage of the experience, you help identify and define the ambitions and challenges for your product or service, and what the experience should feel like for the user.

We mapped the experience statements across the emotional level they should correspond with and divided the statements into three levels:

Hygiene

> The qualifiers that have to be there to ensure the experience is useful, easy, and simple (e.g., receiving an order confirmation, easy to find contact information)

Feel good

> The differentiators that evoke a positive emotional response in the user around the innovativeness and uniqueness of the experience (e.g., getting relevant product recommendations, a product comparison tool that highlights differences)

Delight

> The aspects that bring a bit of euphoria to the experience, thereby energizing the user (e.g., unexpected touches, making setup of new device seamless)

By placing the experience statements across the hygiene-to-delight spectrum, you start to see a flow that corresponds to the emotional level that the user might be going through, just as in Nancy Duarte's analysis of great speeches, Vonnegut's shapes of stories, and Booker's seven basic plots.

Not everything can be on the delight level, nor should we aim to position everything there. Good needs bad, rain needs sunshine, and just as the boat won't sail by moving backward and forward, "delights" and "feel goods" wouldn't exist unless they were put in contrast with each other and the hygiene factors. Additionally, there are certain things that users will never be ecstatic about and that, if given the choice, they would rather not do—like filling in forms, or remembering and entering their password.

There are, however, things we can do to make these experiences more pleasurable. Experience goals combined with the pain and pleasure points we've identified can help us define what these things should be. Perhaps we can break a long form into more bite-sized sections to foster a sense of ease and progress. Or perhaps we can provide contextual help and validation throughout to assist in the completion process and give the feeling that someone is there with the user, guiding them through it.

Through defining your experience statements and mapping them across the three levels, you get a better understanding of whether the narrative structure you had in mind is suitable for your product and for your user's journey. Additionally, with clearly defined overarching experience goals as well as statements, you should, at any given point throughout the experience of a website or app, be able to say how that point in the experience translates as an emotive feeling. It's a little like the exercises I sometimes do with my partner, practicing his lines from random starting points to see if he knows where in the script he is and where to go next.

How to go about it

In terms of how to go about defining and mapping experience goals, I recommend the following five steps:

1. *Brainstorm experience goals*

    Using any identified objective and/or key success factor for the experience, brainstorm experience goals for the product and write them down on individual sticky notes. These experience goals should be written from the user's point of view. For example, imagine that you ask the user, "How would you describe the experience of using Sonyericsson.com?" A possible answer is, "It's easy to find what I need."

2. *Identify patterns and write down keywords*

    Review the brainstorm output and group the sticky notes into clusters of statements with a common theme. Write down some keywords for each grouping; for example, "Intelligent, tailored, personalized."

3. *Formulate three to five overarching experience goals*

    Based on the keywords and the associated brainstorm statements, formulate three to five overarching experience goals. Just as in step 1, write them in a way that a user would express them and then shorten them; for example, "It feels like the website knows me and what I want" becomes ".com knows me and what I want." Use different-colored sticky notes for each overarching goal.

4. *Define and map detailed experience goals*

Identify key experience statements for each experience goal and map them over the three levels (hygiene, feel good, and delight) for each stage in the life cycle. These become your detailed experience goals. Just as in steps 1 and 3 write these in a way that a user would express them; for example, ".com gives me relevant recommendations" for the consideration stage.

5. *Review the output*

With the three to five overarching experience goals divided into experience statements that are mapped across the three levels, review the output.

- Is the emotional journey realistic? Are there too many on the delight level?

- Does the output correctly reflect where key barriers are, and where key differentiators are or should be in relation to competitors?

- Does it correspond with a likely emotional experience for the user?

I advise working with sticky notes and a big wall space to begin with so that it becomes a collaborative exercise in which key stakeholders and team members can participate, and so that it's easy to move things around.

Once you're happy with the output, assign someone to make a digital version that can be shared with the wider team and clients. This digital version can be included in any presentations as well as be printed out and put on a wall to ensure that people keep it in mind during the rest of the product design process.

MAPPING THE HAPPY AND THE UNHAPPY JOURNEY

When working through the experience of our products and services, it makes sense to start with success. Our focus should, after all, be to provide as good of an experience as possible. But the blue sky scenarios we often define in user journeys seldom reflect reality, or what is the likely reality. And that's fine. We use these success scenarios to help identify what we aim for and want the experience to ideally be like. But we should also think about worst-case scenarios and what the experience would look like if everything went haywire.

Ideas often come from seeing things that can be improved, and identifying what would be a bad experience helps us put "good" into perspective. By plotting out the unhappy journey in addition to the happy one, we're forced to think through, for each step or stage, what a bad experience at that point would be. It helps us identify what we should avoid both then and there and as an extension of that (e.g., automatically turning on sharing check-ins to Twitter, as we covered in Chapter 7). Considering the unhappy journey also helps us identify where we need to offer support and guidance to a user, or where we could improve; for example, ensuring that we add a way to track an expected delivery in a "product dispatched" confirmation email.

In summary, the value of mapping out both the happy and the unhappy journey lies in the following:

- Helping us being clear about what would constitute both "good" and "bad" outcomes or aspects from a user's point of view at each step or stage of our product experience

- Identifying opportunities for improvement

- Identifying areas where things could go wrong and where we need to offer help, support, and/or guidance

How to go about it
As for for how to map the happy and unhappy journey, I recommend the following four steps:

1. Identify the experience to work through. This can be a specific journey or an overall experience life cycle.

2. Define and map out the happy journey.

3. Define and map out the corresponding unhappy journey.

4. Arrange each point in the happy and unhappy journey along an emotional spectrum.

While these cover how to use the happy and unhappy journey, other ways of using it include the following:

- For planning out campaigns and product launches across touch points

- As a customer service blueprint with references to (other) guidelines and documents at each stage

When and How to Visualize an Experience

As with most things in UX and product design, what to do and how to do it depends on the value that it adds to a project. However, scriptwriters use the methods we covered in Chapter 5, at the beginning of their writing process for a reason: it helps with the narrative structure of the story. Similarly, the two methods we've discussed for visualizing the shape of an experience add the most value if they are carried out at the beginning of a project, before any wireframing, prototyping, or visual design has taken place.

As for how you visualize the narrative shape of the product experiences you design, you can use the following questions to guide you to the right level of fidelity:

Who do the narrative shapes need to be shared with?

If the narrative shapes are mainly being used internally, then pen and paper, a whiteboard, or sticky notes might be all you need. Translating it into a digital document may not necessarily add any more value to the project, but instead take up time that could be better spent elsewhere. However, if you don't have access to wall space where the narrative shape of the experience for all to see, or if you have additional internal stakeholders or clients that benefit from seeing the output, then translating it into a digital format could be worthwhile.

How are they being used in the project?

The benefit of design tools like narrative shapes is that you can keep developing and adding to them as the project progresses. If you intend to do so, ensure that the narrative shapes are accessible so that they're easily updated. At times, this works perfectly well with pen and paper, sticky notes, or a whiteboard. At other times, it may result in a lot of rework that would be quicker and easier to complete in a digital format. If the latter is the case, develop the first version of the narrative shapes in physical form and from then on work on it digitally, and if possible, print out the output in large format.

How important is the visual presentation?

I've seen and been part of teams that have included sketches in presentations shared with clients, to great success. For some companies and clients, this works. For others, it doesn't, and a more designed and visually pleasing output is needed. Most people can substantially improve their visual presentation style with some simple styling tips and tricks. While I'd generally recommend that you practice this because you will learn and become better at it, at certain times, getting the help of a designer can be a better use of everyone's time overall.

Summary

There is a lot of power in bringing something to life and making it more tangible. Visualizing the shape of a product experience is one way to help see, and show others, how the different parts of the experience come together to make up a whole. It also helps create shared clarity of what that experience might feel like in terms of emotional highs and lows for the user. Visualizing the shape of a product experience can help spark ideas, or help us spot where we might want to make small adjustments to ensure that the experience resonates better, emotionally, with our users. And it can help us plan out for all eventualities, the happy and the unhappy ones.

The kind of exercises we've covered in this chapter are also a great way to get people from different parts of the organization to work collaboratively on how something is and how something should be. As with all the methods in this book, you are encouraged to adapt and make them yours so that they work even better for your specific project.

While all products and all projects are different, commonalities exist between them, and visualizing their shapes forms a good foundation for the part we'll cover next: working with main plots and subplots in user journeys and flows.

[10]

Applying Main Plots and Subplots to User Journeys and Flows

The Ideal Journey

MOST OF US HAVE worked on a project requiring us to define key user journeys or flows. The user journeys may be either *functional*, focusing on what the user does, or *functional-emotional*, including what the user thinks and feels as well as does. Whichever format these user journeys have taken, our focus is often on a few key ones related to some of the main user goals or business objectives. Although at times alternate journeys are defined, more often than not the user journeys focus on the ideal scenario. We abstract steps or generalize what the user thinks and feels. Although these journeys at times depict that the user leaves the product or service in question to visit another website or do something offline, they most commonly focus primarily on what happens when using the product or service in question.

There is nothing wrong with that, per se, but also nothing particularly right about it either. As shown in Figure 7-2, a user's journey rarely follows a linear path. Instead, it's a mixture of online and offline and shifts from searching wide and far to narrow and deep. For user journeys to add the most value, they need to more accurately reflect what actually happens, or is likely to happen, no matter how complex this is. As much as we like to abstract to the ideal and the simple, the reality in which our products and services are going to be used, when and where as well as by whom, is complex, and we do best in embracing this complexity. It's part of the beauty of what we're designing for but also what ensures that the products and services we design actually work for people.

As with every deliverable, tool, or method we use on a project, user journeys should be used in such a way that they add the most value. At times, adding more detail won't bring the work forward in the most valuable way for the project. It may stop key internal team members and clients from understanding and buying into what's presented. Or, perhaps using user journeys only doubles the effort if some other more detailed work is being carried out; for example, through detailed flow diagrams.

We shouldn't, however, shy away from adding in complexities for the fear of making things complex. *Complex* is, after all, an accurate description of the context in which our products will be used, and that complexity can be presented in multiple ways that are easy to understand. Adding in some of these factors that differentiate between different users (such as drivers, handoff points, touch points, key search terms, etc.) can help provide a clearer and more accurate picture of a potential user's experience with our product or service. And at times, defining more than just the ideal and some key happy journeys is needed to really get under the hood of, and be able to account for, all eventualities. It's by actively designing for these scenarios, too, that we make sure our product or service both supports and tells the right product experience story, no matter the outcome. This is where drawing on the concept of the main plot and subplots in traditional storytelling can really help us.

The Role of the Main Plot and Subplots in Traditional Storytelling

In traditional storytelling, more than one storyline often runs through and makes up the narrative. Just think of, for example, *The Lord of the Rings*: the main story revolves around Frodo going back with the ring, but at the same time minor stories take place around the adventures of Legolas and Aragorn who are trying to protect settlements while destroying the Orc armies. Another storyline revolves around Merry and Pippin and their escape from the Orcs. All three of these minor stories, which weave into the main plot by the end, are called subplots.

Subplots are branches of a story that either support or drive the main plot. The Cambridge Dictionary defines *subplot* as "a part of the story of a book or play that develops separately from the main story." By including subplots, you add realism to the story you're telling. Just as events unfold in real life, the reader or viewer doesn't expect a story to unfold in an exclusively linear manner, but instead to jump around somewhat. That's what happens when you have a story with subplots.

For the storyteller, the subplots play an important role as a storytelling mechanism. Together with the secondary characters, subplots can be used to do the following:[1]

- Advance the story in increments

- Unleash transformative forces upon your main character; for example, gain or loss, growth or corruption

- Introduce new information to your main character or the reader

- Pivot the story or provide twists

- Speed up or slow down the story

- Patch holes or solve other problems with your main plot

- Induce mood such as comedy, pathos, triumph, or menace

- Insert or challenge a moral lesson

In many instances, the subplot is tied to the main plot and character by putting an immediate effect on situations or characters. Another way of using subplots is for these secondary stories to run parallel to the main story. Used this way, they add contrast and can, for example, explain decisions made by the main character. They can also be used to add a reminiscing element or backstory without it affecting the main plot. Subplots make the story real and add to the main plot.

The Role of the Main Plot and Subplots in Product Design

Solving problems in the main plot might make you think of main journeys, and alternate ones that users may take if things don't go as planned; for example, through a forgotten password link, or the need to contact customer support for help. For the product experiences we work on, these subflows and journeys add realism, just as they do in traditional storytelling. They take into account the reality of what it's

---

1 Guest Column, "7 Ways to Add Great Subplots to Your Novel," *The Writer's Digest*, December 17, 2012, *https://oreil.ly/pUCZX*.

like when people use our products. People might forget passwords or need different things from our website, and those users will need to jump between sections to find some background or contact information while learning about what we offer.

In both stories and product experiences, the user or character will also often have more than one thing that requires their time and attention. It's one of the reasons users seldom complete a task in one go. They might get disrupted or distracted, or intentionally navigate away from our website or app to do research, only to return later. This multitasking is an accurate reflection of how life actually is, so incorporating these details, subflows, and alternate journeys is a necessity for making sure that our product experiences will work and cater to what people need, and what might happen as they use our product or service.[2]

The need for a user or customer to get in contact with customer support because of a problem is an obvious subplot. But, increasingly, subflows and alternate journeys are also about understanding different combinations of content, touch points, entry and exit points, and how to make the product experience work best no matter the mix. As we covered in Chapter 5, each overarching product experience story is made up of many smaller mini-stories, and each subflow or alternate journey is a story in itself. A story where the "why it began" is a key part.

For the purpose of this book, we'll use the following definitions for plot and subplots when it comes to product design:

Main plot

> The primary journey, either high level or detailed, associated with the desired user journey for the product or service. This plot has to take place for there to be a product or service experience. This can be either the full end-to-end experience journey or parts of it related to a sequence; for example, getting a new phone (full end-to end-journey) or researching buying a new phone (part of the full end-to end-journey).

---

2 Kathy Edens, "How to Use Subplots to Bring Your Whole Story Together," ProWritingAid, May 17, 2016, *https://oreil.ly/jQBE1.*

Subplots

> All minor journeys that branch off from the primary journey, either high level or detailed. These can result from the user encountering a problem in relation to the product, being distracted, or making a deliberate decision. These are often referred to as edge cases, alternative paths, non-happy paths, or non-ideal paths; for example, a forgotten password, shopping cart abandonment.

In traditional storytelling, each subplot should impact the main plot, or that subplot doesn't have a place in that story. In product design, the same is true: all alternate paths, whether happy or unhappy, should have a connection to the main experience.

Types of Subplots

In traditional storytelling, subplots have various types (e.g., romantic, conflict, and expository subplots). Other ways of defining subplots are by the way they relate to the main plot. Here are some examples:[3]

Mirroring subplots

> These mirror the main plot but don't duplicate it (e.g., a romance that takes place between two secondary characters).

Contrasting subplots

> These show the opposite type of progress to the main plot (e.g., a secondary character has the same weakness as the main character, but refuses to go on a journey or through personal development, which in turn benefits the growth of the main character).

Complicating subplots

> These represent change and cause problems in the main plot. Contrary to mirroring subplots and contrasting subplots, complicating subplots might not directly relate to the main theme of the story but instead intersect with the main plot in such an important way that they are inextricable from the main plot (e.g., the main character has a task to complete, which is not directly related to the main plot).

---

3 Jordan McCollum, "Types of Subplots," Jordan McCollumn (blog), September 11, 2013, *https://oreil.ly/PAoA9*.

What type of subplot you choose should both be relevant to and depend on your main storyline.

Subplots can also consist of different subtypes. For example, there can be a romantic subplot to the main plot, a mystery subplot, a vendetta subplot, or similar. However, some genres don't lend themselves well to being subplots. Adventures are one example as these tend to be quite large stories in and of themselves and as such are better as main plots.

Having an understanding of the subplot type is important in product design, to help inform the product experience design. While there can definitely be different kinds of subplots, the types used in traditional storytelling aren't as relevant to product design. Instead, in product design, we propose alternative, unhappy, and branched journey subplots.

ALTERNATIVE JOURNEYS

Alternative journeys in product design resemble mirroring subplots. In mirroring subplots, the main plot is mirrored but it isn't duplicated. Here, the key lies in the word *alternate*, which Cambridge Dictionary defines as "one that can take the place of another." Alternative journeys are alternative routes that a user may take to reach the same end destination (Figure 10-1).

Alternative journeys depict variations in the way the user comes to making a decision about a purchase. The main plot and journey might be based on what data shows are the key steps that the majority of users currently take from; for example, from first hearing about a product to making a purchase. A subplot will be a secondary or tertiary route that users may take; for example, doing most of their research offline or starting from a secondary or tertiary entry point and proceeding from there.

FIGURE 10-1
Alternative journeys

A great way to starting thinking about alternative journeys is to define the ecosystem of the product or service. By having a clear understanding of all the touch points that might be involved, the various routes a user's journey could take start to become clear. Here are some examples of typical alternative journeys:

- Alternative entry points to the same page. For example, one user might start with search and another with social.

- Alternative paths within the product or service. For example, one user might go directly to a product page from the home page, while another might go via Mens/Womens pages and then on to a category page like Jackets and then to a specific jacket's product page.

Exercise: Alternative Journeys

For your product or service, using the concept of mirroring subplots:

- Think about alternative journeys to the main plot.
- Where and how do the alternative journeys differ from the main journey?
- Where and how is the alternative journey similar to the main journey?

UNHAPPY JOURNEYS

In product design, we always want the outcome to be a happy one. We want to fulfill the user's need or goal, even if the result is an unhappy outcome for the product, such as canceling a SaaS subscription. If that is what the user wants to do, then completing canceling their subscription constitutes a happy outcome and, hopefully, a happy journey.

When we talk about *unhappy journeys* as a subplot type in product design, we are referring to those that don't go the way the users would like them to (Figure 10-2). An unhappy journey may include minor obstacles and frustrations throughout, such as CTAs not being 100% clear, trouble finding what they are after, or a page taking a little too long to load. Or the journey might include a more major event, such as not being able to complete the task they set out to do, the website or app displaying an error, or accidentally ordering the wrong thing.

FIGURE 10-2
Unhappy journeys

Whether minor or big, unhappy journeys in product design resemble contrasting subplots. The essence of contrasting subplots is that they show the opposite progress, growth, or change than the main plot. Thinking in terms of the opposite of a happy journey/outcome is a great way to identify the unhappy journeys and the major and minor moments they can contain.

While identifying the ideal happy journeys in product design is important for understanding desired paths and outcomes, identifying the alternative paths and unhappy journeys is just as important. As much as we'd like them to, things don't always go as planned, and for every happy story there is usually at least one possible unhappy outcome, even if just ever so slightly unhappy. To help us avoid the unhappy outcomes as much as possible, it's important to identify what might lead to an unhappy outcome. Additionally, unhappy outcomes can't be completely avoided, and for our product and service experiences to deliver, they need to do so under all circumstances, ensuring that we're always looking after our users and customers.

Exercise: Unhappy Journeys

For your product or service, using the concept of contrasting subplots:

- Think about what a happy journey and main plot would be.
- Think about what an unhappy journey and subplot would be.

BRANCHED JOURNEYS

In traditional storytelling, branched narratives are often present when some type of interactive element is present (Figure 10-3). CYOA books are good examples, though defining these as branched narratives is a little too simplistic (because there is more to these types of narratives than that). In video games, the user is faced with making a decision and that decision will then influence the next part of the game experience.

Many of the more functional or interactive types of product or service experiences we work with include elements of *branched journeys*. To define them, you often need to work with decision tree–based structures to map out the flow of each branch. When working on VUIs and products and services that involve chatbots, decision tree–based structures are a crucial tool for capturing all the scenarios. Bots and voice-based experiences in particular often fall flat when there isn't a relevant or valuable answer to a user's query.

FIGURE 10-3
Branched journeys

The more functional a website or app is, the greater the need for mapping out the full flows, including all the user and system decision points, as well as their results (e.g., a certain screen, error message, etc.). Some of these will result in unhappy journeys/flows, and others in alternative journeys/flows.

Some examples of typical branched journeys are VUIs, bot interfaces, and hotel- and travel-booking websites and apps.

What Storytelling Teaches Us About Working with Main Plots and Subplots

Traditional storytelling teaches us a few key things about plots and subplots that we can apply to product design, including defining and building out subplots as well as visualizing main plots and subplots.

DEFINING AND BUILDING OUT SUBPLOTS

Just as the main plot should have acts and a clearly defined plot, all subplots should follow a narrative and have all the same elements as the main plot (e.g., an inciting incident and a climax). Rather than happen "on stage" however, subplots occur off stage, and the reader or viewer is often left to put the pieces together themselves.[4]

---

4 Shawn Coyne, "The Units of Story: The Subplot," *Story Grid*, *https://oreil.ly/mMMs1*.

In general, subplots will be simpler and not have as many steps involved. They can also vary with regard to when they are introduced and when they are solved (e.g., one subplot being introduced in one chapter and solved in the next), whereas another can run throughout the whole of the main plot. What's important is that the subplot does get solved and that it impacts the main plot. If it doesn't, then it shouldn't be included in the story, as it will then be a separate story altogether.[5]

When you identify and start to work on subplots, one important point to keep in mind is creating too many subplots will be confusing. There are various ways to come up with your subplots, but one of the most suggested ways is to brainstorm characters who can propel the plot. *Writer's Digest* suggests seven ways to come up with your subplot. The following are three ways that have some applicability in product design:[6]

The isolated chunk

Tell your subplot as a story-within-a-story in an isolated chunk. Don't worry about transitions, and just start a new section or chapter. This technique can be particularly useful when you write in first-person, as your character can experience only one thing at a time. An example from traditional storytelling is *Adventures of Huckleberry Finn*. In product design, this approach can be useful for subplots in the experience that are independent from the main plot and journey. Unhappy journeys that occur as the experience branches off into a separate journey are one example.

The parallel line

Write a subplot that weaves alongside the main plot. The advice here is to start with your main plot and focus on the main characters, particularly the protagonist. Once it comes naturally, insert the beginning of your subplot, and from there on switch back and forth as evenly as you can, as this will emphasize their symmetrical nature. An example from traditional storytelling is the cat-and-mouse classic *The Day of the Jackal* by Fredrick Forsyth. In product design, this approach can be applied to alternative paths in

---

5 Edens, "How to Use Subplots to Bring Your Whole Story Together."

6 Guest Column, "7 Ways to Add Great Subplots to Your Novel."

particular; though there may be one main path to making a purchase, for example, the different routes can be fairly equal in terms of importance.

The in-and-out

The main plot focuses on one set of characters while the subplot involves other characters. Let your subplots shuttle in and out as needed. For example, a mentor might appear in one chapter, offering some advice, and then disappears on a different journey until returning later in a different chapter. If you write in first-person, it's perfectly fine for the chapters involving the mentor to be in third-person. In traditional storytelling, an example of this approach is Harper Lee's *To Kill a Mockingbird*. Applied to product design, this approach could be applied to any kind of product or service that has recurring characters making an appearance throughout different stages of the experience (see Chapter 6). Ongoing support and unhappy journeys can be one example, but this approach can equally be applied to happy journeys.

How to go about it

If you've been involved in defining an overall end-to-end experience, or even just a primary user journey, you'll have experienced how, inevitably, branching-off points appear. You'll often know the starting point or the end point and can work your way from there. As with all things, what to do and how to go about it depends on what benefits your project the most. A good starting point is to look at the type of subplot and main plot you're working with, and based on that, try to identify whether the subplot is best treated as an isolated chunk, a parallel line, an in-and-out. However, keeping to a specific approach is not what's important. It's that you're able to define the subplot.

The preceding approaches from storytelling are simply methods that can help you focus and identify your subplot and how it, if applicable, connects with the main plot.

VISUALIZING MAIN PLOTS AND SUBPLOTS THROUGH STORYMAPS

We can also turn to traditional storytelling for inspiration when it comes to visualizing the main plot and subplots. Numerous examples can be found online. These storymaps are commonly used to capture the following information:

- An overview of all the subplots

- Where the subplots and the main plot intersect

- What characters are involved in which subplot

Some storymaps, like the one in Figure 10-4, are beautifully done and can both help inform and inspire how we might visualize main plots and subplots in product design. Other provide low-fidelity ways to bring key information to the forefront, something we can also benefit from in the work we do and the way we present it in product design.

The Hunger Games

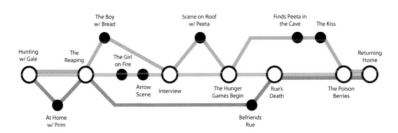

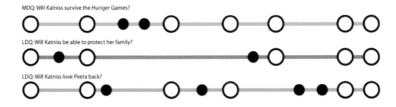

FIGURE 10-4

Storymap of *The Hunger Games* by Gabriela Pereira DIY MFA[7]

How to go about it

What to visualize and how will depend on your specific project and what will benefit it the most, but here are some general steps:

---

7 Gabriela Pereira, "How to Create a Story Map," DIY MFA, May 15, 2012, *https://oreil.ly/ FbY4p*.

- Identify the role and value that visualizing subplots may have. For example, you may use a storymap to show where subplots intersect or to map out the actors and characters involved in each subplot.

- Identify whether this visualization is intended to help you and the team as part of the thinking and defining process, or whether it's for the client or key stakeholder. This will determine the level of fidelity that you create.

- As with most deliverables, look for inspiration in how others have done it and adapt based on what best benefits your project.

Summary

To some extent we, and more so the users we're designing for, are lucky that chatbots and VUIs are making an appearance in the products and services that we work on. These types of experiences mean that we have to carefully think through and design for as many eventualities as possible. We're not quite at the point where we can create a good experience for the user, because dead ends still exist, but these dead ends are opportunities for learning.

Though the primary journey and use case is where we're placing most of our emphasis, the secondary journeys—alternative paths toward the same destination or unhappy outcomes that have to be dealt with—add realism to the products and services that we design. It's by actively understanding those that we dig into and understand our users and help root for them to succeed. By capturing what these secondary journeys and subplots are—and where relevant, visualizing how they are all connected—we better understand what's needed to make the experience come together. That understanding is a prerequisite for what we'll talk about next: theme and story development in product design.

[11]

Theme and Story Development in Product Design

Using Real Content

MANY OF US HAVE worked on projects that included no actual content in the wireframes, design, or prototype before the build was pretty much complete and the website or app about to go live. We all know how that story ends and what happens to the carefully designed modules and pages. They break, and it looks horrible. Even worse, if content isn't carefully considered or covered by the teams involved in building the product, what ends up being included may not be what users or the business actually need.

Throughout my years as a UX designer, I've come across clients or internal stakeholders numerous times who insist on putting the actual content into the wireframes and/or the prototype. Usually, however, it's never really the actual content. It's draft content, which means it needs to be revised and updated, and then added into the wireframes again. In addition, the way the wireframes are laid out may not be the way the page ends up looking in the final design and build and, as a result, further amendments to the content will most likely be needed.

I'm sure there are teams and projects out for which where this process has worked. In my experience, I find that placing real copy and amending it in wireframes causes more hassle and time wasted than value added. It does, however, raise an important issue: we need to get the content into the pages and views we're designing and building in order to really see how it works. Content and design do, after all, need to evolve hand in hand.

Far too often we're designing for only the best-case scenario. Everything lines up neatly. There are no stragglers on a new line, no long words that get cut off in the middle or jump down to the line below, leaving a gap above. No titles that span two or perhaps even three lines, not to mention paragraphs that are simply too long.

Designing with fake content is easy, or at least easier. Designing with and for real content is less so. But that's what's going to happen with the wireframes and designs we create: content is going to go in them. And when that happens, it shouldn't break things. It should fit like a glove, or perhaps more appropriately, what we've designed and how we've designed it should fit like a glove on the actual content.

I'm all for using *Lorem ipsum* when used in conjunction with notes about the content that should go in there. Writing real content is hard and takes time. What I might write in my wireframes or prototypes, if I attempt to write real content, will without a doubt be wordier and less to the point than what my fellow copywriter colleagues would write. It'll also take me substantially longer. That doesn't mean that I don't consider the content. I carefully plan out the story that the page and each module should tell, and include an approximation of the amount of copy that should go in, as well as notes on the details that I believe the copy should cover.

Which way you and your product team approach content on your project is up to you. Numerous designers and product people end up writing copy, and there's no problem with that, as long as it works for the project and as long as the copy is well written. The important thing is that content is considered from the start and that the back-and-forth process of content influencing design, and vice versa, takes place. Everything is connected, and when it comes to good content in product design, everything should be there for a reason, just as in a good story.

The Role of Theme and the Red Thread in Storytelling

When you think about a story and what it is about, whether it's a book or a film, one of the first things you consider is the plot—what happens in the story and the characters it happens to. If you take it one step further and think about what the story is *really* about, that's the theme.

Theme was Aristotle's third principle behind good storytelling. Lexico defines theme as "an idea that recurs in or pervades a work of art or literature." Though the theme of a story is often described with words such as *love and honor*, as is the case with the *Hornblower* books, in the words of author Robert McKee:

> A true theme is not a word, but a sentence—one clear coherent sentence that expresses a story's irreducible meaning...it implies function: the controlling idea shapes the writer's strategic choices.[1]

Theme, in other words, is about what the story means. It's what the story is about, but through "a different experiential context," as journalist Larry Brooks puts it,[2] and it impacts the story itself.

Most stories have multiple themes. In *Harry Potter*, for example, the main theme is about good versus evil and the power of love, but there are also themes around friendship and loyalty. You may have a theme that stretches across the whole narrative, and themes that appear in only certain chapters or parts of the story. The strongest stories tend to have themes that interconnect and complement or contrast one another. Although a theme can be obvious, it can also be more nuanced and harder to identify, as is the case in *Batman Begins*, which features one man's struggle with his own identify and duality.[3]

1 Robert McKee, *Story: Substance, Structure, Style, and the Principles of Screenwriting* (New York: ReganBooks, 2006).

2 Larry Page, *Story Engineering* (Cincinnati: Writer's Digest Books, 2011); Courtney Carpenter, "Exploring Theme," *Writer's Digest*, April 30, 2012, https://oreil.ly/N7X8k.

3 Melissa Donovan, "What Is the Theme of a Story?" *Writing Forward*, October 15, 2019, https://oreil.ly/DYgc_.

Even if the writer of the story doesn't explicitly think about its theme, most stories tend to have one. Themes are so closely related to human nature that it's almost impossible to tell a story without one; the theme can be considered the glue that binds the narrative all together.

When you think about it, in all good stories, things happen for a reason, and in one way or another, everything is connected. Some time ago, my partner D and I watched a horror movie. In one of the scenes, the main character was getting something from a closet. There were two spray cans in the scene, and somehow we just knew that those would play a role later—and sure enough, they did. Walt Disney, as we talked about in Chapter 2, was famous for paying attention to these small details. They are also one of the things my dad really enjoys about being a writer.

One of the books my parents would read to us when we were kids was the Swedish book *Historien om Någon* (*The History of Somebody*) by Åke Löfgren and Egon Möller-Nielsen (Figure 11-1). On the cover of the book is a keyhole with two eyes peering out from inside it, and on the first page of the book, a red piece of string appears. This red string runs through the whole book, guiding the narrative along the events that have taken place, including a fallen vase, and through an open door. As a child, I'd follow that red thread with anticipation of what would be revealed at the end, and I was so pleased when it turned out to be a small kitten.

While the red thread in that childhood story is a very literal one, in Swedish we talk of a red thread, or *röd tråd*, as the thing that binds the narrative together. Not as a visual line, like the one that you can see in the book, or that you can follow if you go exploring caves, or that you can use to find your way out of a labyrinth as Theseus did in Greek mythology with the help of Ariadne. No, this red thread is an invisible one that runs through it all, a through line. In rhetoric, it's used as an expression that means that any recitation, particularly longer ones, should have coherence. In storytelling it's become symbolic for a coherent story, and if it's not present, or we forget what we were supposed to say when we tell a story or give a talk, we refer having "lost the thread" ("tappat tråden").

In traditional storytelling, this red thread, or through line, is connected to the plot or theme of the story. It can also be connected to a character and forms the larger and more important aspect of how everything is connected. As producer Barri Evins says:

> Using theme as your 'decider', from big choices to small ones, is a powerful tool. It empowers you to infuse theme into every aspect of your story, creating a rich and resonant reading experience.[4]

FIGURE 11-1
Historien om Någon by Åke Löfgren and Egon Möller-Nielsen

Exercise: The Role of Theme and the Red Thread in Storytelling

Thinking about a movie you've watched or a book that you've read recently, what was the theme, or red thread in it?

---

4 Barri Evins, "The Power of Theme," *Writer's Digest*, August 17, 2018, *https://oreil.ly/tDdHr*.

The Role of Theme and the Red Thread in Product Design

In product design, we often have an idea about what we're working on when we start. This concept hopefully gets further developed and supported by a clearly defined strategy before any UX, design, or development work begins. In the best of scenarios, a red thread runs through it all (Figure 11-2). Perhaps we've even started developing experience goals (as covered in Chapter 9) as well as design principles, which help us put words to what the experience should look and feel like. These tools start to connect the pieces of the project." If the run project is really well run, we've also started to work on the content strategy. As the project progresses, this mutually informing relationship between UX, design, content, and development is evolving. If not, we may find ourselves in one of those scenarios where we're starting, and even completing, the UX, design, and development process before content is properly thought of, and we end up with a website or app that may have looked great on paper but is an absolute disaster when it's made a reality.

FIGURE 11-2

The red thread in product design

Having a theme, or many themes, that everyone is absolutely clear on is essential for good product design. Without a theme, essentially anything goes, and the offering and experience can become a car crash. Too often, people resist working through content strategy at the same time that UX design begins—not to mention before UX design begins. This resistance leads to an unclear picture of the content you have to include, and how, as well as why. Just as everything happens for a reason in a good story, everything included in product design should be there for a good reason—because it's connected, or at least should be. This connection is also what sets great product design and content apart from just good or average product design or content.

With the help of experience goals and design principles, we can ensure that carefully considered and planned-out red threads exist throughout the experiences we design—even if our red thread is not as visible as it was in my childhood book, or the connection isn't as obvious as it was in that horror movie.

Exercise: The Role of Theme and the
Red Thread in Product Design

With your product or service in mind, identify the main theme of the product experience.

Approaches to Developing Your Story in Traditional Storytelling

There are numerous ways to write a script or a book, from the way you choose to you begin to the bulk of the writing process itself. Some authors and scriptwriters will simply sit down and write. Others use an outline to help structure the narrative and the writing process. The way to go about it will, to some extent, depend on how writing the script or book has come about.

For books like this one, authors are usually asked to put together an outline to help the publisher assess whether the book is, in fact, for them. It's also a great way for authors to help think through and structure their thoughts. After O'Reilly contacted me about writing this book, I outlined the book as requested. Some authors find outlines to be incredibly helpful, and others find it limiting or even a blocker for their writing process.

When you search for advice on how to go about writing, for example, a novel, the advice is often to just sit down and write. A writing blog called The Write Practice recommends you write your first draft in as short a time as possible: a sitting if it's a short story, or a season (three months) if it's a novel.[5] While writing this first draft, the consultants don't recommend worrying too much about plotting or outlining. That can come once you know you have a story to tell. The purpose of that first draft is very much a discovery process, in which you figure out what you actually have. Many writers will write three or more drafts:

The first draft

This is often a rough draft, sometimes called the "vomit draft." It's not to be shared with anyone. It's your own draft, and it's there to help you figure out what it is that you're writing.

The second draft

Though this tends to be more refined, it is not for polishing. In the second draft, you carry out major structural changes and you clarify the plot and the characters, or the idea for your nonfiction book.

The third draft

This is the one for deep polishing and where, according to The Write Practice, the fun begins.

While this certainly holds true for how this book has come about, others would disagree with this approach. There is also some debate around whether writers should worry about identifying their theme: some say not until after writing a first draft, and others say the theme is such an integral part that it should be present throughout the story development. One can argue that it doesn't matter how you go about writing your book or whether you lead with characters, or a theme, or whether you have a clear structure—as long as you write and a page-turning story comes out at the end.

DEVELOPING YOUR CONTENT AND PRODUCT EXPERIENCE STORY

For product design, the equivalent of how to go about writing your story is how to go about defining what that product should actually be and the content and features it should contain. Chapter 6 noted that some projects are led by the big idea rather than the needs of the characters. In film, the equivalent is a particular scene or use of the latest special

---

5 Joe Bunting, "Ten Secrets To Write Better Stories," The Write Practice (blog), *https://oreil. ly/1U1s3*.

effects that drives the story in a particular direction. How you come up with your story or your product idea doesn't really matter, as long as it resonates with its intended audience.

Unfortunately, this is often where many products fall flat because what's being designed and developed is not based on the priority of actual user needs. Or, although the idea is good, the project lacks a clear information architecture and content strategy to make it happen and give users the type of content that they need in a way that makes sense to them.

The number of projects in which an amazing-looking website or app has been created in Photoshop, Illustrator, or Sketch only to be developed and then look nothing like it is far too many. And it's not due to poor development. Most of the time, it's due to a lack of content planning, creation, and governance combined with a lack of collaboration between the design team and those responsible for creating or adding in the content. It doesn't matter how great the website or app looks in design, or how good the idea is, or how well it meets the research findings if what actually goes into the website or app in terms of content doesn't match the basis on which it has been designed.

Just as an outline and defined theme will help some authors plan out their books, and help publishers assess the relevance and value that such books can provide, there are a number of tools and methods that product teams should work with to help plan out and assess the value of a website or app. Three of these are sitemaps, card sorts, and content plans.

In addition to these, in this book we've covered methods from traditional storytelling (such as the index card method in Chapter 5), which helps you plan out the overall narrative and start to identify the different parts of the experience from sequences, scenes, and plots. We covered experience goals in Chapter 9, which help define the theme of the product experience, and we talked about main plots and subplots in the previous chapter. All of these, combined with the tools and methods we are used to using, such as sitemaps, help provide reference points and a framework for ensuring that our product experience has a theme running through it all, working as a guiding northern star for the product experience's story development.

What Storytelling Teaches Us About Theme and Developing Your Product Story

To tell a great story, you need to know what you're saying and to consider who you're telling it to. Chapter 5 described the plot as what you're going to tell your audience when; defining the plot of your product experience will help form a better understanding of the full end-to-end experience. Just sitting down and writing rather than preparing a full outline may have some advantages in traditional storytelling. But for product design, we risk becoming too focused on the detail, such as specific screens, before having a solid understanding of the bigger picture. By working through the narrative structure in one of the ways covered in Chapter 5, you'll have a solid foundation for going into both content strategy and information architecture. While in UX design it is about delivering the right content at the right time, on the right device, it's also about having the right content in the first place. As Joseph Phillips writes for GatherContent, "A huge part of content strategy actually has nothing to do with content itself. It's about people."[6]

IDENTIFY YOUR THEME

Journalist Larry Brooks argues that there is an important distinction between concept, idea, premise, and theme. These terms are often used interchangeably, he says, but in the wrong way, as they are different. Using *The Lovely Bones* by Alice Sebold (Oberon Books) as an example, he explains the differences as follows:

The idea

> To tell a story about what heaven is like

The concept

> To have a narrator who is already in heaven narrating the story and then turn it into a murder mystery. Or, if put as a question: "What if a murder victim can't rest in heaven because her crime remains unsolved, and chooses to get involved to help her loved ones gain closure?"

---

6 Joseph Phillips, "A Four Step Road Map for Good Content Governance," GatherContent (blog), October 1, 2015, *https://oreil.ly/vIQcr*.

> "What if a 14-year-old girl cannot rest in heaven, and realizes that her family cannot rest on earth, because her murder remains unsolved, so she intervenes to help uncover the truth and bring peace to those who loved her, thus allowing her to move on?"

The theme

> What does the story mean?

Brooks conveys that an idea is always a subset of a concept, and a concept, in turn, is a subset of a premise. What makes something a concept is the qualifier. This qualifier can be expressed using a "What if...?" proposition. By simply adding this, you open the door to a story. You then have a premise when you throw a character into the mix and you, so to speak, expand the concept. In *The Lovely Bones* example, this is done by adding the hero's quest into the "What if...?" proposition. The theme, on the other hand, is completely different and raises the question of what the story means to you; what does it make you think about and feel? It's about the relevance of your story to life.[7]

How to go about it

In a nonliterary sense, a concept can still be called an idea, according to Brooks, and that fits well with how we're at times using the terms *idea* and *concept* interchangably in product design. An idea can also come from the realm of a theme, just as an idea for a product can come from a theme such as financial planning. Just as writers may not always be clear about what their theme is, in product design, it can be the same thing. The Writing Forward blog gives the following tips on developing theme:

Learn to identify themes

> Identify themes when watching movies and reading novels, as this will help you become better at bringing themes into your own work.

Don't stress

> A theme will usually emerge by itself as you work through your first draft.

---

7 Carpenter, "Exploring Theme;" Larry Brooks, "Concept Defined," *Writer's Digest*, November 22, 2010, *https://oreil.ly/ENHEp*.

Strengthen the theme

After you've identified the theme, make a list of related themes that you could weave into subplots.

Check your work

Make a list of all the themes in your story.

Whether you start by having a clearly defined theme or developing it as you start to explore and define the product or service doesn't matter too much. The important thing is that you have a theme.

Exercise: Identify Your Theme

Take one of your favorite movies or one that you've watched recently and identify the following:

- What is the idea of the movie?
- What is the concept of the movie?
- What is the premise of the movie?
- What is/are the theme(s) of the movie? What does the story mean?

Now, do the same with your product or service in mind:

- What is the idea of your product or service?
- What is the concept of your product or service?
- What is the premise of your product or service?
- What is/are the theme(s) of your product or service? What does the story mean?

EXPLORE MENTAL MODELS

One of our jobs as product and UX designers is to ensure that the right content appears in an appropriate order and is suitably structured and labeled so that finding our way around it is easy and makes sense. This should be based not only on needs, but also on mental models. Without thinking about it, we, and our users, organize information and items every day in our lives. Certain groupings just feel right or make sense, and others are ones that we've gotten used to. Making sure we meet these expectations is a critical part of structuring and organizing the content that we've defined. One of the best-known tools for organizing information is *card sorting*, a method used to help define or evaluate the information architecture of a website, app, or platform.

But it's not just about making sure that the labeling and organization of information and content makes sense. When we work through and define our content and our information architecture, we should evaluate whether the structure that we've defined tells the story that the user is expecting. The tools we covered earlier in this book, (particularly Chapters 5 and 10) provide us with a good starting point for the different steps and the order in which a user would typically go about an experience. However, as we covered in Chapter 3, a user's journey is seldom linear nowadays, nor does it necessarily start from the beginning that we've so carefully crafted. This means that we need to think about the overarching narrative across pages and views, and the narrative within each of those pages and views, as well as how they fit into the overall experience, no matter when or how a user ends up on them.

Exercise: Explore Mental Models

As you develop your product's story and the content to go with it for each part of the product experience, think about the following:

- Does the content fit with the users' mental models?
- Have you clearly named the content and groups in alignment with your users' expectations?
- Have you grouped content in line with your users' expectations?

Summary

While all of us will have different preferences for the ways we work and come up with the ideas for our product, there is something to be said about having a process or strategy. Processes give us a structure to follow. As the start of any project is usually chaotic (whether it's related to product design or writing a book, play, or screenplay), processes—however light they are in their form—can help ensure that we're on the right path and stay on it.

Chapter 5 defined *plot* as what you're going to tell your audience when. The role of theme and story development is about defining the red thread, or through line, that binds the parts of the plot, and the whole product experience, together, and then developing the content strategy and information architecture to go with it.

As we've covered in this chapter, in all good stories, things happen for a reason, and all the content of the product and services that we design should be there for a reason as well. To achieve that, we have to make sure that through everything we do and say, we're clear on why and how to refer to that content so it best resonates with our users.

Choose-Your-Own-Adventure Stories and Modular Design

One Page for Every Athlete

In 2011 I was working with a very talented team at my most memorable project to that point, the BBC London 2012 Olympics website. Our job was to work with the rest of the BBC Olympics team and create one page for every athlete, every sport, every country, and every venue, and then of course there were the results and the schedules. It was a massive project with a very hard deadline. I was part of the team that worked on the country, venues, and athlete pages.

The athlete pages in particular formed a challenge in terms of making sure they'd work for every single athlete. The template we defined for athletes had to work for the likes of Usain Bolt, who has participated and won medals in previous Olympic Games, and was likely to win medals in the London Olympics too. News stories were written about him frequently, and he was mentioned in other stories about his country and the events he was competing in. On the other end of the spectrum, we had athletes who'd never come close to winning a medal, and who most likely wouldn't win any during the London Olympics either. Some of them came from countries with so few athletes that there may not be a single news story about them or their country. These were just some of the complexities we were working with.

When we started working on the BBC Olympics project, the redesign of BBC Sport was coming to an end. We had to work within the core templates already defined by BBC Sport, but had freedom, within the guidelines, of what modules we could show and, to some extent, where. This was the first dynamic build project for the BBC, and by keeping the core templates the same and setting rules for when to display the various content modules and the variations, we were able to design and build something that would adapt to every single country, sport, venue, and athlete. This was not a small undertaking, but a rather magical one.

It was by no means a simple project, but it was made possible by minimizing variations and having clearly defined rules. The enormous scope of the BBC coverage, the sheer number of website visitors of varying ages, digital and tech savviness, as well as interest in and knowledge of the Olympics and its sports, made this project an incredibly fascinating one.

A lot has happened in technological developments since then, and more devices have also come to market. We're now at a point where experiences that are tailored and personalized to the individual are more possible than ever before. We, as the authors of the experiences, have the ability to tailor our story to a specific user based on who they are, where they physically are, what they know, what we know about them, and where they are in their journey. That specificity is incredibly powerful, opening possibilities to design and deliver experiences that can help users in their everyday lives, as well as to provide moments of delight. It also offers great possibilities when it comes to modular design in a multidevice landscape. With no two users' journeys being the same, and their backstories, needs, worries, and more all slightly different, we also have an opportunity to allow users to choose the kind of experience they want. This is similar to CYOA books.

CYOA Books and Modular Stories

When you think about the nature of our experiences online, rather than being akin to a traditional linear story, they resemble that of gamebooks. Gamebooks—also called CYOA stories, after the *Choose Your Own Adventure* series that made the genre popular in the 1980s and 1990s—contain multiple storylines and possible endings. In the *Choose Your Own Adventure* series published by Bantam Books, the stories are written in second person, and readers take the role of being the protagonist (Figure 12-1). After reading a few pages, they're faced with two or three options for actions the protagonist could take. Based on that choice, the reader will jump backward or forward to a particular page where they're faced with yet more options, all of which will determine the plot's outcome and lead to an ending. The number of possible endings isn't set, but varies from as many as 44 in the earlier books to just 8 in the later adventures.

FIGURE 12-1

The Cave of Time by Edward Packard, the first book in the *Choose Your Own Adventure* series published by Bantam Books

CYOA has also given rise to *hypertext fiction,* which is a form of electronic literature. In hypertext fiction, users move through the story by clicking hyperlinks that take them from one node to the next in the narrative. The term hypertext fiction is sometimes also used to refer to traditional nonlinear literature, in which internal references provide a kind of interactive narrative. Collectively, the term *interactive fiction* (IF) can also be used, though that also refers to a type of adventure game in which the entire interface can be text only, or text with some accompanying graphics.

The main thing about all of these slight variations or CYOA is that they allow the user to participate in the story. Unlike novels, where the reader is passive and the author has decided in which order the narrative will be told, CYOA stories (like games) enable the reader to be active, making choices about characters and which way the story will unfold. In this sense, the reader of CYOA stories becomes more of a "user" than a "reader." The fact that they are in charge of how they want to experience the story makes CYOA very relevant to the context of product design.

CYOA and Product Design

The multiple storylines, decision points, and possible endings in CYOA stories are similar to the way users experience our products and services. As we covered in Chapter 3, users will increasingly land in the middle of the experiences that we create rather than right at the beginning. Any given page generally has more than one CTA (whether a primary or secondary one), that when clicked or tapped takes the user to a different page or view in the experience. Just as in the CYOA books, this action may take the user to an earlier page or view—for example, the home page—or to a later one, based on the way we've planned out that a user ideally should move through our website. In product design, however, we need to make sure that the storyline and the experience still delivers no matter where the user lands when they first come to us, as well as subsequently based on what they choose to click or tap.

Chapter 10 covered branching narratives in the form of main plots and subplots, and in Chapter 11 emphasized the importance of knowing the story you're telling and ensuring that a red thread runs through it. CYOA brings to product design a good metaphor and framework for thinking through the now somewhat chaotic experiences that we design for. Increasingly, we should be able to let the user determine how the product experience story should unfold.

In CYOA books, the content is planned out so that different storyline combinations can work. Though there are fewer variations compared to the range of possible combinations of entry and exit points for the products and services we design, and possible journeys in between, the need to define these variations is something that we see in product design too. On the BBC Olympics project, we weren't directly involved in defining the rules and possible variations of content for the different pages (e.g., athlete pages). As with most things, product design should ideally be a collaboration across disciplines. The main point is that someone on the team owns the job of ensuring that content is thought through and that the right "rules" are set, related to what to show when, where, and for whom. That way, the experience works in all instances and the narrative comes together no matter what choices the user makes, just as in CYOA books.

The Case for Modularity in Product Design

When you think about how CYOA stories are structured, you can see they're made up of multiple parts just like website and app pages and views. When we worked on the BBC Olympics website in 2011, responsive design wasn't yet common practice, but even so, we approached the design in a modular way. We took this approach to allow the pages to be published dynamically. Whether it's for building dynamic pages or simple responsive websites, approaching design in a modular way has to do with standardizing how content and features are presented as well as ensuring that the content can be displayed on as many devices as possible.

Web designer and consultant Brad Frost writes, "Get your content to go anywhere because it's going to go everywhere."[1] We're not yet at a point where "everywhere" is possible, at least not in the fluid and seamless way that we've seen in various movies like *Minority Report* and concept videos like "A Day Made of Glass." As Urstadt and Frier wrote, it's not difficult to imagine what the future will be like; the difficult part is getting there.[2] While we can't future-proof anything, Frost writes,

---

1 Brad Frost, "For a Future-Frienly Web," Brad Frost (blog), October 2, 2011, *https://oreil.ly/lqubX*.

2 Urstadt, Frier, "Welcome to Zuckerworld."

we can make sure that we make is as future friendly as possible, and part of that is ensuring that what design can go on as many devices as possible.

The future of apps might lie in them sitting in the background, pushing content in the form of cards to a central experience, says Paul Adams, SVP of product at Intercom. The apps would be like notifications rather than working as they do today, with each app having to be opened on its own.[3] As Adams mentions, cards are already a big pattern in design. From Pinterest to Google Now, cards are used to deliver bite-sized content, and the benefit of their modular design is that they can be displayed on a large array of devices. You can also easily imagine what these cards would look like in smart mirrors, interactive surfaces, car interiors, windows, smaller devices like those we've seen in movies like *Her*, or even the prototypes of devices as well as tattoos that allow UIs to be displayed on our skin.

The developments we're seeing—including detail views in notifications and Glance on smart watches and phones—are an early taste of what we'll see more and more of. Twitter Cards and Facebook's previews are also a glimpse of what the future of the web and apps as we know them might be. While these are far too restrictive at the moment and require the content owner to choose from a few predefined templates, they trigger an interesting idea that increasingly we'll be designing our content for everywhere else it's going to go rather than for our own websites and apps.

The Grid attempted to do this with its AI website builder (Figure 12-2). The site will automatically adapt the content you add based on the styling rules that you have defined as well what is best for the device and the content in question.[4] Though v2 of the Grid is currently not available, and v3, according to the website at the time of this writing, is in progress, the Grid provided what may be an early taste of how websites and apps will be built in the future.

---

3 Paul Adams, "The End of Apps as We Know Them," Inside Intercom (blog), October 22, 2014, *https://oreil.ly/T3UCw*.

4 Frederic Lardinois, "The Grib Raises $4.6 Million for Its Intelligent Website Builder," *TechCrunch*, December 2, 2014, *https://oreil.ly/IU8Xh*.

FIGURE 12-2
Some of the Grid's earlier page views

Imagine taking any link from any website and pasting it into another website, and for the content that came with that original link to automatically take the shape and form of the new website. That's essentially what Facebook previews and Twitter Cards do, in a very basic way. The information we see in various types of card-based designs, such as those in the Google app and the websites previously created with the Grid, are similar. However, with Google cards, no link is required. The information that is shown can be based on scraped data, a feed, or an API call. This kind of content fluidity places yet another level of complexity around the content we design, as we lose even more control of how users first come across it, experience it, interact with it, and potentially how it's displayed. In addition, we're now also increasingly designing for VUIs, and the user in some instances will have no visible UI at all. However, even in these instances, the interface is about modularity, not the least because VUIs return one result at a time, and from here, the user makes a decision on how to proceed.

Websites and apps as we know them probably still have a fairly long life span, but the fact that we're increasingly experiencing them in parts rather than wholes is something we have to design for. From a storytelling and content strategy point of view, this change places even more emphasis on understanding the various contexts in which our content might be experienced (as we discussed in Chapter 7). This modularity is also about how it can tell and form part of a story together with content from other apps and websites.

Differences will always exist between device types in terms of their suitability (or lack thereof) to be used in certain situations and locations, and the role they play in our day-to-day lives. However, with a clearly defined content strategy, defined templates for pages and modules, and conditional if-this-then-that rules to inform dynamic publishing, we're in an incredibly exciting position to deliver experiences and content in a way that not only works for as many devices and sizes as possible, but also as many different and unique users as possible. This is one way in which we can better tell stories that resonate with users, specifically.

The Need to Focus on the Building Blocks Rather Than the Page or View

Before we can tell that story to users, we also need to tell it internally and to any clients. In the past, we presented one view of one page. Whether we had a wireframe or a glossy JPEG, we could say with certainty to clients and internal stakeholders what their website would look like, with a few differences between browsers. It was kind of like flipping through and showing pictures in a book or a brochure. The introduction of the first iPhone in 2007 that started to change that. We started to optimize the experience for mobile devices, mostly with custom mobile websites. With that mobile view added to the picture, the "one view" went out the window, and the more devices that appeared on the market, the more diverse and different that view of what the website would look like became.

As the challenges and costs involved with maintaining custom mobile websites grew, and as users' expectation of being able to find the same content and the same functionality irrespective of the device increasingly became the norm, we started to design differently. Rather than focus on the pages, we started focusing on the building blocks, or *modules*, of those pages. Modular design and pattern libraries had been around for many years, as an attempt to streamline both design and development efforts, and to ensure more consistency in the UI that users were presented with. But it became more of a "thing" in 2010 onward,[5] together with responsive design. Today, modular design through module and pattern libraries is something that is widely talked about and used.

When you work with *modular design*, each piece has a purpose and forms a part of something bigger, but also something that can adapt. As a starting point for responsive websites, we should aim to keep the core content and functionality the same and make sure that we can adapt it to the device and the screen in question. While we're not at a point where our experiences are as fluid as John Underkoffler's vision in *Minority Report*, in responsive design the content flows and adapts to the device in question.

Trent Walton, a web designer and founder of Paravel, talks of this flow as something we as designers and developers need to coordinate and calls it *content choreography*. It's a beautiful expression that describes our job in a lovely way. Just like the choreographer of a beautiful ballet performance, we need to steer the movement of the content pieces so that, as he says, "the intended messages are kept at any device and at any width." Through a methodology called *content stacking*, we define the order and the priority of the content across devices and screen sizes and, as we hit one of our defined breakpoints, how it should reflow into the new layout that we've defined. Seamlessly. To make this work, we need to work with modules within modules.

Approaching the UX, design, and the development phase in a modular way is the only way we'll be able to ensure that our content can flow onto as many devices as possible, both current and future ones. It's also the most rewarding and efficient way to both design and build, and it's vital for ensuring that we can use dynamic publishing as a way to deliver content. This is so that what we design works, but more importantly, so that we can make sure it works for each of our users, no matter what entry point they come from, what they've seen or done before, and no matter what choices they make on where to go next. As with all

---

5 Erin Malone, "A History of Patterns in User Experience Design ," *Medium*, March 31, 2017, *https://oreil.ly/ikWIe*.

things product design, there is value in finding ways to visualize these complexities, and here's where turning back to CYOA can help inspire the product design process.

Common Patterns in Choice-Based Stories

Just as Kurt Vonnegut and Christopher Booker identified typical shapes and narrative structures in stories, various analyses have been made on the typical patterns of CYOA books and other choice-based stories and games. Sam Kabo Ashwell, a game creator, identifies a nonexhaustive list of eight patterns and structures. Many works will fall straight into one pattern, but others may involve elements of multiple patterns.[6]

[NOTE]

For the purpose of this book, the terms *playthrough(s)*, *game(s)*, and *player(s)*, as used by Kabo Ashwell in his post, have been changed to *story/stories* and *reader(s)*, respectively.

TIME CAVE

The *Time Cave pattern*, the oldest and most obvious CYOA pattern, involves extensive branching (Figure 12-3). CYOA stories of this type tend to have relatively short storylines, and each choice leads to a different outcome, without any rejoining of the storylines. This pattern strongly encourages the reader to re-read the story.

This pattern has a lot of similarities with product design. The pattern has multiple endings, just as there are multiple endings and exit points in product design. Some are bad (marked in red), just as some endings in product experiences are unhappy. Though readers will re-read the story, they're likely to miss a good deal of the content, just as users of a website are likely to engage and view only part of what that website holds. One main difference is that in the Time Cave pattern, all the choices the user makes are of roughly equal significance, which is not the case in the majority of product experiences.

---

6   Sam Kabo Ashwell, "Standard Patterns in Choice-Based Games," These Heterogeneous Tasks (blog), January 26, 2015, *https://oreil.ly/wL0Yf.*

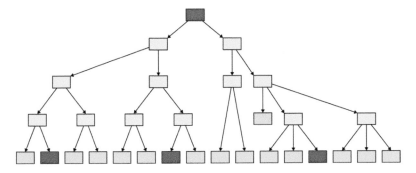

FIGURE 12-3
The Time Cave pattern

Examples of this pattern from traditional storytelling are *The Cave of Time* (Skylark Press) and *Sugarcane Island* (Vermont Crossroads Press), both by Edward Packard, as well as Emily Short's game *A Dark and Stormy Entry*.

GAUNTLET

In contrast to the Time Cave pattern, in the *Gauntlet* the central thread is long rather than broad, with branches that end in either dead ends, backtracking, or rejoining the central thread (Figure 12-4). Some branches have multiple endings, but in these instances they often stem from one final choice that the reader must make.

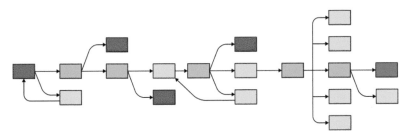

FIGURE 12-4
The Gauntlet structure

As Gauntlet structures usually tell one central story, they can be created in similar ways to a linear story. Most readers will also come across most of the important content, and it's usually apparent to them that they are on one constrained path. Because of this, the presentation of the side branches are of great importance. In CYOA stories of this kind, the Gauntlet pattern can create an atmosphere of a hazardous or difficult world with uncertainties around whether going down one branch may lead to death, just a wrong answer, traveling back in time, a blocked path, or just some scenic details. This uncertainty is naturally not what we're trying to evoke in most of the product experiences that we cover. However, this pattern holds a lot of similarities with more linear product experiences, such as task-based applications in which errors are illustrative of the dead ends, or "deaths" as referred to in the Gauntlet pattern.

Examples of the Gauntlet pattern in traditional storytelling are *Zork: The Forces of Krill* by Steve Meretzky (Doherty Associates) and *Our Boys In Uniform*, a game by Megan Stevens.

BRANCH AND BOTTLENECK

In the *Branch and Bottleneck* structure, the story branches off but regularly rejoins, usually around common events that all versions of the story share (Figure 12-5). What makes this structure different from the Gauntlet is that it relies heavily on *state tracking:* a record of past choices and actions are tracked and used to determine what to present next. If there isn't any state tracking, then you're most likely dealing with a Gauntlet pattern.

This type of pattern in CYOA is often heavily governed by time and used to reflect the growth of the reader/character, allowing the reader to create a fairly distinct story while still keeping a quite manageable plot.

In general, Branch and Bottleneck stories tend to have quite similar storylines to begin with, and for the later state tracking to work, they need to be fairly large as well as involve enough time. This is in order to accumulate the changes that need to happen before it's possible to show the result of those changes reflected in the storyline. This is similar in product design to needing enough usage and the right data around what users have seen and interacted with in order to deliver contextual, tailored, and personalized products.

An example of the Branch and Bottleneck pattern is the *Long Live the Queen* game; the pattern is also a guiding principle of Choice of Games and non-IF games.

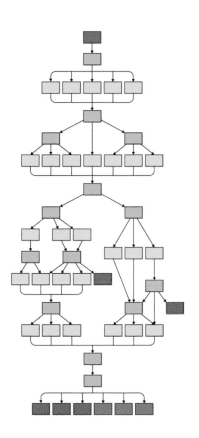

FIGURE 12-5
The Branch and
Bottleneck structure

QUEST

In the *Quest pattern*, distinct storyline branches are formed based on the decision the user makes (Figure 12-6). These branches tend to rejoin a small number of winning endings, often only one, and have a modular structure to each branch, with small tightly grouped clusters of nodes. There is generally no backtracking, and re-emerging is quite common. Quest structures tend to be large and include some form of state tracking, or they do poorly.

The tightly clustered nodes result in multiple ways to approach a single situation within one cluster, and there is a lot of interconnectedness. However, because the narrative is often fragmented or episodic, some parts of the story may not have any impact on the big picture. This is something we're increasingly seeing in product design, with the number of possible entry points growing but without the specific touch point in question having much of an impact on the product experience itself, though each touch point is connected in terms of messaging and desired CTA.

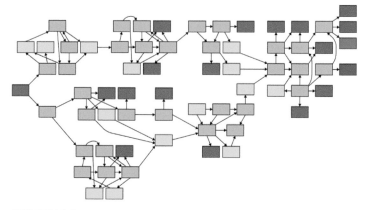

FIGURE 12-6
The Quest structure

The Quest structure category involves some of the biggest CYOAs and is well-suited for stories that involve purpose-led journeys of exploration and those that focus on setting, as they tend to be organized by geography rather than time. Examples of this structure are the *Fighting Fantasy* books by Steve Jackson and Ian Livingstone.

OPEN MAP

In the *Open Map* structure, travel between the nodes is reversible, creating a static geography and a world in which the reader can explore and play indefinitely (Figure 12-7). Though time still plays a role, this pattern is structured by geography. This geography is often literal and relies on extensive state tracking, both explicit and secret, for the narrative to progress.

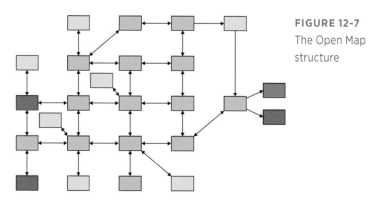

FIGURE 12-7
The Open Map structure

This pattern is often used to imitate the default style parser IF, and the narrative tends to become slower paced and less directed. There is plenty of time for reader to explore the world, and often they spend less time advancing the story. Thinking of product design, this resembles products of a social nature. An initial part requires learning about the platform before signing up. Thereafter, however, the main focus is on getting familiar with the platform. As that happens, exploration of the content and the different sections the platform contains takes over, and the narrative of the experience slows down.

An example of this structure in traditional storytelling is *Chemistry and Physics* by Caelyn Sandel and Carolyn VanEseltine.

SORTING HAT

In the *Sorting Hat* structure, the story branches heavily in the early game and rejoins heavily too, often transforming it into a Branch and Bottleneck structure where it's determined which major branch the user gets assigned to. Often these major branches are quite linear, at times looking like Gauntlets. Other times they are choiceless, straight paths. Sorting Hat structures rely heavily on state tracking in the early game and bottlenecks when it comes to the decision points.

With its Branch and Bottleneck structure early on and the more linear structure in the second half, games with a Sorting Hat structure are a compromise between the breadth of the more open structures and the depth of the linear ones. Generally, the reader has a lot of influence over the way the story unfolds. Although it may feel like all choices will lead to the same thread, the author may at times end up having to write several different games.

Examples of this structure from traditional storytelling are the visual novel *Katawa Shoujo* (Four Leaf Studios) and the game *Magical Makeover*.

FLOATING MODULES

The *Floating Modules* structure is possible only in computer-based works. In this structure, there are no trees, no central plot, and no through line, though there may be scattered twigs and branches. Instead, modular encounters become available to the reader either randomly or based on state.

In this structure it's hard for the author to make assumptions about prior events and it's generally a hard structure for the author to grasp. In order for the Floating Modules structure to work, it needs a large amount of content, or it tends to turn into a linear structure. When it comes to the play mechanics, these are largely about exposing stats to the reader.

LOOP AND GROW

In *Loop and Grow* structures, the narrative revolves around a central thread of some kind that loops around over and over and comes back to the same point (Figure 12-8). Because of state tracking, however, each time around, new options may be unlocked and others closed off. This pattern is very general and can coexist with many others.

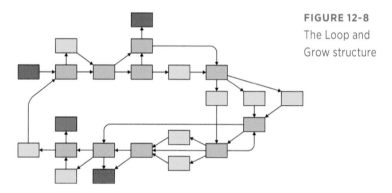

FIGURE 12-8

The Loop and Grow structure

In Loop and Grow structures, the regularity of the world is emphasized while still maintaining a narrative momentum. There generally has to be some kind of justification for why whole parts of the narrative repeat, and these are often related to the reader performing routine activities, engaging in time travel, or performing tasks. Because of the regularity of this structure, many stories of this kind involve a struggle against stagnation or confinement. Applied to product design, this structure resembles task-based applications and software with online banking examples. Looking at traditional storytelling, the games *Trapped in Time* by Simon Christiansen and *Solarium* by Anya Johanna DeNiro are some examples.

Exercise: Common Patterns in Choice-Based Stories

With your own product in mind which pattern most corresponds to the narrative structure of the product experience?

Key Principles from CYOA Structures Applied to Product Design

The preceding CYOA structures and accompanying diagrams are a lot smaller and simpler than the actual works (Figure 12-9). What they illustrate, however, like the typical shapes of stories (as covered in Chapter 9) is the basic pattern of different types of CYOA stories. These provide a foundation for understanding, defining, and working with different types of CYOA stories.

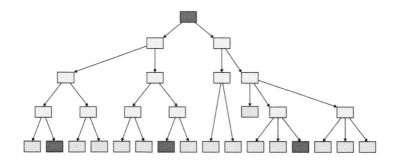

The Cave of Time (Edward Packard, 1979)

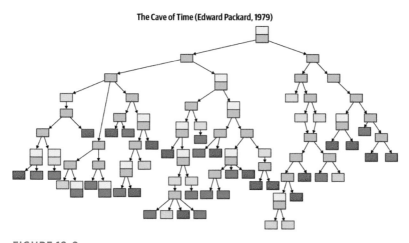

FIGURE 12-9

The Time Cave pattern (top) and map of the book *The Cave of Time* (bottom)[7]

---

7 Sam Kabo Ashwell, "CYOA structure: The Cave of Time," These Heterogenous Tasks (blog), August 5, 2011, *https://oreil.ly/Jvdaf.*

Though there'll always be exceptions, these CYOA patterns help identify some key principles that can guide authors in terms of how best to make their CYOA story work, as well as provide inspiration that sparks the imagination. Some of the principles are also of particular relevance to product design.

BRANCHING NARRATIVES

One of the main things about CYOA stories is the *branching narratives* that form from story nodes and the subsequent choices the reader makes. In some instances, the story has main and secondary branches, but in others, no branch of the story is more important than any other.

Applying it to product design

While all CYOA stories have to start from one central point, what makes product experiences so complicated is that they can start, and end, anywhere. Additionally, at any point the user can choose to go elsewhere, both through the CTAs that we've deliberately defined and designed into the experience, and also based on their own desires. The onward journey may involve using the main navigation, searching on the website or app, or even leaving it altogether.

The job for us is to, as much as possible, define and design the branches of the product experience narrative in such a way that they keep the user on track, for as long as it benefits them. Our goal is not to keep the user on our website or app just for the sake of it, or for the sake of an engagement metric, but to provide actual value and steer the user the best we can, even when that means off and away from our website or app.

Exercise: Branching Narratives

For your product or service, define the following:

- What are the main branches of the product experience?
- Are there branches that haven't been carefully thought through?
- What can you do to help make the branched narrative even clearer?

A CENTRAL THREAD

Some CYOA structures, like the Gauntlet, are structured around a *central thread*. Others have more branching structures, but in some instances, those branches can, in turn, have their own central thread.

Applying it to product design

In most product experiences, there is still a dominant branch, at least to begin with. Chapter 10 defined main plots and subplots; types of sub-plots are alternate journeys, unhappy journeys, and branched journeys. Here, the dead ends that some of the branches in CYOA stories lead to are most akin to unhappy journeys, whereas branches that rejoin are most akin to alternate journeys.

No matter what type of main plot and subplot we have in the product experiences that we define, a red thread should always be present, that through line that connects it all. Sometimes it's more connected in the product narrative, and other times it's more disjointed, but with a clear connection between the different parts nonetheless.

Exercise: A Central Thread

For your product or service, what is the central thread, or red thread, that runs through the experience narrative?

STORY NODES

Though some CYOA structures don't have a central thread, all have nodes that bind the story branches together, and from where the reader makes a choice. These *story nodes* make up the backbone of the sto-ryline and form a big piece of the CYOA narrative puzzle. Even if they aren't directly linked through linear narrative, they connect to each other in a disjointed way. If you change something in one part of the CYOA story, it might affect a story node elsewhere.

Applying it to product design

In product design, there are always some key parts of the experience that bind it all together. Being able to see these pieces and how every-thing fits together is key for both CYOA stories and product experience design. When we talk about modular design and pattern libraries, we often talk about main modules and module variations.

A simple example is a hero module that when used on the home page has a certain layout, but when used on a secondary page has a slightly different and less "hero" layout (e.g., just showing a title and a CTA, while on the home page a description is included). Additionally, some key modules that are reused again and again make up larger parts of the pages and views, and these modules play a big part in pushing the user's experience forward. Related posts are one such example.

Just as changing something in a CYOA story may have an effect elsewhere, often changing something in a module that is used on one page or view may also (involuntarily) change something on another page or view where that same module is being used. This brings us to the next principle, which is interconnectedness.

Exercise: Story Nodes

For your product, think about the following:

- What are the key points in the product experience? Think back to plot points and opening and closing scenes from Chapter 5.
- Identify some of the main modules that your product's pages and views are made up of. Think about these as the story nodes that help push the product experience narrative forward.

INTERCONNECTEDNESS

In order for the CYOA narrative to work, something needs to connect the story nodes to one another and to connect the reader to the nodes, or the story will fall apart. Many of the structures identified by Kabo Ashwell have a high level of *interconnectedness*. The one that stands out the most in relation to product design is the Quest structure, which provides numerous ways to approach a single situation.

Applying it to product design

This interconnected structure is similar to the multiple entry points we work with in product design: often numerous routes exist into the same page or view. Additionally, in product design everything is connected. As with the connected story nodes, each module that is being used to tell the story of the product is connected to other parts of the product experience through the same use of that module, as well as to the bigger picture. A change on one end might have an impact on the experience elsewhere. In addition, in order to ensure that you don't end up with too many pieces in your content module puzzle, the general approach is to reuse the same module pattern and page or view layouts wherever it makes sense from a content, user, and business point of view.

Exercise: Interconnectedness

With your own product in mind, what are the things that connect the various parts of the product experience?

STATE TRACKING

In order to know which part of the story should be told to the reader next, and even to advance the story at all, many CYOA structures rely on *state tracking*. In turn, for the state tracking to work, the CYOA story itself needs to be fairly large and to allow some time to pass so that the change that is required can be produced.

Applying it to product design

State tracking is of particular importance because of the trends we're now seeing in product design and marketing. As covered earlier in this book, and particularly in Chapter 3, there are growing opportunities for using data as part of the product experience to deliver more value to users. In order for this to work, we need to know what data to look at and what that content, in turn, should result in.

With the advances in IoT, smart homes, chatbots, and VUIs, we'll increasingly become accustomed to interfaces that we talk to using more natural language, and those experiences will feel more personal. The rise of the tap-of-a-button expectations, providing access to everything at the tap of a button, is also doing its part in increasing users' expectations of getting what they want, when they want it. Instant gratification is a thing, and soon that'll start transcending our experiences on websites too, beyond what is already in place today.

The possibility to delivering tailored experiences through dynamic publishing is in one way quite similar to the CYOA books, only multiplied. At almost every single key point in the experience, there's a possibility to give users what's relevant to them specifically. That doesn't mean that we'll all necessarily have completely different experiences of the same website, but that what we see and how much we see of it will be tailored to us, based on where we are and what we're using at that point in time.

Exercise: State Tracking

With your product in mind, give some examples of the following:

- How state tracking is currently being used, if at all.
- How it could be used (more/differently) to add value for the user.
- How it could be used (more/differently) to add value for the business.

FLOATING MODULES

As mentioned earlier, the Floating Modules structure is one that is really hard for the author to pull off and one that's possible only in computer-based works. *Floating modules* are mentioned only in the Floating Modules structure, so it's not really a general principle. Still, it's one that's important to bring up in the context of product design because it reflects the way we increasingly are having to think about product experiences.

Applying it to product design

As we covered earlier in this chapter, increasingly we're having to prepare for our content to go anywhere and for our user to be coming from and going to anywhere. As more product experiences take place away from the traditional page or view that we've so far been used to, we'll need to think about product experiences as branched narratives made up of story nodes and floating modules with a high level of interconnectedness. Though we're still able to, and even have to, visualize and define these branched narratives through the possible main plots and subplots that the product experience can take, we won't be able to define all the possible variations. And that's not required. However, having a framework for approaching these new types of experiences benefits us immensely, and this is where we can take some inspiration from how CYOA stories are worked through.

Exercise: Floating Modules

With your product in mind and thinking of the metaphor of floating modules, give some examples of the following:

- What are some parts of the product experience that could be experienced as floating modules?
- Where could these floating modules live or be experienced? (e.g., as part of a VUI, as a card displayed on social media, in a feed).

What Product Design Can Learn from CYOA

The core idea behind CYOA books is that the user will choose how the story unfolds. It's based, of course, on predefined options, but nonetheless, what happens next is in the hands of the user. As much as we try to design the path that the users of our products and services should take, it's almost always in their hands to determine when and where to begin and when and where to end. Naturally, there are points of no return where users are met with errors or unclear interfaces that cause an unwanted stop rather than a continuation of their journey, but overall, it's up to the users to choose in which order, when, where, and how they'll experience our product or service.

As we've covered so far in this chapter, there are a few similarities and shared challenges between CYOA and product design. Some of the challenges are the same, as well as some of the approaches that are taken to help with those.

IDENTIFYING BRANCHING NARRATIVES

In CYOA stories, the basic concept is to give the reader preselected choices for what will happen next. In some instances, there'll be fewer choices, and in others, there'll be more, just as in product design.

Much of what we've covered earlier in this book should help with identifying branching narratives. Working through the plot as covered in Chapter 5, and using something like the index card method, will help identify the points where the product narrative starts to branch off. Once you get into working with journeys and flows, and look at the main plot and subplots as covered in Chapter 10, even more detail is added. There are however, instances where the branches of the narratives are on more equal terms, if not equal, with each other similarly to the choices that the reader makes in CYOA stories. As one example of branched narratives, we work with machine learning and dynamic content that swaps out elements, whole modules, or in some instances whole pages based on active and passive choices that the user has made before, or not made, as well as based on data. Bots and conversational interfaces are also prime examples of experiences with branched narratives based on the choices that the user makes.

Applying it to product design

In product design, we don't always take a systematic approach to identifying the different branches of the experience. However, working through key aspects can help you identify the branches and define the experience around it. Speaker Cassie Phillipps outlines four facets of branching stories and advises that you approach them in the following order:[8]

Story

> Make sure you have a meaningful and impactful story and that you aren't distracted by offering too many choices, as this can slow the story process and hurt the end result. Instead, focus on the outline to begin with and make the story loose enough to change but tight enough so you know the beat of the story works. Applied to product design, we must ensure that we have a clear understanding of what the experience narrative should be and that we don't confuse the user of that experience with too many choices.

Branches

> Your major branches should lead to a changes in scenes or characters as a result of the choice that is being made. The branches could also provide unique ways of reaching the same goal. Two ways to identify branches are to work backward from major conflicts or goals and to reorder scenes. Applied to product design, it's particularly applicable to look at how the experience works if the user goes through it in a slightly haphazard way; for example, landing on a product page rather than the home page.

---

8 Cassie Phillipps, "All Choice No Consequence: Efficiently Branching Narratives," Game Narrative Summit, 2016, *https://oreil.ly/qdV2A*.

Dialogue

In meaningful story branches, the dialogue makes a difference. As much possible, it should be kept succinct because attention spans are short. In addition, to further the narrative, the characters should have unique voices and there should be clear consequences and goals tied to key parts in the dialogue.

Choices

When it comes to presenting choices in branching narratives, these can often be found in the characters' possible reactions (e.g., will they respond X, Y or Z?). Other areas where choices often present themselves are in character defining traits like attitudes, and in unavoidable consequences. Creating choices requires paying attention to details, including giving each option appropriate weight, ensuring that each choice has a clear consequence, and avoiding bad choices. Bad choices may have the following characteristics:

- *False*—The player-character immediately negates the choice.

- *Bad*—The story interprets a different meaning than what was presented.

- *Vague*—The player doesn't fully understand the options.

The same guiding principles can be applied to product design and, again, particularly to bots and conversational interfaces. The first aspect about choices can often be found in character reactions, is a useful one to keep in mind and tie back to the emotional response to a product experience.

VISUALIZING CONTENT AND BRANCHING NARRATIVES

As a reader of CYOA books, it can be quite hard to keep track of where you've come from. In the republished versions of the *Choose Your Own Adventure* books, the Chooseco publishing company included maps of the hidden narrative structure of the stories (Figure 12-10). Each arrow represents a page, a circle represents a decision point, the squares represent endings.[9]

---

9 Sarah Laskow, "These Maps Reveal the Hidden Structures of 'Choose Your Own Adventure' Books," *Atlas Obscura*, June 13, 2017, https://oreil.ly/rNO2C.

Other than being lovely visualizations, these mappings show that the books don't follow the same structure and that at times readers will have two, three, or even just one option at a decision point. Fans and bloggers such as Kabo Ashwell have been creating these visualizations for years. Another approach is to visualize the type of ending the different branches lead to, which is something that the computer scientist Christian Swinheart has done (Figures 12-11 and 12-12).

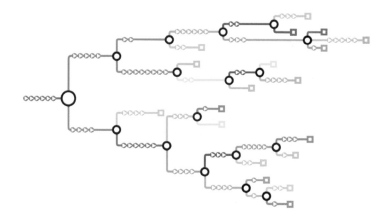

FIGURE 12-10

The hidden narrative structures in the CYOA book *The Case of the Silk King*, courtesy of Chooseco

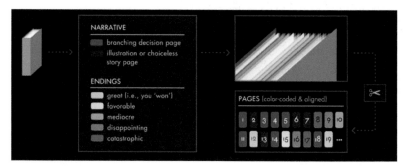

FIGURE 12-11

Visualization by Christian Swinehart where every page in the CYOA book has been color coded based on the number of choices offered and the goodness of the ending (*http://samizdat.co/cyoa/*)

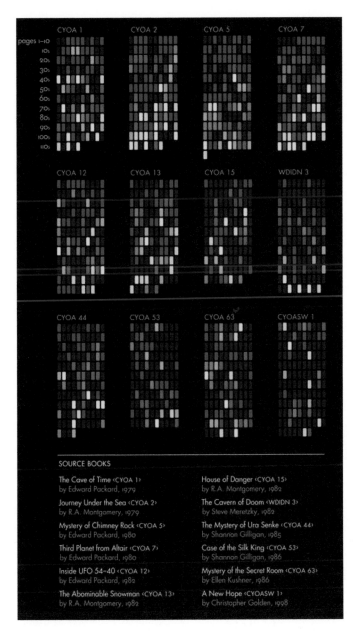

FIGURE 12-12
Visualization by Christian Swinehart of 12 CYOA books laid out next to each other with the oldest at the top, showing a gradual decline in the number of endings in the newer books (*http://samizdat.co/cyoa/*)

Applying it to product design

Many of the structures covered earlier in this chapter relied on state tracking to a lesser or greater extent to identify what the next part of the story should be. In product design, particularly when dynamic elements are included, having defined the criteria for swapping out one module for something else is key. This criteria might mean that just one module is changed and the rest of the product story remains the same. Or it may be that the product experience branches off from there based on data about the user as well as actions, or lack thereof, that they've taken.

When we think through and plan out content for the experiences that we design (websites, apps, bots, voice-based, or physical experiences), we can draw a lot from CYOA and visualizations of these stories. Those who have worked on a complex piece of software or website know how beneficial flow charts are for both defining and designing for each eventuality. The more complex the software or experience, the more value in and need for ensuring that all eventualities are captured, from what a user might do, to the response of the system, including error messages and pages.

Summary

Users' journeys to, with, and onward from our products are becoming less linear and often start in the middle rather than at the home page, which we'd previously considered the beginning. As a result, the need to ensure that the UX works no matter what is ever more important.

As we've covered in this chapter, branching narratives will always exist in product design, just as they do in traditional storytelling. With the number of devices and connected homes on the rise, the complexities of what we're designing are increasing. But the opportunities are increasing, too. Though we'd like to think that we can control how the user moves from one part of the experience to the next, the best thing we can do is to embrace our loss of control. It's up to the users to choose how and what they interact with and for us to ensure that the experience works no matter what their selections are.

CYOA stories teach us about the power and beauty of letting the user define how the story is told, and show us that being clear about our choices helps us ensure that the experience story comes together. CYOA also provides useful references for visualizing the complexities and seeing how the various parts of the experience come together. It can also help us define what content to show next, or what module to show instead of a default one based on who the user is, their context, and which part of the product narrative that they've so far experienced.

In the next chapter, we'll take a look at using storytelling to bring all of this together into pages and views that tell a clear and valuable story to the user.

Applying Scene Structure to Wireframes, Designs, and Prototypes

The Things That Didn't Fit Above the Fold

DURING MY FIRST YEARS at Dare, we frequently had conversations with clients about getting content *above the fold*. This phrase was originally used to refer to the upper half of a newspaper page. It has since come to mean the part of the web page that is visible without scrolling and that contains the most important content. All our wireframes had a nice dashed line indicating where the fold was likely to be, to both help us and to preempt questions from clients. It worked, but the question usually still came up about getting even more to fit above the fold. It wasn't just at Dare that we had these conversations. Numerous discussions arose in articles and blog posts, and although I didn't go to any UX meetups or conferences at this time, I'm sure plenty of discussions took place there too.

At one point, the trend was to design websites that didn't go below the fold. They extended down only as far as the browser screen would go, and all the content would fit within the visible area of the screen. On those projects, there weren't any discussions about the fold. Instead, we discussed right and left navigation as well as big canvas-style websites, almost like a big flat lay of pages that you'd move up and down, and left and right. Gradually, however, more and more research started suggesting that users do actually scroll, and though the fold is still important to consider, all the content doesn't have to go above the fold.

With the introduction of the iPhone in 2007 and the iPad in 2010, just how much we could fit above the fold shrunk. We also started to see a new shift from users rarely navigating all the way to the bottom of the page to them glancing over the middle and spending more time at the bottom. As with most things, the reason for this and how it came to be was an intricate play involving multiple factors. It was a mixture of the ease of swiping all the way to the bottom with the flick of a thumb, and the fact that we started to place some navigation links at the bottom of mobile views to address the decreased amount of space that was available to show top navigation. Last, but not least, the use of "more like this" style content at the bottom of pages on both desktop and mobile devices became more common.

Together these started to establish patterns of learned behavior among users. As they increasingly found more and more useful content at the bottom of pages, the expectation that this would be present on other pages grew. The more users expected it, the more we supplied it, and so on. As a result, when you look at reports of how users now engage with longer pages, the focus is still at the top, but rather than trickling off toward the end of the page, we're now seeing an increase in activity there and less so in the middle of pages.

With the introduction of responsive design and the insurgence of one-page websites, the concern for the fold went right out the window for many designers and some clients. Still, today we see many of websites that have the majority of their content below the fold. Full-width imagery that automatically fills the browser window became popular and led to a substantial page weight increase. Among many startups in particular, the big statement is what leads the experience, and the focus is on that first impression and a "wow" reaction rather than being able to find the most critical content or functionality above the fold.

The debate and the importance of the fold is, however, still a valid one. While many of us, as well as clients and internal stakeholders, are now more confident that users do scroll, we still need to make sure that we choreograph the story of the page. We should draw the user in, make it clear that there is more below the fold, and then keep their attention and direct them where we and they want to go. We need to choreograph the opening scene of each page and how the rest of that scene will play out, as well as link to the other scenes in the story.

THE ROLE OF SCENES AND SCENE STRUCTURE IN STORYTELLING

In traditional storytelling, scenes are considered the building blocks of the story. In a scene, the character(s) will act and react to the events that are taking place, the places they visit, and the people they meet. Just like a larger sequence in a film, a scene is made up of a beginning, a middle, and an end, and it should focus on a definite point of tension that takes the story forward.

When defining the scenes of your story, it's useful to think of them as "an unbroken flow of action from one incident to another."[1] No major time lapse or leap from one setting to another should take place. The characters may well walk from one place to another without breaking the scene and, when you think of it in film or TV terms, the camera would just follow along. At times, writers get caught up with deciding whether something should be one scene or two—whether a small time gap or change of location constitutes a new scene or can be considered part of one scene. The general advice here is that if it feels like the same scene, treat it as such. Another useful way of thinking about what makes for a scene is that in a scene, something changes, so something has changed when the scene is over.

These changes indicate, again, that each scene should have a beginning, a middle, and an end. Just as with any other story, the order in which you tell the story of the scene will impact how it's perceived, as well as how the rest of the story hangs together with earlier and subsequent scenes.[2] The way to position a scene depends on where in the story it's placed. It also depends on the type of story you're writing and how long it's going to be. Novelist C.S. Lakin provides these guidelines for the types of scenes a story should include:[3]

- *Opening scenes* should set up your promise and be loaded with character. This is where you want to introduce the backstory.

- *Middle scenes* should carry the conflict and raise the stakes. It's also where the twists should take place.

1 Ali Luke, "What Is a Scene?" Aliventures (blog), March 21, 2016, https://oreil.ly/wplr9.

2 Martha Alderson, "7 Essential Elements of Scene + Scene Structure Exercise," Jane Friedman (blog), August 29, 2012, https://oreil.ly/2iEqT.

3 C.S. Lakin, "8 Steps to Writing a Perfect Scene—Every Time," Jerry Jenkins (blog), https://oreil.ly/UWewi.

- *Climactic scenes* should build to a riveting climax. These scenes may be shorter and filled with both action and emotion.

If a writer struggles with a scene, or if it simply doesn't work, it's usually not because the dialogue is poor or because the setting is poorly explained. It's more often than not due to the scene structure and a lack of pacing. Further ahead in this chapter, we'll look at ways to plan and structure scenes.

Exercise: The Role of Scenes and Scene Structure in Storytelling

Think about a book that you've read recently, or a series or movie that you've watched:

- What scenes stood out for you?
- Why would you define them as scenes?
- What was the beginning, middle, and end of the scene?
- What was the tension point that caused the change?

The Role of Scenes and Scene Structure in Product Design

When we think about scenes in product design, it's closest to our hearts to think of these as the pages and views of our product or service. These are the building blocks of our product story. While scenes no doubt could include external factors of the specific time and setting in which the action related to the product experience takes place, in this chapter, we'll be using scenes in relation to the pages or views of our product experience and focusing only on the on-screen aspects. As for what goes on outside of the screen, this is what we covered in Chapter 7.

As presented in Chapter 5, scenes are part of the building blocks of a story, smaller than sequences and acts but larger than shots.

This is how we defined the building blocks:

Acts

The beginning, middle, and end of an experience

Sequences
> Life cycle stages *or* key user journeys, depending on what you work with

Scenes
> Steps *or* main steps in a journey *or* pages/views

Shots
> Elements of a page/view *or* detailed steps of a journey

Setting
> The environment and context in which the product experience takes place

Many times things are a bit backward when it comes to the pages and views we present to our users and customers. As the New York–based web and development agency Kanz writes on its blog, "We're selling information to people at the wrong time, in the wrong order,"[4] resulting in experiences that are both confusing and overwhelming. Just as traditional storytellers at times struggle with defining a scene—more precisely, where it begins and where it ends—in product design we at times struggle with defining what content belongs on one page versus another. Sometimes we include too much content, resulting in a confusing page experience for the user. Other times we include too little, and the user is left to click or tap more than should be necessary to get more content. As Kanz says, we don't always present the right information at the right time.

Just as scene structure matters in traditional storytelling, it matters in product design. A wireframe or design, no matter how low or high fidelity, always tells a story. It should be an inspiring story that clearly helps the users on their way to achieve their goal, whatever their quest might be. When we don't get the hierarchy of information right, we also don't get the story right. In this context, it's also important to look at pages and views as mini-stories. Each page or view will have an opening scene that sets up the new page that the user has come to. As they scroll further down, they go through the middle scenes and the closing scene.

---

4 "Cinematography in User Experience Design," Kanze (blog), *https://oreil.ly/HI718*.

Next, we'll look at the role of scenes and scene structure in relation to the pages and views of our products.

[NOTE]

In this chapter, we are talking about wireframes, designs, and prototypes, but when what we refer to applies across all three, we'll refer to the *page* or the *view* instead.

THE STORY OF THE PAGE OR VIEW

Earlier in this book, we talked of sequences in film and in relation to product design (e.g., user journeys) as being mini-stories with their own three acts. That concept can also be applied to wireframes, designs, and prototypes. Together all of the pages or views will make up one story, and each page or view will be part of that story. But each page or view also tells a story in and of itself with a beginning, a middle, and an end.

Just think of the role of opening scenes in films and TV series, which we referenced in Chapter 5. This is the scene that "sets the scene" for what is to follow.

In product design, the opening scene of any page or view is what the users see above the fold. This is the beginning of your page story. No matter where the users have come from, this is what they see first. This opening scene sets the expectations for the rest of the page and what user will judge the page on. Does it appear to be what they are looking for? Does it look interesting? Do they want to find out more?

The job of the rest of the page or view is to guide the user through the content and to get the balance right. As Xinyi Chen of the Nielsen Norman Group states, "Relevant information is 'signal,' while irrelevant information is 'noise.'"[5] The goal for any UX designer or visual designer is to ensure that there is a high signal-to-noise ratio, in terms of content and page design, and CTAs showing how to continue the journey. Just like the *Finding Nemo* example in Chapter 5, the way in which we tell our story will impact how the audience understands it

---

5 Xinyi Chen, "Signal-to-Noise Ratio," *Nielsen Norman Group,* September 9, 2018, *https:// oreil.ly/0uO-V.*

and what they take away from it. Further on in this chapter, we'll cover how to go about defining the narrative structure of your page and why it's beneficial to test and think about whether the page still tells a story if you strip away all the styling.

Exercise: The Story of the Page or View

With your own product in mind, or one that you use on a regular basis, think about the home page:

- What story should the page tell new users? Make this assessment without looking at the page.
- What story should the page tell the user as it currently is? This time, looking at the page.

THE STORY BELOW THE FOLD

We tend to be so focused on the things we and users will see immediately that we forget about the opportunity to deliver something wonderful, and perhaps even unexpected, as the user starts to move down the page. During the summer of 2012, I worked on a big redesign of a global makeup brand's website. One of the objectives of the new site was to educate consumers about choosing the right makeup.

We defined a content structure: after a set number of products in the product grid, we'd feature a short but aesthetically pleasing piece of advice related to the kind of products the user was looking at. We also defined that after a set number of rows, we'd feature a full-width product module to break up the grid (Figure 13-1). Both of these variations in the grid were defined to keep engaging users by capturing their attention and providing them with a reason to keep on scrolling to see what was coming next.

My boss at the time, Mark Bell, went through a period where he pulled up Swedish online newspapers, like that of Aftonbladet.se, as great examples for feeding the browsing experience. As you scrolled to the end of a news article, you didn't have to click back to the home page; but instead, the website would automatically show you the home page again so you could just keep on scrolling.

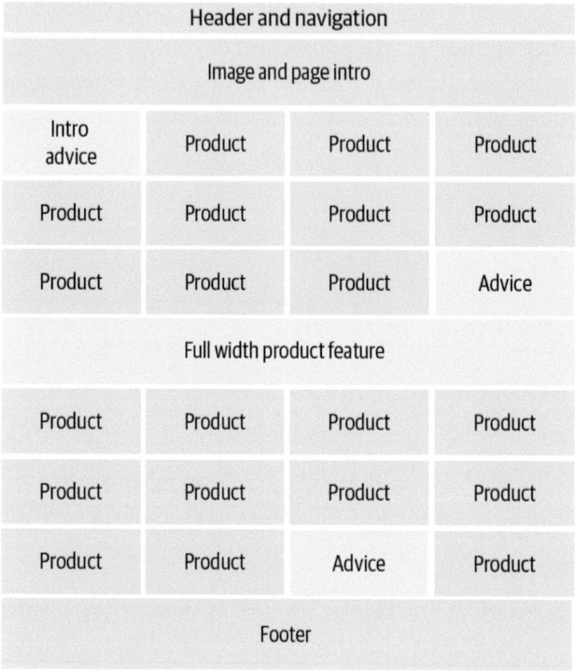

Header and navigation			
Image and page intro			
Intro advice	Product	Product	Product
Product	Product	Product	Product
Product	Product	Product	Advice
Full width product feature			
Product	Product	Product	Product
Product	Product	Product	Product
Product	Product	Advice	Product
Footer			

FIGURE 13-1

Deliberately breaking up the grid

In some cases, like a news site, that's exactly what you want users to do: you want to keep them on the website, exploring and engaging with more articles. In other instances, like an ecommerce site, you want to move them along the purchase funnel from discovery to checkout with as few clicks and interruptions as possible. In other cases, you want to connect pieces of either informative or aspirational content at the right time to what's being shown on the page. Whatever the purpose of our pages, we need to keep flow and the storyline of the page in mind.

The *New York Times* was the first to come out with interactive content pieces like that of "Snow Fall" (Figure-13-2). As you scrolled down the page, additional pieces of the story are introduced through the use of parallax scrolling. This approach builds a fascinating narrative that draws you in and leaves you wanting more.

These kinds of experiences are great for certain types of content, but we need to make sure that we're not distracting the users from what they are trying to do, or from what we would like them to do. Having these goals identified is critical when you start to work through your pages and views. We should also have defined experience goals to help provide a reminder of what's important when, as well as what level the experience should be at. Defining the purpose of the page or view, as well as what a first-time and returning user should be able to do, is also useful, as we'll cover shortly.

FIGURE 13-2
The interactive news story "Snow Fall"[6]

As a guiding principle, think of what's *above the fold* to be the opening scene of your page. Applied to traditional storytelling, this is the "scene" that needs to grab the audience's attention and draw them in so they continue reading or watching. That's how you should think about it for product design too. What's *below the fold* is the main content of the story you're telling. Make sure it's an exciting one, a full-on story that draws the user in at the right point, tying in to the desired action you want the user to take as well as the emotional response you're hoping to evoke.

THE PAGE OR VIEW AS ONE PART OF THE STORY

Though the user of the finished product will see only one page or scene at a time, the way we structure a page should also help users create a mental picture of how this page or scene fits in with the rest. No matter if this is the first or the last page or view that they experience, it should contain enough to make sure that it works as either the beginning of the story, or the middle, or the end.

---

6 John Branch, "Snow Fall," *The New York Times,* 2012, *https://oreil.ly/gb0u_.*

Chapter 3 described how fragmented user journeys have become and how, more often than not, the only context the user has as they land on our website for the first time is what accompanied the link they clicked or tapped. In the majority of cases, this will be what they see in their search results, or what accompanies the social post that they interacted with. Here it helps to think back to CYOA books (as covered in Chapter 12), and how to plan out the narrative so that it works no matter in what order the user experiences it.

In Chapter 10, we talked about substories and alternative journeys. These jumping-off points should be clear to users, no matter what page or view they are on. We should help them anticipate what they'll get if they click or tap that link or button, as well as what they'll see if they choose to go back or to a different section or page. This is where the importance of playing to users' mental models is so important, as we talked about in Chapter 11.

THE STORY OF THE WIREFRAME AND UX PROTOTYPE

The story we tell with our design isn't just for the intended users. A big part of what we do before our design gets to the user is to tell stories internally and to clients. When telling the story of the page or view to this audience, wireframes and prototypes play a big role.

Compared to traditional storytelling, *wireframes* are similar to screen-plays. Wikipedia describes a screenplay as a unique literary form; just like a musical score, it is "intended to be interpreted on the basis of other artists' performance, rather than serving as a finished product for the enjoyment of its audience."[7] The same applies to wireframes. They aren't supposed to be a direct reflection of the finished products, and for the visual designers to just "color it in." Similar to how a screen-play describes the scenes in which the story takes place and provides stage directions, a wireframe describes the hierarchy of content. A wireframe describes content goes where, the intended length, features and functionality, and so forth in order to help not only designers and developers bring it to life, but internal stakeholders and clients as well.

Chapter 8 showed how storyboards are sometimes used as inspiration to help define the plot of the movie. Other times they are used as the deliverable to help demonstrate how that story should be told

---

7 "Theories on Writing a Screenplay," Wikipedia, *https://oreil.ly/h3hD4.*

and brought to life. Here, we can draw some parallels to prototypes. *Prototypes* serve as a way for the team to test out interactions and flows in order to help shape and define the product experience. Prototypes also serve as a tool for capturing how that product experience should be told.

When it comes to their role and story that wireframes and prototypes tell on your project, the deciding factor should be based on what will help the project, the team, and the client or internal stakeholders the most. How we use them, what level of detail we go into, the number of notes and annotations, as well as how high-fidelity both the wireframes and the prototype are, should all be based on what purpose they help to serve.

Thinking about the overall page or view as one part of the story, as well as a story in and of itself, forms a good foundation for both identifying and defining the story of the page or view. There are, however, more specific lessons we can draw from traditional storytelling, and that is what we'll be looking at next.

Elements of a Scene

There are various definitions of what a scene should include, depending on whether you're writing a novel, a script, or a play. The definition also varies within the same form. Author Jane Friedman refers to seven layers in a scene:[8]

Time and setting
This first layer grounds the reader in the "when" and "where."

Dramatic action
This second layer unfolds moment by moment.

Conflict, tension, and/or suspense
This is embedded in the second layer, and though the conflict doesn't have to be overt, it has to be present.

Character
The heart of the story is the character's emotional development and it's what motivates action.

---

8 Alderson, "7 Essential Elements of Scene + Scene Structure Exercise."

The protagonist's goal
> This is the fifth layer, which looks at the specific goal the character hopes to achieve in the scene. If that goal is clearly understood, the audience is left asking the question, "Will they succeed?"

Characters and their change or emotional development
> This is the sixth layer and addresses the essential emotional change that the character must go through to keep the audience interested.

Thematic significance
> This final layer covers the overall theme and your reason for writing the story. If the details you use in your scene match what you want your readers to take away from your story, then you've created meaning and depth to the overall plot.

Author Ali Luke has another take, and defines the following elements of a scene:[9]

Characters
> At least one character that takes action.

Dialogue
> If there are more than one character dialogue should occur.

Surroundings description
> Where are they, and how do the surroundings affect the action and/or dialogue that is taking place?

Conflict or complication
> This leads to the point of tension.

Rising emotion or tension
> Let the emotion build in the scene rather than start at the highest point.

Ending
> Close it with a strong ending rather than letting it gradually stop.

Link to the next scene
> This can be a clear continuation of the current scene, or less direct.

---

9 Luke, "What Is a Scene?"

APPLIED TO PRODUCT DESIGN

Both Friedman and Luke provide good reference points that we can draw on in product design. Luke's elements have the closest connection to product design and can be almost directly applied to defining the story of the page or the view:

Characters
> This is your main user and the one who is about to take action (or no action).

Dialogue
> This is the brand messaging.

Surroundings description
> This is any accompanying messaging and content that is present on the page or the view and that serves to provide context and enough background information to help the user make a decision relating to the action.

Conflict or complication
> Let this rising emotion or tension emotion build in the scene rather than start at the highest point.

Ending
> Close it with a strong ending rather than letting it gradually stop.

Link to the next scene
> This can be a clear continuation of the current scene, or less direct.

Exercise: Elements of a Scene

Using Luke's list of elements of a scene, work through one, two, or all three of the following exercises:

- Take a scene from your favorite movie and define the elements of that scene as per Luke's definition.

- Take a page or view related to your product or one you use on a regular basis and define the elements of that page or view by using the list adapted for product design.

- Take a page or a view for that hasn't yet been designed or built and define the elements of that page or view by using the list adapted for product design.

Elements That Help Tell the Story of a Page or View

In product design, it's easy to think of the basic modules that a page or view are made up of as the elements of the page. Of course, these also play a role: how we use and combine them, and the order in which we present them, shape the story we're telling. They form a key part of the story and can be broken down as follows:

The building blocks
> The modules and the elements that make up the modules (e.g., images, headings, text, buttons, form fields)

The visual presentation
> How these are brought to life, how they are used to draw attention to certain parts of the page or view, and what their aesthetics tell the user about the page, view, and product as a whole

However, more can be considered elements of page or a view, which we can draw from traditional storytelling:

The characters or users
> Any given page or view is aimed at specific users who we want to take action. A good page or view should be clear in who it's aimed at and why.

Primary and secondary CTAs
> Just as one scene should contain a link to the next scene, a page or view should provide a clear way to continue through primary CTAs, in particular, to the next page; as well as less prominent links onward through secondary and more contextual CTAs.

What Scenes Teach Us About How to Define the Story of the Page or View

When writers start working on their scenes, they write. It may seem obvious, but it's a simple thing that also applies to product design. And it doesn't mean that they necessarily start writing the actual story. There is a lot of "structural" or planning writing that, just as in design, is helpful for the steps ahead.

There is so much power in writing, and as we've covered, each page or view tells a story. The first step of telling that story is to identify what the story actually is, and who it's primarily being told to.

The following seven methods take inspiration from traditional storytelling and are great ways to help define the story of your page or view. They are organized so that they can either be worked through as a step-by-step guide, or used individually in the way that adds most value to your product, team, and project.

DEFINE THE PURPOSE OF THE PAGE OR VIEW

According to Jerry Jenkins's blog, one of the first things you should do when you start working on a scene is to define its purpose in one or two sentences. The argument is that the general advice that a scene should advance the plot, reveal the character, or both, is good but too vague. The blog says you want your scene to have strong pacing, and rather than tell, you want to show and create empathy for your protagonist. You also want to make sure that the reader will want to keep turning the page to read more. We process what happens and decide on a new action, so "action-reaction-process-decide-new action." The advice is that you should write one sentence that encapsulates each scene, and that if you can't come up with a purpose for a scene, you should throw it out and come up with one that works.[10]

I do something very similar before I start sketching or wireframing. I've made it a habit to always start by defining the purpose of the page or view that I'm about to do a sketch or wireframe for. I tend to begin with the overall statement and then further refine it and break down what a first-time visitor and what a returning visitor should be able to do, as well as do this for both mobile and desktop, respectively. By doing this, not only do you force yourself to be clear about why this page is needed and what its main purpose is, but you also have to think through the needs that it should meet and how they may be slightly different on mobile versus desktop devices.

Many times, UX designers and the rest of the team aren't able to answer these simple questions, neither before they begin wireframing, nor after the wireframe is "done." Instead, they jump straight into

---

10 Lakin, "8 Steps to Writing a Perfect Scene—Every Time."

sketching, wireframing, designing, or prototyping. However, by doing so, you miss an important step that risks sending you down the path of "just doing" instead of making clear the "why," "what," "for whom," and "how." Just as putting the purpose of a scene in writing helps create clarity, doing it for pages or views serves as a good check-in with yourself (Figure 13-3). If you struggle to pinpoint just what the purpose is, then there's more work to be done, either to define it, or perhaps to rethink the whole page, just like the Jenkins blog's advice for writing.

Home page—large

The purpose of the home page is to:
Communicate what the site is about
Clearly direct users where to go next
Feature what's recommended today

FIGURE 13-3
Defining the purpose of a page or view

How to go about it

The best way to go about this is in whichever way works best for you. You should be able to just sit down and write a sentence or two about the purpose of the page. However, some people think better while, for example, sketching. So if it helps you to better grasp what you're working by sketching, then sketch.

I tend to write out a list of bullet points following the intro phrase "The purpose of this page/view is to." Most of the time, writing will help ensure that you gain clarity as to what the page should focus on, rather than just let your ideas for that great page layout lead you. If you start by sketching or wireframing, make sure you go back over your visualization and can complete the statements about the purpose of the page.

Exercise: Define the Purpose of the Page or View

Take one of the pages or views for a product you're working on at the moment, or one you use on a regular basis:

- Define the purpose of the page or view by completing the sentence "The purpose of this page/ view is to..." and list out the answers as bullet points below (see Figure 13-3).

This is also a useful exercise to do retrospectively for a page or view that is already designed or even built. In this case think about the following:

- Is it clear and easy to articulate what the purpose of the page is based on what you can see?

IDENTIFY WHAT THE PAGE OR VIEW SHOULD INCLUDE TO MEET FIRST-TIME AND RETURNING USERS' NEEDS

When you start working on a scene, you should write down three to seven bullet points that describe what's going to happen. This helps ensure that you don't have too much or too little happening in the scene. It also helps ensure that you stay on track as you start writing that scene.[11]

We should use a similar process in product design. It's easy to just start sketching, wireframing, designing, or even building without having identified all the content, features, and CTAs that should go on the page. We think we have all those elements clear in our heads, but when we actually begin to write down what that content is, it isn't usually as clear as we'd thought. Setting aside time to define what the page or view should include for first-time and returning users is a useful step to help you identify what should go on the page (Figure 13-4). It is also a useful exercise to go back over, just as it is in traditional storytelling, to ensure that you're staying on track.

---

11 Luke, "What Is a Scene?"

Home page–large

The purpose of the home page is to:
Communicate what the site is about
Clearly direct users where to go next
Feature what's recommended today

As a first time visitor, I should be able to:
Understand what the site is about
Easily find what I'm looking for

As a returning visitor I should be able to:
Quickly find a way back to where I left off
See what's new since my last visit

FIGURE 13-4
Including first-time and returning user needs

How to go about it

I tend to write this in two columns—one column for first-time user needs and one for returning users—and position it under the purpose statement. The purpose statement then acts as the overarching anchor that applies to all and summarizes why the page exists. Then I write a phrase at the top of each column: "As a first-time user, I should be able to" and "As a returning visitor, I should be able to." This kind of language and the subsequent bullet points describing what a first-time user and a returning user should be able to do helps me identify each of their needs and priorities.

Exercise: Identify What the Page or View Should Include to Meet First-Time and Returning Users' Needs

Take one of the pages or views for a product you're working on at the moment, or one you use on a regular basis:

- Define what a first-time user should be able to do by completing the sentence "As a first-time user, I should be able to..." and list the answers as bullet points below (see Figure 13-4).

- Define what a returning user should be able to do by completing the sentence "As a returning user, I should be able to..." and list out the answers as bullet points below (see Figure 13-4).

This exercise is also useful to do retrospectively for a page or view that is already designed or even built. In this case, complete the previously mentioned sentences and then evaluate the page or view in question in light of your answers:

- Does the page or view meet the needs of first-time visitors?

- Does the page or view meet the needs of returning visitors?

IDENTIFY THE DESIRED TIME A USER SHOULD SPEND ON THE PAGE OR VIEW

Another good guiding principle for defining the story of your pages or views, deciding what content and functionality to include, and creating its structure is to be specific about what you believe is a good duration of time for a new or returning visitor to spend on each page. A clearly defined time frame gives you another checkpoint that can help you assess whether you are supporting the users in their direct journey or distracting them.

Sometimes a planned, or unexpected, stop is a nice thing. Other times, like when we're short on time or have a task to complete, they become a frustration and are best avoided. It's a great exercise to do this before you begin defining and sketching out the content so you can keep it at the back of your mind together with the purpose and role of the page or view.

How to go about it

The actual time users spend on a page or view will always depend on multiple factors and will vary based on their familiarity with the subject and with the product, how tech savvy they are, and so on. However, as with anything measurable, you can use general ranges. The most beneficial is to just break it down based on first-time and returning visitors.

If your product is already live, and you're improving pages or doing a redesign, a useful starting point is to look at the analytics indicating the amount of time that new and returning visitors on average spend on the page. Most analytics platforms, such as Google Analytics, will allow you to view this data. However, it's best to always use both quantitative data, like analytics, together with qualitative data so you'll get insight into both the "what" (quantitative) and the "why" (qualitative).

The current behavior of users may not be ideal or the most optimal, so supplementing a quantitative assessment with qualitative insight will help ensure that you understand what drives the behavior. Analytics combined with tools such as Hotjar, which allows you to assess where users are looking and how they are scanning the page in a less moderated, biased way, can help you assess what story the page is currently telling, perhaps nondeliberately.

If you're working on a new product, looking at data from similar websites in the same industry, or pages and views of noncompetitors that serve the same kind of purpose, can provide a good benchmark. However, it's recommended that you have a go at defining the desired time on your own as a first step, regardless of whether you're working on a redesign, improvement, or brand-new product. This is to ensure that you don't get too biased or steered in a particular direction but instead keep the purpose, role, and the needs of your first-time and returning visitors at the front of your mind. If you're really unclear on how long a good indicative duration is, run a couple of tests internally with people who aren't directly involved with the project to help assess how long first-time and returning visitors will likely spend time on-site. These durations can then be further refined based on the benchmark data we've previously discussed.

Whichever way you go, it's recommended to keep the desired time as a ballpark figure rather than try to pinpoint the exact milliseconds. The key is that the desired time on the page should help serve as a reference point based on the purpose of the page and the context of use. Additionally, this estimate should help make the product design team more conscious of how the design impacts the user's navigation.

IDENTIFY AND PRIORITIZE CONTENT ACROSS DEVICES AND SCREEN SIZES

Putting the content itself into words and identifying the content that should go on each page and view is also a great way to work through what you might need on mobile versus desktop options. I often advise those who attend my workshops or classes to write down the content that they think they'll need for their desktop pages and mobile views and then go through and prioritize it for each (and add devices as applicable). It's a quick and easy way to get your head around the priorities and to identify whether you really need that specific piece of content on mobile. As a starting point, if you don't need it on mobile you probably don't need it that much on desktop either (unless there's a really good reason for it, hence the exception).

How to go about it

Once you have defined the purpose of the page and view together with what a first-time-user and a returning user should be able to do, the easiest way to figure out the content is, with these in mind, to grab a pen and paper and in one column write down the content the user would need on desktop and in the other, the content they'd need on mobile. Here, it can be useful to think of specific scenarios for your users as the context of use may mean that something is of higher importance on mobile. When looking at restaurants from a desktop, for example, the user is often about planning ahead, so the current location may not be a priority; but when looking for restaurants on a smartphone, the user is more likely to want nearby and open right now.

Exercise: Identify and Prioritize Content Across Devices and Screen Sizes

For one of your pages or views for which you've already defined the purpose, as well as what a first-time and returning user should be able to do, define the following:

- What content would the user need on a desktop?

- What content would the user need on a mobile device?

- Prioritize the importance of the desktop content by numbering each item, with 1 being the highest importance.

- Prioritize the importance of the mobile content by numbering each item, with 1 being the highest importance.

- Compare the two lists. If needed, look into how to adapt the mobile or desktop view so it best meets the user's needs.

DEFINE HOW CONTENT SHOULD FLOW FROM SMALLER TO LARGER SCREENS

When we plan out the story of a page, we need to consider both the flow from top to bottom, and how the sections and the modules within them come together to form a whole. As we talked about in Chapter 12, and in the words of Trent Walton, in order to ensure that the intended message is conveyed on any device, we need to choreograph the content and its flow from a bigger screen to a smaller one, and vice versa. We do this in responsive design by defining breakpoints for where the layout is going to shift from one to another and by defining our content-stacking strategy—that is, how content should be "stacked" in the different views. This is an important aspect in defining the narrative of the page or view.

As a starting point, we should keep the core content and functionality the same. But that's not to say that the story you deliver on desktop and mobile options, respectively, is exactly the same. Take, for example, an experience in which location plays a key role, and you want to use a map to point out certain things on a desktop. On the desktop view, you have plenty of space to include both the map and an accompanying list, similar to what Airbnb or Foursquare do. On mobile it becomes a bit squeezed. Just because the starting point should be to keep the core content and functionality the same doesn't mean that you have to show it exactly the same way, or place as much emphasis on the map on mobile as you do on desktop. In addition, product designers have the opportunity to make use of the user's current location on mobile. These aspects should be considered in light of context of use in the product design process.

When we define the stories of our pages and views across smaller and larger screens, we need to think about the role those screen sizes might play in the experience, and what each device is great at or less suitable for. This in turn helps us define the story of each page or view.

How to go about it

Having identified and prioritized the content, it's easier to sketch out the flow of that content on the page and views. Most definitely, without any exception, start by sketching, before you do any work on the computer. Even if you just spend 15, 30, 45 minutes, or an hour, spending a bit of time up front sketching will make you understand the flow and story of the page and will save you time. It's also really good for putting the prioritization of content into something a bit more concrete, as Figure 13-5 shows.

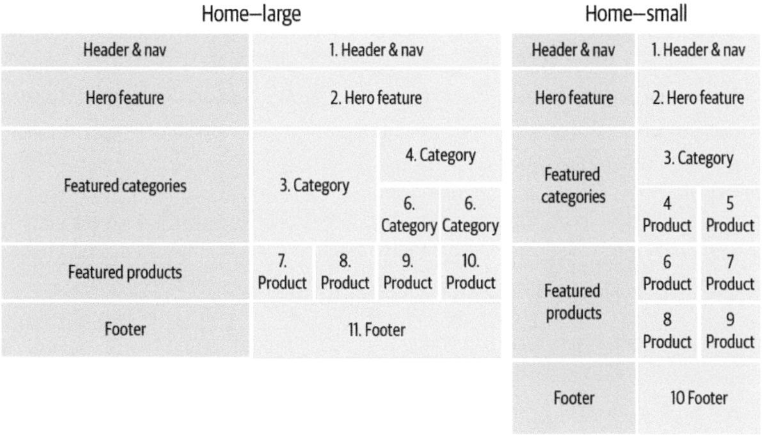

FIGURE 13-5
Prioritizing content across devices and screen sizes

When thinking through the content and how it's going to flow from one device to the next, the key is to consider the breakpoints. If you imagine that you decrease your browser window by dragging the bottom right corner to the left, at a certain point, the layout of the page is going to change. That's when you've hit a defined breakpoint. These breakpoints are essentially what we're defining our content-stacking strategy for, so that we know how the content is going to reflow to fit within the new dimensions.

There is no need to sketch to perfection, or until you've done all the main page and view templates, in all the sizes that you need. Stop when you have a good understanding of the content, the flow of each page, and how the pages and views are similar as well as different from each other, including based on screen size.

There is a lot of talk of "mobile first," and in some instances it's mentioned as the approach that *has to be taken* for the wireframing process too. Mobile first is a critical approach to the way we develop our designs, but not for how we go about thinking through the content and its layout.

Whether you start sketching out your smallest device first or your largest doesn't make a difference to the end result in most cases. The most important thing is that you work through the content on both smaller and larger screens in conjunction with each other, rather than do all your mobile wireframes first and then those for the desktop. Some people find it easier to start with mobile first and work their way up. Personally, I prefer to start with the most complex screen first, which for me, in terms of the different layout options, is the desktop. The only time I start with mobile is when the experience we're working on is primarily going to be used for mobile.

I don't believe in right and wrong ways. If someone tells you that you have to do wireframes for mobile first, I'd challenge it unless they have a very good reason. What matters is getting to the end result, and since we shouldn't complete one set of wireframes first and then do the next one anyway, it really doesn't matter which way you start.

Exercise: Define How Content Should Flow from Smaller to Larger Screens

With your list of prioritized content for one of your product's pages or views, take two pieces of paper, one for desktop and one for mobile, and sketch out the outline of the appropriate screen on each. Then do the following:

- Starting either with mobile or desktop, draw a high-level wireframe following the content prioritization you've defined. This can be on a modular level, as in Figure 13-5, or with more detail. The key is that you work through the content layout.

- Do the same for the other screen size, constantly keeping what's most appropriate for the respective screen size in mind; for example, three columns are hard to fit on mobile.

- Review and revise ter you've completed both before going into more detailed wireframing/design.

USE PRIMARY AND SECONDARY CTAS TO HELP TELL THE STORY

Mark Bell, who I've mentioned previously, had an idea that a well-designed website doesn't need any main navigation. Instead, users should be able to navigate through the content and story of a page on its own. This is a really great principle to have at the back of our minds when we define and structure pages and views.

Each page should tell its own story through the visual hierarchy of the content and primary calls to action, but also through the supporting and secondary links. The main navigation should be the ticket that we always have in our back pockets, our personal elevator, or teleporter if you wish, that with a click/tap or two, magically takes us from one place to another. No wait, no confusion, just straight there.

Contextual navigation through links and calls to action within content of the page/view itself, on the other hand, provides a more casual browsing experience. We're less in a "take-me-there-now" kind of mood, but instead out to explore and let the content and the story of the page guide us on our journey. Contextual navigation is an often overlooked opportunity, and the result is that users have to fall back to the main navigation, or search, to get to where they want to go.

How to go about it

Defining the primary and secondary CTAs, as well as contextual links, is very much about knowing the story the page itself should tell, and what part of the overarching story the page or view in question plays. Navigation is about ensuring that there are doors that take the user on the right onward journeys, supporting either the main plot (main CTA) or one of the defined secondary plots (secondary CTAs and contextual links).

Navigation is, however, also about ensuring that the user isn't given too many options that end up confusing them, and that the goals of the user and the business are kept at the front of your mind. The following exercise is a useful one to work through both before you start wireframing or designing, and while you're at it.

Exercise: Use Primary and Secondary CTAs to Help Tell the Story

For the page or view that you've been working with in the previous exercises, define the following:

- What is the primary action you want the user to take on this page or view?

- What secondary actions do you want them to take?

- How can you support other onward journeys through contextual navigation; for example, if they want to see more of something?

- What, if any, related content should the user be made aware of if what's on this page/ view isn't quite right?

USING STORYTELLING TO TEST AND EVALUATE WIREFRAMES, MOCKUPS, AND PROTOTYPES

All of the previous exercises for defining the purpose, the needs of first-time and returning visitors, as well as the prioritization of content help you plan out and define the story, content, and functionality of your pages and views, whether it's for wireframes, more developed mockups, or the prototypes you put together. They are also great to revisit after the wireframes, mockups, or prototypes are developed, and to check them off with a "yay" or "nay" in terms of whether the defined pages and views meet your initial specifications in terms of purpose and user needs/ goals. Additionally, the exercises provide a great starting point for informing and aligning your key performance indicators (KPIs) and metrics as well as analytics setup, and subsequently measuring against them, as well as for testing the actual pages.

Testing the Narrative Structure of Your Pages and Views

Through the use of clickable prototypes, you can evaluate whether the pages and views are meeting what you've defined they should. You can also visualize the journeys users would take by overlaying wireframes and screen views with highlighted areas, or you can build the structure of a presentation so it takes the audience through it step by step. While the red thread would normally not be visible, these types of visualized journeys can be the time to turn the red thread into an actual presentation and narrative feature, just as in the book from my childhood.

Incorporating User Feedback and Research Findings

A really nice and visual way to play back user testing findings is to add quotes, observations, and feedback from users to this type of presentations. You can also to tie into your personas and highlight what their journey would look and feel like.

Chapter 6 discussed the importance of personas. To ensure that the storytelling tools and principles covered throughout this book aren't just included in the beginning and then left on their own to magically keep on informing and guiding the project, we need to continuously bring them in. We can do this in various ways, depending on which way will best benefit your project and be suitable to your audience.

Summary

The need to identify what goes on a page or view exists no matter whether you're in the camp that sees the value in wireframes or not. A page or view will always tell a story. To ensure that it's the desired one—and a page-turner that encourages the user onward—that story needs to be defined.

Though you could skip the steps and methodologies outlined in this chapter and achieve a decent result by going straight into design or development, going through them provides a great deal of value. Many times it seems like a pointless exercise, as surely we know what we're doing. However, by spending some time up front to define and work through steps for all the main pages and views of our product (before we get heads-down into modules, layout, and code), we help ensure that we have a holistic view of our work to better meet the needs of both the user and the business, and that we spend our time most efficiently. Working through the exercises presented in this chapter and being able to clearly articulate the purpose of each page and how that page or view meets user and business needs also helps ensure that we can present our work and sell it to clients and internal stakeholders.

[14]

Presenting and Sharing Your Story

How Storytelling Helped Save the Day

TOWARD THE END OF 2010, we moved into a new office with Dare, and our experience planning team gained a new addition. Her name was Roz Thomas, and Roz's background was in product design for, among others, what was then called Polly Pocket Group, a line of dolls and accessories. Roz was great at sketching up her thinking in ways that could easily be presented to the client.

At the same time, I was working on a redesign of the Sony Mobile (previously Sony Ericsson) home page in preparation for a new phone campaign. We had received some initial feedback on the first version, and in my view, what our client was asking for didn't meet the needs of the users or the business on a global or local market level. Inspired by Roz, I took to trying to sketch out my thinking.

Exactly how I ended up with what I did, I can't recall, but somehow my scribbles, which were initially done for my own benefit to capture my thinking, turned into a comic-style document with the home page content depicted as superheroes. I used the illustrations to tell the story of why our original version of the home page was along the right lines. Our Sony Mobile team at Dare liked it so much that rather than talk the client through our feedback verbally, I ended up taking them through my comic-style sketches (Figure 14-1). They got a great response, and as far as I can recall, the client agreed with my pitch, and we went with our original recommendation.

FIGURE 14-1

My local home page approach walk-through

Though the outcome of that call might have been the same without the sketches, they helped bring to life the rationale behind our approach in a way that captured the client's attention and allowed them to relate. Presentations, calls, and even conversations often fall on deaf ears because of the lack of emotional connection they evoke, which in turn is often a result of the way they've been presented or told. When something doesn't grab our attention, those two thousand daydreams that all of us have each day start to make an appearance.[1] As a result, we might end up saying "no" instead of "yes" (or receiving a no instead of a yes), all because we simply don't connect and take in what the person presenting is saying. Similarly, the people on the receiving end don't take in what we say when we're presenting.

We had a really good relationship with the Sony Mobile team, and had it not been for that, I wouldn't have been so comfortable presenting my superhero-style sketches to them. My presentation most certainly was a bit unusual, but sometimes that's a good thing. As long as you take

---

1 Jonathan Gottschall, "The Science of Storytelling," *Fast Company*, October 16, 2013, *https://oreil.ly/dekVH*.

the client along on the journey, present the work in the right way, and set the right expectations, most types of deliverables and ways of presenting will work. Reaching your audience is just a matter of how you present them and what story you tell, and that it is the right story and the right focus for the audience.

The Role of Storytelling for Presenting Your Story

Throughout history and various professions, storytelling has been the way when it comes to presenting a tale. There is no separation between them. Telling someone something is storytelling.

All of us who are involved with product design—whether as a UX designer like myself or in a different role—are involved in creating the best possible experiences for our users. When it comes to using storytelling for presenting our work, the opportunity and value lies in how storytelling can be used to create a good experience for the people you present to and work with, be they team members, internal stakeholders and/or clients. Rather than simply present facts, rationale, feedback, or the work that we've done as is, storytelling enables us to turn the "tell," as producer Peter Guber calls it, into an experience for our audience. Using storytelling might seem like overkill when it comes to work situations, but the more we can embrace that everything, including all aspects of work as far down as reading an email, is an experience, the better we can make those experiences.

In most workplaces, we're expected to use logic and reasoning as a way to support and communicate our work. Yet storytelling (as covered in Chapter 1) is one of the most powerful ways to move people into action. Something happens in us when facts and messaging are embedded in a story. Stories help us remember details and events, and moves us emotionally. Reasoning and logic on its own can make the strongest of business cases fall flat, but embedding them in a story can move people emotionally.

In short, storytelling matters. It is such a powerful tool, in part because of what it enables us to accomplish. Next, we'll look at four important ways we can use storytelling.

USING STORYTELLING AS A WAY TO
ACHIEVE A DESIRED OUTCOME

One of the main things to remember when it comes to storytelling is that no matter what type of story you're telling, or how you're presenting it, in the end you're trying to make something happen. Whether you're offering a document, giving a presentation, or leading a meeting, there's always a reason and a desired outcome.

Guber talks of purposeful stories, those that are told with a specific purpose in mind.[2] The secret sauce behind his success has been in telling purposeful stories, he says, and it's something anyone can do and see the results instantly.[3] This is what the troubadours back in the Middle Ages did: they gauged the way their audience reacted and adapted their performances accordingly.

We see it today in journalists who present stories that evolve as they ask their questions. We see it in comedians who build up to a specific punchline, hoping that the audience will laugh, but then quickly adapt and try to save the situation if the joke falls flat. And we see it in great public speakers, who structure a speech for a desired outcome, but continuously gauge the audience reaction and adjust their performance based that.

Being clear on the call to action

With everything we do and everything we communicate at work, we want the person on the other side to do something. The power of storytelling lies first and foremost in telling purposeful stories that bring to life that call to action in a way that resonates with our audience. This applies to our work not only in terms of what it is, but also in how we present it, verbally and on paper. The visual and verbal presentation are critical aspects in making sure that our message resonates with our clients and internal team members. Besides, if we don't know what CTA we want our audience to take, how can they take it?

---

2 Mike Hofman, "Peter Guber on the Power of Effective Communicators," *Inc.*, March 1, 2011, *https://oreil.ly/jxvOC*.

3 Arianna Huffington, "Why Peter Guber's Book Tell to Win Is a Game Changer," *HuffPost*, March 1, 2011, *https://oreil.ly/nklqy*.

Exercise: Using Storytelling as a Way to Achieve a Desired Outcome

Take a presentation or deliverable you're currently working on and think through the following:

- Why are you putting it together? For example: to present a proposed solution and explain the rationale and research behind it.

- Who is it aimed at? For example: senior internal stakeholders who need to approve, the main client contact and the superiors it will be passed on to.

- What are you hoping they'll get out of it? For example: understand the rationale behind what you're proposing.

- What's the action or desired outcome you're hoping to achieve with it? For example: this can be buy-in for something, or something you want someone else to do.

USING STORYTELLING AS A WAY TO GET BUY-IN

One of the main overall desired outcomes we have for whatever we present is a wish for the team members, internal stakeholders, and clients to buy in to what we're presenting. This desire for buy-in applies to concepts and ideas, proposed solutions, ways of working, and more. No matter how good your idea, approach, solution, or argument might be, if you can't convince the team and/or the client, it will never see the light of day. This is true for getting buy-in for UX but also for the work that you do across every single step of the project process, stretching from ideation to post launch, from the first review to that final sign-off and post-launch follow-up. It's one of the reasons that, as UX designers, product owners, and more, one of our key skills is to be great storytellers.

At times, we may have a tendency to think that our work or the proposition we're presenting will sell itself. This is seldom the case. Being able to present the story related to your work is absolutely key for also getting buy-in. As Guber says, "If you can't tell it, you can't sell it."

If you're a writer and have spent the better part of a year or more on your story, but that story is never read, then it's never told. It's the same for startups, small business owners, musicians, etc.: it doesn't matter what you create or how great it is if no one sees or hears it. This also applies to product design.

Other reasons buy-in is important

Besides selling our ideas and work, there are other key reasons buy-in is so important—the user's experience, for example. Many organizations are struggling to change the status quo and to adapt to more agile and collaborative ways of working, as well as to fully grasp requirements for multidevice projects and digital overall. While conferences and the latest and most popular *Medium* articles might lead us to believe that most people "get it," many organizations and many people don't. Beyond making what we do and why it's valuable understandable, and selling our ideas and work, there are other key reasons we should care and focus on getting buy-in. Getting buy-in can help do the following:

- Improve ways of working to ensure collaboration across disciplines and business units

- Break down silos in the organization

- Ensure a better use of budgets and everyone's time

- Ensure everyone is on the same page

Understanding why there is a lack of buy-in

Working toward increased buy-in, whether for UX design or something else, should always start with understanding why that buy-in is lacking. More often than not, whatever the overarching reason might be, the underlying reason tends to come down to three issues, often in combination:

They don't yet understand the value

Whoever is not bought in on, for example, UX design, doesn't yet see or understand the value of UX, the role UX has, and how UX fits into the bigger picture and the project process.

They understand something else better

Whoever is bought in on, for example, UX design, comes from a different discipline and understands that and/or something else better (e.g., development), and as a result, prioritizes that in terms of allocating more budget to development or letting development lead the way.

The budget is focused elsewhere

Whoever influences the budget and schedule has prioritized them elsewhere, for one or both of the previous two reasons.

Who to get buy-in from

Having a better understanding of *why* there is a lack of buy-in is the first step in defining the story you need to tell in order to get the buy-in you need. The preceding three reasons provide a good starting point, though nuances exist. A key part of gaining buy-in is also understanding *who* you should focus on and the role they'll play in ensuring your desired outcome. At a broad level, the "who" can be categorized as follows:

Internal team members

Your closest allies, whom you need to get on board

Clients and stakeholders

People who are in control of budgets and the "yes" or "no"

How to increase buy-in

With a good understanding of why there is a lack of buy-in, and whom to get the buy-in from, the next step is about identifying more about *what* will increase the chances for buy-in. To increase buy-in among internal team members, three main things need to happen:

Understand the story of the team and the individuals on that team

You need to understand the team's backstory in addition to understanding where they are going. Depending on where the lack of buy-in occurs, you may need to look at the individual, the whole team, or a combination of both.

Identify what makes the other person or people the hero(s)

Each team member and each team will always have something that they particularly care about. If you're met with resistance, try to understand why, and what will make the person or people in question shine.

Adapt your approach and your work

Based on what you've learned in the previous chapters, adjust the way you approach a subject, suggest an idea, or similar, so that it better fits with the specific team member or team.

Increasing buy-in with clients and internal stakeholders is similar but should have a clearer focus on the value put in context with what really matters to them. Though it's not about playing games or bending over backward, we can often do little things that help the person in question do their job or look good in relation to someone they report to. Here are some steps you can take to increase buy-in among clients and stakeholders:

Identify the key clients and stakeholders

These will be the people you deal with both directly and indirectly. Understanding who has the decision-making power and controls the budget is the first step in increasing your chances of getting buy-in.

Identify what matters to them

This is about understanding what they respond best to. Using UX as an example again, some clients and internal stakeholders will simply prefer to focus on visual designs over UX deliverables, and that's OK. If that is the case, make sure you place a bit more emphasis on the visual aspect of the UX deliverables.

Assess their current understanding of the subject

Your proposal should always take into consideration their prior knowledge of the topic. You don't tell a story same way to someone who is completely new to the subject as you do to someone who has a good understanding of it.

Tie the value of what you propose to what matters to them

This step is also about making them look good. If buy-in is about UX, tying the value could be about understanding how and where UX sits in the process for them and how it can be used to help and make them look good, not only with regard to what UX adds to the project, but also how each of the UX deliverables helps the client and their project get one step closer to a better end result.

Adapt how you present your work so it resonates with them
Some prefer a lot of details, and others prefer just a high-level summary. Hit the right balance to appeal to the person in question rather than give them a reason to immediately be put off.

Give them something tangible to share with the people they report to
The main client and stakeholder you most often deal with is not always the one in charge of the budget or the power to provide a final "yes" or "no." For this reason, it's important to provide your main stakeholders and clients with something they can pass up the chain of command that makes it easy for them to sell it.

Sometimes, however, when it comes to buy-in, you feel like you've reached a dead end. If the organization you're working with has a very low level of UX maturity, you may need to partner with someone in a more influential position and get them to help tell the story of why and how UX should be involved in the organization.

This doesn't necessarily need to be someone high up. You could team up with someone on the creative team, if the company is led by the big idea; a business analyst, if the company is led by the business; or engineering, if that's what the company is currently most focused on, and so forth. The lone storyteller is often not the best way to go when there is a low level of maturity or buy-in. Instead, this is where you need an ensemble that can grow and grow until eventually the full organization has embraced it. Last but not least, if you want someone to get excited about what you're proposing and the work that you've done, you have to make sure that you give them a reason to get excited, which is directly related to what we'll cover next.

Exercise: Using Storytelling as a Way to Get Buy-in

Take a presentation of a project, idea, approach, or similar that you're currently working on/recently worked on and think through the following:

- Who is your main target audience? These are the people you want to get buy-in from.

- What do you want them to buy in to? Be clear on the specific aspects that you want them to buy in to.

- Why should they buy in to that? Make the value of your proposal clear to your audience.

- How have you structured/can you structure your presentation to build to that? Put a narrative structure together that builds up to that, but also one that makes it clear to the audience what you want.

- What objections, and from whom, might you get? Put yourself in their shoes as much as possible and identify barriers that may stop buy-in from happening, just as we do with personas. Be clear on the points where your presentation story could take a negative turn so you can plan for that and "fill any gaps" before they happen. For example, they might not get the "why" or the main purpose behind what you propose, they might think it'll cost too much or take too long, and so on.

- How can you adapt what and how you present it so it resonates with them? Understand what matters to them, present the right level of detail, and give them something tangible of value.

USING STORYTELLING AS A WAY TO INSPIRE

In every great story, a bit of magic is involved as the storyteller makes us see things differently. Throughout history, great storytellers have had the ability to make this magic happen by capturing the imagination of their audience and transporting them into the world they're describing. Whether inspiring people to action or simply capturing their attention and interest, all good storytellers spark that appetite and desire to hear more, and even to be around that person. In the workplace this type of great storyteller can take the form of a leader, manager, or colleague who always fills others with energy and a "Let's do this" motivation whenever they speak. Or it can be the person who makes the complex seem simple, or makes what's usually boring become interesting.

Guber says all good stories contain a promise of something to come. When that something is grounded in what makes the listener tick, the story becomes inspiring. It almost doesn't matter what subject is being talked about or covered; if it's told in a way that enables the listener to relate, it has the potential to inspire and to move people into action. History is filled with examples of great storytellers who had the ability to inspire others and get them to believe in what they believed in. Very few of us will have the same inspirational impact as these people, nor should we all strive to be great inspirational leaders and speakers. All of us can do little things to help our workplaces and work environments be more inspiring.

The pull of possibility

Storytelling plays an important role in inspiring and motivating others. Chapter 2 introduced Nancy Duarte and her analysis of great talks. Duarte looks at speeches by Martin Luther King Jr. and Steve Jobs in detail and visualizes how they move from What Is to the New Bliss in various ways.[4]

In Steve Jobs's iPhone launch speech, Duarte color-coded where he talked, switched to video, and then demo. She also overlaid audience reactions at various points as well as how Jobs himself deliberately reacted to reflect what he wanted the audience to feel. He marvelled saying things such as "Isn't this awesome," "Isn't this beautiful," and by doing so, Duarte says, he compelled them to feel a certain way.

Martin Luther King Jr., on the other hand, reached into his listeners' hearts by using metaphors as well as by referencing scriptures and songs that resonated with the audience. Through the use of repetition and comparing what currently is to what could be, King connected with people.

Both King and Jobs have iconic lines in their speeches. For Martin Luther King Jr., it was "I have a dream…," which he repeated over and over. For Steve Jobs, it was "Every once in a while a revolutionary product comes along and changes everything." Each one deals with the promise of what's to come, the thing that connects with us emotionally.

---

4 Nancy Duarte, "The Secret Structure of Great Talks," *TEDxEast* Video, November 2011, https://oreil.ly/XSSWO.

They are another take on "Once upon a time" or "In a galaxy far, far away," and however we start or end our stories, when told right, we know that something good is to come.

By structuring our story and its presentation to incorporate the pull of possibility, we increase our chances of creating mental images for the audience of what could be. Just as a comedian builds up to a main joke, we can use narrative structure to identify when and how to build up to the main part and how best to tell the story from there on to make sure we get the desired action. Sometimes, however, something more tangible is needed as well, in order to reach the desired outcome of attaining buy-in or inspiring people—and that's data.

Exercise: Using Storytelling as a Way to Inspire

With what you're presenting in mind, identify the following:

- What currently is
- What the lofty "what if" is

IDENTIFYING AND TELLING THE RIGHT STORY BEHIND DATA

Steven Levitt, author of *Freakonomics* and *SuperFreakonomics*, believes that "data is one of the most powerful mechanisms for telling stories." In fact, that's what he does—he takes huge amounts of data and tries to get it to tell a story, from the one about why so many drug dealers live with their mothers, to the story of how teachers cheat on behalf of their students on tests. His stories from data are what made him famous and eventually won him the John Bates Clark Medal, one of the most prestigious economic science awards.[5]

Economist Dan Ariely says, "Big data is like teenage sex—everybody talks about it, nobody really knows how to do it, everyone thinks everyone else is doing it, so everyone claims they are doing it." Levitt argues that when you look back historically, it's traditionally been business people who have been the experts when it comes to data. It's been their job to ensure that people got what they wanted and knew the answer.

---

5 Anne Cassidy, "Economist Steven Levitt On Why Data Needs Stories," *Fast Company*, June 18, 2013, *https://oreil.ly/IvUlm*.

But with the development in big data, the goal is no longer to know the answer, but instead how to leverage the data effectively. Levitt continues:

> The future of business lies with the companies that understand how to use the data to inform their strategies and personalize their services.[6]

Many organizations sit on a ton of data, but as the quote implies, very few know how to get it, use it, or apply it. No matter what we're using data for, whether it's for part of an interface, findings in a report, or a presentation, the data always has a story to tell. The tricky part is that data can tell us anything, or absolutely nothing, if we don't know how to interpret it. Understanding and working with big data is a discipline in and of itself—one that *Harvard Business Review* called "the sexiest job of the century" in 2012.[7]

The key to untapping the value that lies in big data is, according to Levitt, to break down organizational silos and encourage collaboration across departments and teams. The catalyst for this to happen often lies in a realization of the benefit that comes from doing so. Just as all UX designers don't have to be—or should be—expert coders, neither should we all be data scientists or experts, but it helps to have an understanding of how we can use data in the design process, as part of the design, as well as to both present and evaluate what we've done. But we need to know what to use and how to use it, or we risk basing decisions on the wrong information.

Understanding the story behind data and what data to use

Over the last few years in particular, data-driven design has become such a hot topic that many jump on board without fully understanding the context. Many of us are familiar with Google's 41 shades of blue: the company analyzed the range between two blues used on its home page and the Gmail page, respectively, to find the one that was most effective so it could be standardized across the system. Some companies

---

6 Jessica Davies, "Authenticity is key to multiplatform storytelling, says economist Steven Levitt," *The Drum*, May 29, 2013, *https://oreil.ly/Z4udi*.

7 Thomas H. Davenport and D.J. Patil, "Data Scientist: The Sexiest Job of the 21st Century," *Harvard Business Review*, October 2012, *https://oreil.ly/MXzem*.

have jumped to running similar tests. In one horror story, a company ran tests every single day, and based on the outcome, changed things on the fly, daily.

The risk of becoming this data driven is that you look at the data in isolation and mistake it for telling you a truth, which in fact is a lie. As our interactions and behavior online are becoming more complex and influenced by a growing list of factors, including external nondigital ones, there's a real danger in looking at a single metric and basing decisions on that. These single metrics are often called *vanity metrics* because they don't actually tell us anything or provide a false picture based on a lack of context.

When we incorporate data into the work we do, we might be working with quantitative or qualitative data:

Quantitative data
> This data focuses on a breadth of information to enable us to find patterns and common ground. It's numerical data that is usually focused on answering "who," "what," "when," or "where." Surveys and analytics are quantitative methods.

Qualitative data
> This nonnumerical data is more focused on the "why" or "how." Rather than aiming to get as many responses as possible, we use this data to go beyond just the answer to understand the reason. Common qualitative methods are observations and interviews.

Many vanity metrics are based on quantitative data. Page views and average session duration are two examples of metrics that are often used without context; a higher number is commonly assumed to be a good thing. It can be, but it can also be a bad thing, all depending on the context. As noted in Chapter 5, we need to take into account a growing list of factors in the experiences that we design. This doesn't apply just to the way we consider and incorporate them, but also to the way we measure them.

As UX designers, understanding data and being able to work with it are increasingly important skills. We want to be able to use analytics to inform (or not inform) design decisions, set KPIs, and present insights from data in a compelling and value-adding way. We should also understand what data is available from users, how we can use it and how we shouldn't, and whether we're even allowed to legally use it.

Using metrics and KPIs to help tell your story

When we work through, define, and design websites and apps, there's always something that we want a user to do. As I noted earlier in this chapter, if we don't measure it, we won't know if what we set out to do was a success or not.

KPIs have commonly been something that marketing, strategy, or the suits have dealt with. Far too often, the UX and design team aren't involved in defining what the KPIs should be, or whether they indeed were met.

Your KPIs should, however, be closely related to the goal of the experience. This is where having defined objectives for your pages and views and experience goals really helps. Thinking through what your KPI would be for each experience goal, as well as the overarching one(s), and for your pages and views, is a great way to be specific about how you'll know whether something is successful. As with all things, using KPIs doesn't end by just setting them, but should be followed up on to see if, in fact, the KPIs were met.

Visualizing data

Many of us have sat through a presentation with poorly designed slides showing chart after chart, and as soon as whoever is talking through and explaining them has moved on, we've forgotten all about the details and can't for the life of us figure out the meaning of a slide by simply looking at it. *Visualizing data* might bring to mind various kinds of information dashboards presenting a wealth of data and, hopefully, some meaning around it. While information dashboards can certainly help reduce the dependency on short-term memory by displaying (all) relevant data in one place, the need for and value of visualizing data goes well beyond information dashboards.[8]

Not too long ago, being able to visualize data was a "nice to have." Now it's close to a "must have," particularly the higher up the career ladder you climb. However, basic visual communication skills is a must-have skill across at all stages of your career. As Aristotle wrote, the way we tell a story has a profound impact on the human experience, and in his

---

8 Shilpi Choudhury, "The Psychology Behind Information Dashboards," *UX Magazine*, December 4, 2013, *https://oreil.ly/pDhON*.

seven golden rules of good storytelling, decor plays an important role. Just as design has become a competitive advantage, being able to visualize data and present it is something that will set you apart from, or back from, your competition, whether that's a colleague in the same company, a candidate somewhere else, or a competing website or app.

No matter what you're presenting, the ability to visualize data will help break information into parts that are easier to digest and understand. All data has a story to tell, but we need to get it out in order to be able to tell it. As the data we create and subsequently have access to via, or for, the websites and apps we create, the importance of being able to break it down and present it in a meaningful way for its purpose and audience is critical.

Visualizing data is important because it helps us to do the following:

- Reduce dependency on short-term memory
- Reduce cognitive overload
- Guide the eye of the reader
- Provide information for decision making

Exercise: Identifying and Telling the Right Story Behind Data

With a project you're working on, or have worked on recently, think about the following:

- How is/was qualitative and quantitative data used as part of the product design process?
- How, if at all, is data visualized and how does it benefit the product or project?

What Traditional Storytelling Can Teach Us About Presenting Your Story

Many of the methods and tools covered in this book can help us with the presentation part of our work. As I've said previously, everything is an experience, and though you can never guarantee that someone will experience something in a particular way, you can design the experience to be as optimal as possible. This section explains five steps to using storytelling for presenting your story.

IDENTIFYING THE "WHO" AND "WHY" OF YOUR STORY

All good stories are told with someone specific in mind. In traditional storytelling, that someone may be part of a large and broad audience with diverse needs and tastes, but the plot and the characters for one reason or another resonate with them (Figure 14-2). When presenting our story at work, we might still have a broad-ish audience in mind—the larger company if it's about an approach to work, or the direct team or client if it's about a proposed solution, for example. However, the more we understand about the specific "who" of those we present our story to, the higher the possibility that we're able to tell it in such a way that it resonates and we achieve our desired outcome.

FIGURE 14-2
Identifying the "who" and the "why" of your story

The desired outcome is closely related to the "why" of your story. For most of the work we do and most of the presentations we put together, we have a reason for doing so. But often it's just a high-level "why" that we're aware of and able to articulate. Many deliverables and presentations leave their audience second-guessing about what it is they are looking at, or what the main takeaway should be, rather than the presenter being explicit enough to prevent confusion.

As we've covered previously, characters should ideally come before plot in relation to product design, as it's all about the users in the end (without users, there will be no product). However, most design includes the idea of a plot; that is, a "what" that product should be, before detailed work begins on who the product is for.

Similarly, in presenting our work, there is often a "why" that leads to the "who." Most people will start with a "why" (e.g., to increase sales) or a "what"(e.g., a redesign), and though the "who" is ever present, the details about the "who" often follow as an extension of "why" and "what," and that is absolutely fine. The main thing is that all are clear.

According to Aristotle, plot and character are on par with each other, and that's the case with the "why" and the "who" of the story you're telling too. For example, your team may be working on a client presentation (the "who" being the client) to sell a concept or idea (the "why").

Just as we in product design need to be specific and clear on who our audience is, what their needs are, and why our product and service is for them, when it comes to presenting our story, it's important to do similar up-front work identifying our audience. It's not something that has to take more than 15 minutes, but the impact of going through a simple "who" and "why" can pay off immediately.

In summary, the "who" and the "why" of what you're presenting can be defined as follows:

Who

> Your primary and secondary audience

Why

> Closely related to the "who" of what you're presenting and is about the desired outcome

How to go about it

Principles related to personas, empathy maps, and character maps, as covered in Chapter 6, are applicable as ways to work through the "who" and the "why."

A first step, however, should always be to more precisely define the "who," as it's only then that you can really focus on what the specific people who will be subject to your presentation will care about. Leaving it as *presentation* (what) *to the client* (who) *to sell our latest work* (why) is very nonspecific and doesn't take important details into account. In most instances, you'll be presenting to not only your main client contact, but also their superiors and often the ultimate decision makers and budget holders who the presentation will be passed on to.

Many of the methods and exercises used in this book can be used to also help identify the "who" and the "why" of the story you're telling. Chapter 6 presented a common list of characters in product design. This forms a useful basis for working through which characters apply to the product or service you design. Similarly, a more general list of the "who"s when it comes to presenting your story forms a useful starting point for defining the specifics in your situation.

Just as the characters in product design will differ based on your company and your role, the "who" will differ too. There are, however, various stakeholder analysis techniques and maps that can be used no matter the project. One of those techniques is the "Power/Interest Grid for Stakeholder Prioritization" which identifies which stakeholders need to kept "satisfied" versus just "informed." Another one is stakeholder maps, which goes into more detail about the needs of the respective stakeholder. The latter is similar to a user persona.

Exercise: Identifying the "Who" and "Why" of Your Story

With a project you're working on, or have worked on recently:

- List the all the stakeholders (the "who") that the presentation, deliverable, or work is relevant for.

- For each one, identify why it's relevant and what you're hoping they and you get out of the presentation (the "why").

DEFINING YOUR STORY

The next step after having defined the "who" and the "why" is to plan out and start defining your story. Many of the methods and exercises we've covered in this book that relate to defining your product or service experience also apply to presenting your story. For instance, both the two-page synopsis method and the index card method as covered in Chapter 5, work well for working through the narrative structure.

Whether you're putting together an actual presentation or simply figuring out what you need to define and work through to best meet the brief, I advise the UX teams, strategists, and business people that I mentor and work with to quickly sketch up an outline before getting stuck (Figure 14-3). With a simple framework in place and a clearly defined narrative, plot points, and that last act when everything comes together, you're ensuring that you're clear about what steps you need to take. This outline also becomes a valuable tool and something physical to take to the rest of the team to talk through. If done properly—and this often doesn't take more than an hour—you'll clearly be able to talk through "This is what I recommend that we'd do and here is why."

FIGURE 14-3
Defining your story

Over the last few years, this has become my default way of approaching projects, particularly when I'm working with new agencies that I'm not yet familiar with in terms of their ways of working or how much knowledge they have of UX and more strategic experience planning pieces. This process is also incredibly valuable for more junior UX teams who are developing their strategic and presentation skills, as well as any UX team working on getting more buy-in for UX deliverables in an organization. It's a simple way of storyboarding what you need to cover and how it all fits together. Usually, it takes a couple of sketches before I get it right, but that's part of the process and what makes it so incredibly valuable. Thinking you need to do something to only realize when you have the full story in front of you that you don't, potentially saves a lot of time. Less is usually more, and if you can say something in one diagram/slide, that's generally better than two, three, four, or five slides.

This process is similar to sketching out pages or app views and writing down "The purpose of this page/view is to..." as we talked about in Chapter 13. Sometimes people can be a little resistant to this process, as they just want to get the work done and jump straight into the details. However, taking a step back to first get that full picture— whether for a presentation structure, the kinds of deliverables you need to do, or your pages and views—usually saves a lot of time in the long run, plus makes the information much more to the point. And that's usually a good thing, since no matter how formidable our presentation or deliverables might be, if things can be presented in less time and fewer pages or slides, that's a plus. We can hold our attention for only so long, and there are generally other things to do afterward. After all, even the best stories must come to an end.

How to go about it

Thinking of the metaphor of a presentation, start by working through what slides you need and sketch out each one. Together with the "blank slide," write down the purpose in a few words (e.g., "Persona overview," "Key templates"). If you want to take the process one step further, add the main points each slide needs to make in order to address and answer the statements. The output might look something like Figure 14-4.

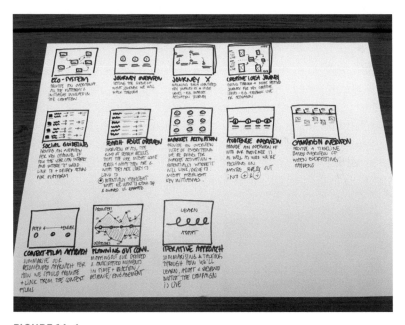

FIGURE 14-4
Sketched-out slides

THE VERBAL ASPECT OF YOUR STORY

The *verbal aspect* of your story is very closely related to the written aspect of your story. But there's a performance element added to it (Figure 14-7). When you're working with just the written word, you don't have the opportunity to conduct the auditory aspect of how that story is told.

Back in the old days, one of the reasons troubadours were so successful and being a storyteller was regarded as a great profession was their ability to adapt to as well as captivate their audience. They paused at planned and intentional times to ensure certain details came across with impact. It was a well-used technique back then, and it is a well-used technique today. How the storyteller or performer approaches it ties back to the overall narrative structure of the performance.

FIGURE 14-5
The verbal aspect of your story

We see this in great speakers, be they motivational speakers like Tony Robbins, speakers at conferences, or internal team members who present something in front of the company or client. What all of these have in common is that they read their audience. By looking at the audience's response, or lack thereof, the speaker adapts accordingly. They pay attention and invite questions to be asked and create both a safe and inspiring environment. With the right verbal presentation style, the most seemingly uninteresting topics can be made interesting. Whether or not you achieve this comes down to how you tell that story and how you engage the audience.

How to go about it

Delivering your presentation starts with knowing the story and what you'd like your audience response to be at each key point. One way of working through this is to draw on the material covered in Chapter 9. Try to map out visually what you'd like the emotional response to each slide to be in your presentation.

You can do this in various ways; for example, by writing an "L" for *low*, "M" for *medium*, or "H" for *high* in the top-right corner of each slide, as sketched out as part of the following exercise. Or you could simply draw lines between each slide, connecting them at the bottom if the emotional response is lower, the middle if it's raised somewhat, or at the top if it's a higher-engagement moment.

With a clearer picture of the presentation as a whole, and the slides"that make it up, it's easier to start thinking about the verbal presentation. You can identify what to say on each slide and what level of detail you want to go into. For the latter, it's useful to come back to the "who" and "why" so you get the balance.

Exercise: The Verbal Aspect of Your Story

Using your sketched-out presentation done as part of the "Define Your Story" exercise as a basis:

- Define the key moments in your presentation where you want to really capture your audience attention and mark these slides with a star. The key moments could, for example, be the inspirational lofty "What if" or a detail that is really important.

- Work through the desired emotional response to each slide by marking each with an "L" for low, "M" for medium, or "H" for high in the top-right corner. Remember that not all slides can be high emotional moments.

- Review the presentation as a whole and make any necessary adjustments to get the flow from low to high right so that there is a bit of back and forth.

- Once you're happy with the flow of the presentation, make notes on how you may want to adjust the verbal presentation based on certain slides and the desired emotional response. This could involve slowing down somewhat for a slide with a lot of detail, or speaking with more excitement on the lofty "what if" moments.

THE VISUAL ASPECT OF YOUR STORY

In traditional storytelling, the *visual aspect* (Figure 14-6) has often played an important role. Chapter 1 described how the Australian Aborigines used cave paintings both as a way to remember the story they were about to tell, and as a way to bring it to life.

When it comes to the work that we do in relation to product design, we sometimes forget about the importance of the visual aspect. Numerous companies don't overlook its importance, and ensure that visual or graphic designers create the presentations that are given. And, of course, there are companies that do forget, and it shows. The visual aspect, however, doesn't just apply to presentations in relation to product design. It applies to every output and deliverable, from emails and project plans to strategic, UX-related, and technical documentations, and everything in between. With everything we do, we tell a story, and the way we tell that story affects the way it's experienced. Whether we want to or not, the way we present something "on paper" impacts the way the intended, or unintended, audience reads and understands the subject, or how they don't understand it.

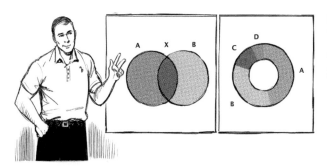

FIGURE 14-6
The visual aspect of your story

Dribble and Pinterest are filled with stunning-looking deliverables. The real world does, at times, look a little different. Some might argue that the purpose of UX deliverables is not to look good—and sure, that's not the primary purpose—but it's not an excuse for not caring about the visual presentation. Our job as UX designers is to bring clarity to experiences, to work with the information hierarchy, and make things easy to use. Yet, many UX designers forget to apply these same principles to the work they produce, sometimes to the point where it's not even clear what you're looking at.

To some extent, the way what you present looks says something about how much love and attention you're giving the project. You don't have to have great visual design skills in order to create nice-looking deliverables, or write clear emails and reports, for that matter. You just have to be clear about the story you're trying to get across, what the desired action is, and apply simple information hierarchy principles to support that. In addition, you need to keep usability, readability, and relevance for your audience in mind.

How to go about it

With a clear "who" and "why," as well as an understanding of the verbal aspect of the story you're telling, the next step is about bringing that story to life. A key thing to remember here is the purpose of the presentation or the deliverable and how it's going to be used. As a general rule of thumb, you should have less text in presentations that are given mainly in person or via video/ phone meeting than if they are simply sent around. In the latter case, more explanatory text is needed.

It's also useful to go back to the desired emotional response and put more visual emphasis on the high moments, where you want to inspire or really draw your audience in. However, depending on who your audience is, perhaps a high moment is one with a lot of data and detail. It all depends on your "who" and "why."

Exercise: The Visual Aspect of Your Story

Using your sketched-out presentation done as part of the "Define Your Story" exercise as a basis, and the further refinement you did as part of "The Verbal Aspect of Your Story."

For each slide, review your initial thoughts (the high-level sketch)about the visual aid or layout that should be used to best convey the message and purpose.

ADAPTING HOW YOU PRESENT YOUR STORY

As we talked about in Chapter 2, Aristotle was the first one to point out that the way we tell a story influences the raw human experience of that story. Just as we aim to adapt and tailor the experience we provide our users based on who they are and where they are in their journey, we ought to adapt what we present and how we present it to the client or stakeholder in question based on what they know, what they care about, and where we are in the project journey (Figure 14-7). This applies to both their understanding of UX and the level of detail we go into.

FIGURE 14-7
Adapting how you present your story

When you think about it, this adaptation is similar to the way we tell stories in our day-to-day lives. You won't talk to a five-year-old child about your day at work in the same way you'd talk a grown-up, or tell a story with the same detail to someone who hears it for the first time and someone who's heard it a hundred times before. Equally, if a client has extensive experience with or knowledge of UX and UX deliverables, there is no need to go through what a sitemap is, what the purpose of wireframes are and aren't, etc., but the background becomes critical if they don't.

How we tell our story in the best way has a lot to do with where we place the emphasis, and this in turn should link back to the "who" and the "why." It's also influenced by a number of other factors, such as these:

- What's the key thing we want to get across?
- What do we need to get input or feedback on?
- How much do they know already?
- What does the person in question care about?

The last question is very much about what makes the person we're presenting to "click" or not "click." Some internal stakeholders and clients want all the details, whereas others want just the key points. Which side of the spectrum they are on makes a crucial difference to how we present our work on paper and verbally, what we include, and how we structure it. Failing to get this right often leads to unengaged clients, or clients who don't give you the feedback that you need.

If the aim is to get buy-in, there are some additional things to consider:

- What is their current understanding of, for example, what UX?
- What is their current understanding of, for example, where UX sits in the organization and process?
- What is their current understanding of, for example, the value of UX?
- What is their current understanding of, for example, how UX could help projects and the organization?

Exercise: Adapting How You Present Your Story

Think about a presentation you've given or attended recently:

- How did you, or the presenter, adapt the presentation to its audience?
- Was this linked to the "who" and the "why" of the presentation?
- If not, how could it have been improved?

Summary

As we've covered throughout this book, storytelling is an integral part of the design process—a practical tool to help narrate, inform, structure, prioritize, and plan out what you work on and how to bring it to life as an experience that fits into the user's own story. But just like storytelling in the good old times was used to educate, entertain, pass on values, and move people into action, the role of storytelling in the workplace serves the same purpose: to unite people around common visions and goals and to get buy-in for projects, ideas, and approaches to work, as well as win new clients and directives, and of course, as a way to better present our work.

No matter what level you're at in your career or how much of your day-to-day work involves presenting in various ways, being a storyteller is part of all of our jobs. Although we won't all become experts, we can all definitely master storytelling to some degree and see the direct benefits as soon as we put it into practice.

Presenting your story requires being both intentional and purposeful with the story you're telling, and knowing why and how to tell it. It's about acknowledging that not everyone will respond to the same thing, but that colleagues and clients are all different, just like the users of the products and services we design. Being a storyteller is a skill that has to do with listening and research. It's about understanding nuances and being able to adapt and respond right then and there to how your audience is reacting. And it's about having confidence in yourself and the material or subject you're talking through. More than anything, it's about creating a good experience for your audience, and although a story told is not necessarily a good one, a story told well has the power to change people's minds and move them into action. And that is, after all, what we're almost always after in work-related situations.

[Index]

Plutchik, Robert: Wheel of Emotions, 101–104
presentations
    buy-in as goal of, 357–362
    data in, story behind, 364–368
    inspiration as goal of, 362–364
    outcome as goal of, 356–357
    similarities to storytelling, 355
    story for, defining, 371–380
    verbal aspect of, 374–380
    visual aspect of, 376–380
    "who" and "why" for, identifying, 369–371
primary emotions, 102
printing press, 8, 8–9
product design. *See also* UX (user experience) design
    buy-in for, 18, 357–362
    character development for. *See* characters
    content in. *See* content
    customer journey maps for, 241–242
    details, importance of, 36–37
    device considerations. *See* devices
    dramatic question in, 34
    dramaturgy in, 29–33, 128–131, 143–144, 146–148. *See also* dramaturgy
    emotional aspect of. *See* emotions
    emotional journey maps for, 260–264
    examples and lessons for. *See* examples
    experience maps for, 229–231, 242–243
    happy and unhappy journey maps, 263–264
    plots and subplots in. *See* plot
    presenting. *See* presentations
    role of stories in, 17–19. *See also* stories
    scenes in. *See* scenes
    setting and context in. *See* setting and context
    storyboards for. *See* storyboards
    storymaps for, 278–280
    technologies supported. *See* technologies
    theme in. *See* theme

user considerations. *See* users
user journeys for, 267–271
product experience
    categorizing emotions in, 108–113. *See also* emotions
    circular nature of, 29–32
    dramaturgy in, 150–154. *See also* dramaturgy
    shape of, 259–266
product experience story
    developing, 288–289
    main and subplots for, 270
    mental models for, 292–293
    methods for developing, 288–289
    modules for. *See* modular stories
    real or fake content in, 281–282
    theme for, 286–287, 290–292
product life cycle, 136–139, 148–149
protagonist's goal, as scene layer, 336
prototypes, 334–336
public speaking, storytelling in, 42–44. *See also* oral storytelling; presentations

Q

Quest pattern, 307–312
The Quest plot, 256

R

Rags to Riches plot, 256
Rail Europe Experience Map, 229–230
Ready Player One movie, 76
Rebirth plot, 258
Reddit, 105
red thread. *See also* theme
    in product design, 286–287
    in stories, 2, 283–285
reflective level of emotions, 101
reflective moments, 111–113
robots, 182
rock art, 7
round characters, 188

S

scenes
    content flow across screens for, 346–349
    CTAs for, 349–350

About the Author

Anna Dahlström is a Swedish UX designer based in London. She's the founder of the UX design school UX Fika. Since 2001 she has worked client side, for agencies, and for startups on a large variety of brands and projects, from websites and apps to bots and TV UIs. She's a regular speaker and holds a MSc in Computer Science and Business Administration from Copenhagen Business School.

Colophon

The animal on the cover of *Storytelling in Design* is a red fox (*Vulpes vulpes*). Fox is originally an Old English word. The red fox is one of five fox species in North America. Their range includes Australia as well, where they are considered invasive. Red foxes prefer open areas with low-lying vegetation, but thrive in desert, forest, and tundra as well.

Their fur can be red, rusty-red, reddish yellow, or multicolored, and is white underneath and at the tip of their tails. Black fur trims their legs, ears, and tails. Their pupils are vertically oriented ovals, and their faces taper off in a disproportionately slender muzzle. The tail of a red fox is longer than half its body length. Red foxes typically have 18 to 33.75 inch-long bodies and 12 to 21.75 inch-long tails. Their weight is highly variable—it's considered normal anywhere from 6.5 to 24 pounds.

At birth, red foxes are brown or gray, blind, deaf, and toothless. Litters of young cubs (or *kits*) typically consist of 4 to 6 individuals, but can be as few as 2 or as many as 12. Red foxes are monogamous, and both care for their young until fall, when kits can support themselves. The average lifespan of a wild red fox is two to four years.

Red foxes eat a variety of small birds and mammals including mice, rabbits, and groundhogs, in addition to fruits and grasses. They bury surplus food. Red foxes hunt before sunrise and late in the evening. Their acute hearing and binocular vision help them hunt small prey in the dark. You can find red foxes during daylight hours as well, though—they're often active during the day and have the distinction of being the most populous canid in the world.

Many of the animals on O'Reilly's covers are endangered; all of them are important to the world.

The color illustration is by Karen Montgomery, based on a black and white engraving from *Le Jardin des Plantes*. The cover fonts are URW Typewriter and Guardian Sans. The text font is Scala; and the heading font is Gotham.

O'REILLY®

There's much more
where this came from.

Experience books, videos, live online training courses, and more from O'Reilly and our 200+ partners—all in one place.

Learn more at oreilly.com/online-learning